ANCIENT INDIAN TRADITION & MYTHOLOGY

TRANSLATED BY

A BOARD OF SCHOLARS

EDITED BY

Professor J. L. SHASTRI

VOLUME 33

ANCIENT INDIAN TRADITION AND MYTHOLOGY SERIES

VOLUMES

ŚIVA PURĀṆA 1-4

LIṄGA PURĀṆA 5-6

BHĀGAVATA PURĀṆA 7-11

GARUḌA PURĀṆA 12-14

NĀRADA PURĀṆA 15-19

KŪRMA PURĀṆA 20-21

BRAHMĀṆḌA PURĀṆA 22-26

AGNI PURĀṆA 27-30

VARĀHA PURĀṆA 31-32

BRAHMA PURĀṆA 33-36

VOLUMES UNDER PREPARATION

BHAVIṢYA

BRAHMAVAIVARTA

DEVĪBHĀGAVATA

KĀLIKĀ

MĀRKAṆḌEYA

MATSYA

PADMA

SKANDA

VĀMANA

VĀYU

VIṢṆU

VIṢṆUDHARMOTTARA

BRAHMA PURĀṆA

PART I

TRANSLATED AND ANNOTATED BY
A BOARD OF SCHOLARS

MOTILAL BANARSIDASS • DELHI
UNESCO • PARIS

© MOTILAL BANARSIDASS
Head Office: Bungalow Road, Delhi 110 007
Branches: Chowk, Varanasi 221 001
Ashok Rajpath, Patna 800 004
6 Appar Swamy Koil Street, Mylapore,
Madras 600 004

UNESCO COLLECTION OF REPRESENTATIVE WORKS—Indian Series
This book has been accepted in the Indian Translation Series of the Unesco Collection of Representative books jointly sponsored by the United Nations Educational, Scientific and Cultural Organization (UNESCO) and the Government of India.

First Edition: Delhi, 1985

ISBN: 81-208-0003-6

Printed in India by Shantilal Jain, at Shri Jainendra Press, A-45 Naraina, Phase I, New Delhi 110 028 and published by Narendra Prakash Jain for Motilal Banarsidass, Delhi 110 007.

PUBLISHER'S NOTE

The Purest gems lie hidden in the bottom of the ocean or in the depth of rocks. One has to dive into the ocean or delve into the rocks to find them out. Similarly, truth lies concealed in the language which with the passage of time has become obsolete. Man has to learn that language before he discovers that truth.

But he has neither the means nor the leisure to embark on that course. We have, therefore, planned to help him acquire knowledge by an easier course. We have started the series of Ancient Indian Tradition and Mythology in English Translation. Our goal is to universalize knowledge through the most popular international medium of expression. The publication of the Purāṇas in English Translation is a step towards that goal.

PREFACE

The present volume contains the *Brahma Purāṇa* Part I (Chapters 1-40) in English Translation. This is the thirtythird volume in the Series on *Ancient Indian Tradition and Mythology.*

The project of the series was planned in 1970 by Lala Sundar Lal Jain of Messrs Motilal Banarsidass, with the aim to universalize knowledge through the most popular international medium, viz. English. Hitherto the English translations of nine Purāṇas, namely Śiva, Liṅga, Bhāgavata, Garuḍa, Nārada, Kūrma, Brahmāṇḍa, Agni and Varāha have been published by us.

The present volume (*Brahma Purāṇa,* part I) contains 40 chapters. Chapter 1 opens with a dialogue between Sūta Romaharṣaṇa and the sages of Naimiśa forest. Here as usual Sūta is the chief speaker who on enquiry from the sages describes, in detail, the origin of Devas and Asuras. Ch. 2 narrates the birth of Pṛthu from Vena and his installation on the throne as the lord of subjects. Ch. 3 mentions 14 Manus—six in the past, one in the present and seven in the future. Chs 4-6 review the evolution of Vaivasvata Sun and kings of the solar race. There are references to the Haihaya race which comprised the following well known tribes : Vītihotras, Śaryātas, Bhojas, Avantis, Tuṇḍikeras, (or Kuṇḍikeras), Tālajaṅghas, Bharatas, Sujātyas, Yādavas, Śūrasenas, Ānartas and Cedis. Mention is made of Śakas and Yādavas who helped the Haihaya kings in their war with Paraśurāma. Further, references are made to Pahlavas, Pāradas, Yavanas, Kambojas, Dāradas, Śakas and Cīnas. The chapter refers to some unknown tribes such as Kālasarpas and Daryas who are not identifiable. Chs. 7-8 narrate the birth of Soma and the dynasties of kings of the Lunar Race. Chs. 9-11 recount the genealogy of ancient Kṣatriyas with the narrative of king Yayāti in detail. Chs. 12-15 relate to the family of Vṛṣṇis, the birth of Śrīkṛṣṇa in that family and the episode of Syamantaka jewel. Chs. 16-22 deal with the seven continents with particular reference to Jambūdvīpa. They survey the magnitude of oceans, continents and nether regions. While describing the upper and lower worlds, they present the dreadful portrait of hells as well as the precise position of the pole star.

Ch. 23 relates to the holy centres of pilgrimage and describes their efficacy. Chs. 24, 25 describe the glory of Bhārata through the mouth of Brahmā. Chs. 26-31 prescribe the worship of Sun-god, his one hundred and eight names, his glory and nativity. Chs. 32-36 describe the marriage of Umā-Maheśvara and their departure from the Himālayas. Chs. 37-38 recount the story of Prajāpati Dakṣa and the destruction of his sacrifice by the gaṇas of lord Śiva. Chs. 39-40 describe the holy centres—Ekāmra and Utkala.

This Purāṇa is related to Brahmā, because Brahmā is the chief speaker. The Purāṇa states about a Sūryakṣetra, at Koṇārka, near the holy place of Puri. This throws light on the place and date of composition of the chapters related to Sun-god. The Sun-temple was built at Koṇārka and the deity installed therein in the year 1241 A.D. Similarly, the holy places of Orissa seem to have been described by one who was well acquainted with Orissa. Moreover, there is a special treatise in this book on Orissa. The remaining chapters are not important from the point of view of fixing the place of composition inasmuch as they deal with the general topics.

Acknowledgement of Obligations

It is our pleasant duty to record our sincere thanks to Dr. R.N. Dandekar and the Unesco authorities for their kind encouragement and valuable help which render this work very useful. We are also grateful to Shri T.V. Parameshwar Iyer for his valuable assistance in the preparation of this work. We should also express our gratitude to all those persons who have offered suggestions for improving the same.

—*Editor*

CONTENTS

PART I

PREFACE vii

ABBREVIATIONS xi

INTRODUCTION xiii

Purāṇa : Definition xiii

The Nomenclature xiv

Extent xv

Transmission of tradition xvi

Text-criticism xvii

Date of Composition xvii

Place of Composition xix

Religion and Philosophy of Brahma Purāṇa xx

CHAPTERS

1. On the Origin of Devas and Asuras 1
2. Origin and glory of Pṛthu 19
3. Manvantaras 29
4. Evolution of Vivasvat Āditya 33
5. Review of the Solar Race 37
6. Kings of the Solar Race 45
7. Birth of Soma 53
8. Kings of the Lunar Race 56
9. Genealogy of Ancient Kṣatriyas 61
10. The Narrative of Yayāti 65
11. Dynasty of Yayāti 69
12. Birth of Śrīkṛṣṇa 84
13. The Family of Vṛṣṇis 88
14. How the Syamantaka jewel was brought back 93
15. Akrūra obtains Syamantaka 97
16. Seven Continents 100
17. Jambūdvīpa 105
18. Magnitude of Oceans and Continents 108
19. Magnitude of Nether worlds 114

20. Hells in nether regions 117
21. Upper Regions 121
22. Pole Star 124
23. Holy Centres : Their Greatness 126
24. A Dialogue between Brahmā and Sages 132
25. Bhārata Subcontinent 135
26. The Glory of Koṇāditya 140
27. Efficacy of Devotion to Sun-god 145
28. Glory of Sun-God 150
29. Names of Sun-god 157
30. Nativity of Sun-god 160
31. One Hundred and Eight Names of Sun-God 170
32. Penance of Umā 174
33. Testing of Pārvatī 183
34. Pārvatī weds Śiva 189
35. Hymn in Praise of Śiva 201
36. Umā and Śaṅkara leave Himālayas 205
37. Destruction of Dakṣa's Sacrifice 209
38. The Prayer by Dakṣa 217
39. The holy Centre of Ekāmra 230
40. The holy centre of Utkala 237

ABBREVIATIONS

Common and self-evident abbreviations such as Ch(s)-Chapter(s), p—page, pp—pages, V—Verse, VV—Verses, Ftn—footnote, Hist. Ind. Philo—History of Indian Philosophy are not included in this list.

ABORI	*Annals of the Bhandarkar Oriental Research Institute*, Poona
AGP	S. M. Ali's *The Geography of Purāṇas*, PPH, New Delhi, 1973
AIHT	*Ancient Indian Historical Tradition*, F. E. Pargiter, Motilal Banarsidass (MLBD), Delhi
AITM	*Ancient Indian Tradition and Mythology* Series MLBD, Delhi
AP	*Agni Purāṇa*, Guru Mandal Edition (GM), Calcutta, 1957
Arch.S.Rep.	Archaeological Survey Report
AV	*Atharva Veda*, Svādhyāya Mandal, Aundh
Bd. P.	*Brahmāṇḍa Purāṇa*, (MLBD), Delhi 1973
BG	*Bhagavadgītā*
Bh. P.	*Bhāgavata Purāṇa*, Bhagavat Vidyapeeth, Ahmedabad
Br.	*Brāhmaṇa* (preceded by name such as Śatapatha
BS. P.	*Bhaviṣya Purāṇa*, Vishnu Shastri Bapat, Wai
BV. P.	*Brahma Vaivarta Purāṇa*, GM, 1955-57
CC.	*Caturvarga Cintāmaṇi* by Hemādri
CVS	*Caraṇa Vyūha Sūtra* by Śaunaka; Com. by Mahidāsa
DB	*Devī Bhāgavata*, GM, 1960-61
De or GDAMI.	*The Geographical Dictionary of Ancient and Mediaeval India*, N. L. De, Orienta Reprint, Delhi, 1971
Dh. S.	*Dharma Sūtra* (preceded by the author's name such as Gautama)
ERE	*Encyclopaedia of Religion and Ethics*—Hastings.
GP	*Garuḍa Purāṇa* Ed. R. S. Bhattacharya Chowkhamba, Varanasi, 1964

GS	*Gṛhya Sūtra* (preceded by the name of the author such as Āpastamba)
HD	*History of Dharma Śāstra*, P. V. Kane, G. O. S.
IA	*The Indian Antiquary*
IHQ	*The Indian Historical Quarterly*
JP	*Purāṇa* (Journal of the Kashiraj Trust) Varanasi
KA	*Kauṭilya Arthaśāstra*
KP	*Kūrma Purāṇa*, Veṅkaṭeśvara Press Edt. Bombay, also Kashiraj Trust Edt., Varanasi 1971
LP	*Liṅga Purāṇa*, GM, 1960; also MLBD, Delhi, 1981
Manu.	*Manusmṛti*
Mbh.	*Mahābhārata*, Gītā Press, Gorakhpur, VS 2014
MkP	*Mārkaṇḍeya Purāṇa*
MN	*Mahābhārata Nāmānukramaṇī*, Gītā Press Gorakhpur, VS 2016
MtP.	*Matsya Purāṇa*, GM, 1954
MW	*Monier Williams Sk. English Dictionary* MLBD, Delhi, 1976
NP.	*Nāradīya or Nārada Purāṇa*, Veṅkaṭeśvar Press, Bombay
PCK	*Bhāratavarṣiya Prācina Caritrakośa*, Siddheshwar Shastri, Poona, 1968
Pd. P.	*Padma Purāṇa*, GM, 1957-59
PE	*Puranic Encyclopaedia*, V. Mani, English, MLBD, Delhi, 1975
PR or PRHRC	*Puranic Records on Hindu Rites and Customs* R. C. Hazra, Calcutta, 1948
ṚV	*Ṛg-Veda*, Svādhyāya Mandal, Aundh
Śat. Br.	*Śatapatha Brāhmaṇa*
SC or SMC	*Smṛti Candrikā*--Devanna Bhaṭṭa
SEP	*Studies in Epics and Purāṇas*, A.D. Pusalkar, Bharatiya Vidya Bhavan (BVB), Bombay

INTRODUCTION

Purāṇa : Definition

The Purāṇa, as a class of literature, represents different phases and aspects of life lived by the people in diverse ages. It is not possible to adopt a standard definition for the class of literature that contains heterogeneous phases and aspects of life. Literally the word Purāṇa means 'old'. A Purāṇa is therefore, the record of ancient tradition. According to the lexicographer, Amara-Siṁha (c 500 A.D.), a purāṇa should treat of five subjects, viz (1) Creation, (2) Dissolution and Re-creation (3) Genealogies of gods, patriarchs and illustrious monarchs, (4) Epochs of Manus and (5) the history of ancient dynasties.[1] The definition is applicable to the Brahma Purāṇa as well as to the other Purāṇas. To illustrate: Chapters 1-3 treat of Sarga (Creation) and Pratisarga (Dissolution). The latter is taken up again in Chs 122-125. Chs 4-11 treat of Vaṁśa (dynasties) and Vaṁśānucarita (the history of illustrious monarchs). Ch. 3 deals with the fourteen Manvantaras (ages of Manus), viz. Svāyambhuva, Svārociṣa, Uttama, Raivata, Cākṣuṣa, Vaivasvata, Raibhya, Raucya, Tāmasa and five Sāvarṇi-s—Sūrya, Dakṣa, Brahmā, Dharma and Rudra.

But the definition was found inadequate even in the early age of Purāṇas. It could not cover the entire contents of the Purāṇa. The scope of definition was therefore enlarged even at the stage when the Purāṇa literature was in the offing. The Bhāgavata Purāṇa added five more characteristics to the Pañca-lakṣaṇa Purāṇa. They were *Vṛtti* (means of livelihood), ***Rakṣā*** (incarnations for the protection of the people), ***Mukti*** (final release), ***Hetu*** (unmanifest primordial nature) and ***Apāśraya*** (Brahma).

---

1. Sargaś ca Pratisargaś ca Vaṁśo Manvantarāṇi ca /
Vaṁśyānucarıtaṁ caiva Purāṇaṁ pañcalakṣaṇam //
BD. P. 1.1.1. 37, 38

But even this daśa-lakṣaṇa[1] definition could not fully cover all aspects. Hence, the Matsya Purāṇa[2] provided a definition approaching nearer to the description of the extant Purāṇas. According to this definition, the Purāṇa included the glorification of Brahmā, Viṣṇu, Sūrya and Rudra, as also of Dharma (righteous conduct), Artha (economics and polity) and Kāma (erotics).

But neither the Pañcalakṣaṇa nor the Daśalakṣaṇa nor the Matsya Purāṇa definition of the Purāṇa could cover such topics as Tīrtha-yātrā (pilgrimage) etc. With changes in the peoples' mode of behaviour, the Purāṇa introduced various other subjects which could not be covered by any definition. However, this class of literature was definable only by the etymological meaning of the word 'Purāṇa' that is 'old.'[3]

Nomenclature

The Padma Purāṇa[4] classifies Brahma Purāṇa as Rājasa and assigns it to Brahmā, the god of rajas quality. This conforms to

---

1. *Bhāgavata* : 11.7.9-10
Sargo'syātha visargaśca vṛttirakṣāntarāṇi ca /
Vaṁśo vaṁśyānucaritaṁ saṁkhyā hetur apāśrayaḥ //
Daśabhir lakṣaṇair yuktaṁ Purāṇaṁ tadvido viduḥ /
Kecit pañcavidhaṁ brahman mahadalpavyavasthayā //

2. *Matsya* : 53.66.7
Brahmaviṣṇvarkarudrāṇām māhātmyam bhuvanasya ca /
Sasaṁhārapradānañca Purāṇe pañcalakṣaṇe /
Dharmaścārthaśca kāmaśca mokṣaścaivātra kirtyate //

3. *Vāyu* : 1.203
Yasmāt purā hyanatīdaṁ Purāṇaṁ tena hi smṛtam /
Brahmāṇḍa: 1.1.1. 173
Yasmāt purā hyabhūccaitat Purāṇaṁ tena tat smṛtam //

4. *Padma*, Uttara 283. 81-84
Mātsyaṁ Kaurmaṁ tathā Laiṅgaṁ Śaivaṁ Skāndaṁ tathaiva ca/
Āgneyaṁ ca ṣaḍ etāni tāmasāni nibodha me //
Vaiṣṇavaṁ Nāradīyaṁ ca tathā Bhāgavataṁ śubham /
Gāruḍaṁ ca tathā Pādmaṁ Vārāhaṁ śubhadarśane/
Sāttvikāni Purāṇāni vijñeyāni śubhāni vai //
Brahmāṇḍaṁ Brahmavaivartam Mārkaṇḍeyaṁ tathaiva ca/
Bhaviṣyaṁ Vāmanam Brāhmaṁ rājasāni nibodha me //

the statement of Matsya[1] that the rājasa Purāṇas are assignable to Brahmā or Agni, sāttvika to Viṣṇu, tāmasa to Śiva. The Purāṇas are classifiable as sāttvika, rājasa and tāmasa on the strength of quality which they possess predominantly. But as the study reveals, the Brahma is more sāttvika than rājasa. A considerable portion of this Purāṇa is devoted to the glorification of Puruṣottama Vāsudeva, Śrīkṛṣṇa, Sun-god and Śiva. The Purāṇa speaks of Ekāmra-kṣetra and Puruṣottama-kṣetra as sacred to Śiva and Viṣṇu respectively. Viṣṇu and Śiva are paramount lords while Brahmā occupies the third position. Brahmā himself speaks highly of Viṣṇu and Śiva.

But the Purāṇa takes its name after Brahmā. It is because Brahmā is the main speaker here. It is Brahmā who narrates this Purāṇa to the sages on mount Meru.[2] That version with certain modifications was repeated by Vyāsa to the sages at Kurukṣetra[3] and by his disciple Romaharṣaṇa to the sages at Naimiśa.[4] The Purāṇa derives its name merely because it has appeared through the mouth of Brahmā.

Extent

According to the Nārada Purāṇa,[5] Brahma Purāṇa contains 10,000 verses. This is corroborated by Liṅga, Varāha, Kūrma and Padma Purāṇas. The Matsya Purāṇa (printed edition), however gives the number as 1300, though some of the mss of the Matsya Purāṇa read this number as 10,000 (daśa-sāhasra). In fact, if we divide the Brahma Purāṇa into 2 parts, arbitrarily, (although there is no mention of this division in the Purāṇa itself), part 1 containing 138 adhyāyas comprising 10,000 verses and part 2 comprising Gautamī māhātmya containing 4000 verses, the number comes to 14000 verses which

1. *Matsya* 53. 68-69
Sāttvikeṣu purāṇeṣu māhātmyam adhikaṁ Hareḥ/
Rājaseṣu ca māhātmyam adhikaṁ Brahmaṇo viduḥ //
Tadvadagneśca māhātmyaṁ tāmaseṣu Śivasya ca/
Saṅkīrṇeṣu Sarasvatyāḥ pitṛṇāṁ ca nigadyate //
2. *Brahma*. 24. 27-28.
3. *ibid*. 24. 6-9.
4. *ibid*. 1. 4 ff.
5. *Nārada* IV. 92. 31.
tad vai sarvapurāṇāgryaṁ dharmakāmārthamokṣadam /
nānākhyānetihāsāḍhyaṁ *daśa-sāhasram* ucyate //

is supported by Devībhāgavata. But, whether Gautamī māhātmya is a part of Brahma Purāṇa or an independent work has always been an open question. The Nārada Purāṇa excludes Gautamī māhātmya from the contents of Brahma Purāṇa. This shows that Nārada Purāṇa did not recognize Gautamī as a part of Brahma Purāṇa. From this we can conclude that the original Brahma Purāṇa must have comprised 10,000 verses approximately.

Tradition of transmission

According to Brahma Purāṇa it was Brahmā who narrated the story of Brahma Purāṇa to the sages on mount Meru.[1] That version with certain modifications was repeated by sage Vyāsa to the sages at Kurukṣetra.[2] Again, the same version with further modifications was repeated by his disciple Romaharṣaṇa or Lomaharṣaṇa to the sages at Naimiśa.[3] The extant Purāṇa is the version of Lomaharṣaṇa curtailed or enlarged in the process of transmission from one Sūta (reciter) to another.

The tradition is pretty old. Though the reference to the installation of image of Viṣṇu at the Puruṣottama kṣetra by king Indradyumna brings the date of this section to a very late period, say 1200 A.D., there are references to the sanctity of the region long before this period. For instance, Ch 43 records a dialogue between the divine pair—Viṣṇu and Lakṣmī to have occurred in the hoary antiquity, on the peak of Meru on the said topic.

1. *Br. P.* 24. 27-28
   Vyāsa uvāca :
   śṛṇudhvaṁ munayaḥ sarve vakṣyāmi yadi pṛcchatha /
   yaḥ saṁvādobhavat pūrvam ṛṣiṇāṁ brahmaṇā saha //
   Merupṛṣṭhe tu vistīrṇe—
2. *ibid.* 24. 6-9
   Kurukṣetre samāsīnaṁ Vyāsaṁ matimatāṁ varam /
   .. ..
   draṣṭum abhyāyayuḥ prītyā munayaḥ śaṁśitavratāḥ //
3. *Ibid* 1. 4 ff.
   supuṇye Naimiṣāraṇye .. .. /
   satre dvādaśavārṣike .. .. /
   tatrājagāma sūtas tu matimān Lomaharṣaṇaḥ //

Text: Criticism

The present English translation of Brahma Purāṇa is based on the Veṅkaṭeśvara edition which is available in two forms which for convenience sake may be called A and B. 'A' contains the complete text of Brahma Purāṇa but instead of placing the Gautamī māhātmya after adhyāya 69 as existing in the Ānandāśrama edition, it places the same at the end. B consists of Gautamī māhātmya alone which in 105 chapters describes the various holy places on the bank of Godāvarī and is the same as appended to A. The Gautamī māhātmya is a later addition. Hence, the Veṅkaṭeśvara edition is justified in placing it at the end. It is decidedly later than the chapters on Orissa, because the Nārada Purāṇa which gives the contents of the Brahma Purāṇa text includes the māhātmyas of Ekāmra, Puruṣottama and Viraja kṣetras but omits Gautamī. Though the Gautamī māhātmya is a part of Brahma Purāṇa it constitutes a unit by itself.

Date of Composition

According to the consensus of opinion, it is not possible to assign a particular date to a complete Purāṇa text. Any agreement in favour of a particular date is conclusive only for isolated chapters and not for the whole Purāṇa. This being the majority view of Purāṇa scholars, the date of composition of the Brahma Purāṇa cannot be fixed to a definite period, but will have to be spread over a long time.

In most of the Purāṇas where the names of Purāṇas occur in serial order, the Brahma Purāṇa tops the list. The Nārada Purāṇa[1] which gives the contents of the Purāṇas in brief regards this Purāṇa as 'ādi', placing it at the head of the list. This shows that the Brahma Purāṇa was completed before the completion of the Nārada Purāṇa. A comparison of the Puruṣottama māhātmya contained in the Brahma and Nārada Purāṇas shows that the latter borrowed from the former. The Nārada Purāṇa which gives the contents of the Purāṇas might have been

1. *Nārada*, 92.30
Brāhmaṁ Purāṇaṃ tatrādau sarvalokahitāya vai /
Vyāsena Vedaviduṣā samākhyātaṁ mahātmanā //

composed when the kernel of the Purāṇas had taken their structural shape. Moreover, the Nārada Purāṇa refers to the twofold division of the Brahma Purāṇa,[1] consisting of Chs 1-39 and Chs 40-138 respectively. The contents of the Br. P. as given in the Nārada Purāṇa corresponding to the chapter numbers of the Brahma Purāṇa show that the Nārada Purāṇa was acquainted with the kernal of the Brahma Purāṇa long before the latter was completed.

Part one of Brahma Purāṇa (according to Nārada Purāṇa) includes	*Brahma Purāṇa*
Origin of Devas, Asuras, Prajāpatis, Sun-god and solar race	1-6
Life of Rāma	6
Lunar race	7-15
Continents and Subcontinents	16-18
Nether regions	19
Upper regions	20
Hells	20
Eulogy of Sun-god	26-31
Birth and marriage of Pārvatī	32
Legend of Dakṣa Prajāpati	37
Description of Ekāmra kṣetra	39

Part 2 of Brahma Purāṇa (according to N. Purāṇa) includes	
Description of Puruṣottama	40
Life of lord Kṛṣṇa	70-103
Description of the world of Yama	105
Ritual for the manes	110-112
Castes and stages of life, their duties	114
Legends of Viṣṇudharma	118-121

1. *Nārada* IV. 92
Etad brahmapurāṇaṁ tu bhāgadvayasamanvitam /

Dissolution	122
Yoga, a way of life	127-136
Sāṁkhya system	137
Praise of Brahma Purāṇa	138

The study of the contents of Brahma Purāṇa as stated in the Nārada Purāṇa indicates that the kernel of the Brahma Purāṇa, consisting of ten thousand verses was known to the author of the Nārada Purāṇa, that a substantial part of the Brahma Purāṇa, viz Gautamī Māhātmya which contains 105 chapters, did not exist, at least as a part of Brahma Purāṇa when the author of the Nārada Purāṇa wrote the contents of the Brahma Purāṇa. Had he known of Gautamī māhātmya, he would have divided the Purāṇa into 3 parts, and would also have mentioned the demarcating line between the second and third parts. This shows that the author of the Nārada Purāṇa was acquainted only with the earlier version of the Purāṇas than the extant Purāṇas which were completed by the tenth century A.D. The earlier version of the Purāṇas known to the author of the Nārada Purāṇa must be earlier at least by half a century.

But there are evidences to fix up certain parts of this Purāṇa to a definite date. The mention of the Sun-temple at Koṇārka[1] shows that these chapters are later than 1240 A.D., as the sun-temple was built in the thirteenth century A.D. by Narasiṁha-deva 1. The portion of this Purāṇa dealing with the glory of Puruṣottama Kṣetra could not have been earlier than the end of the ninth century A.D. because there is a mention of Śiva-temple[2] at the end of the Mārkaṇḍeya lake which was built in 800 A.D. by Kuṇḍalakesarin, king of Orissa.

Place of Composition

The Purāṇas have not been composed or compiled at one place, by one hand, and in one period. Different episodes or glories of regions may have been written by different authors at different places and incorporated in the text. For ascertaining their places of origin, a number of chapters will have to be grouped subjectwise. To illustrate : Chapters on the holy

1. Br. P. 26
2. *Br.P.* 53. 67-68

places of Orissa such as Ekāmra, Puruṣottama and Viraja could form a group which might have been written by a person who was sufficiently acquainted with the regions or who lived there. Again, Ch 23 of this Purāṇa describes holy places of Northern India, outside Orissa. It has no link with the foregoing or proceeding chapters. It might have been interpolated in later times, by a person who lived in Northern India.

Again the Purāṇa praises the region, north of Sahya mountain, where flows Godāvarī, as the most charming place in the world.[1] The section may have been composed there and appended to the text. Again, the largest group of one hundred and five chapters on the glory of Gautamī may have been written by one who lived on the bank of Godāvarī, because it betrays the author's thorough acquaintance with that region.

Religion and Philosophy

Generally, the Purāṇas present a polytheistic creed. A considerable number of gods and goddesses have entered these treatises and settled there. We find Brahmā, Viṣṇu, Śiva, Indra, Yama, Sūrya, Agni, Varuṇa, Kubera and the rest being eulogized or worshipped ritualistically. An elaborate paraphernalia connected with their ritual is also ear-marked. Further, we witness the important role the tantra played in shaping the religious modes of the people in the Pauranic age.

A large portion of the present Purāṇa deals with the topics of religious nature. Chapter 104 narrates the legends of Viṣṇu's incarnations. Chs 105-106 take up the narrative of Yama and his hells. Ch. 108 deals with Dharma and the problem of rebirth. Ch 109 glorifies the gift of food. Chs 110-112 relate to Śrāddha (food-offering to the manes). Ch. 114 describes the duties of castes and stages of life (Varṇāśramadharma). Ch. 115 expounds Ethics. Chs 122-123 deal with prognostics.

The Brahma Purāṇa is predominantly Viṣṇuite. Though Brahmā is the chief speaker here and though the author of the Padma Purāṇa calls it rājasa (rajas being a quality assigned to

1. Br. P. 25. 43.
Sahyasya cottare yastu yatra Godāvarī nadī /
Pṛthivyām api kṛtsnāyāṁ saḥ pradeśo manoramaḥ //

Brahmā), this Purāṇa glorifies Viṣṇu predominantly. Viṣṇu incarnated in various forms: Matsya, Kūrma, Varāha, Nṛsiṁha, Vāmana, Paraśurāma, Rāma and Kṛṣṇa. Moreover, he is worshipped in different forms in different continents. In Bhadrāśva he is worshipped as Hayaśiras, in Ketumāla as Varāha, in Bhārata as Kūrma, in Kurupradeśa as Matsya and in the form Viśvarūpa everywhere.[1]

Not less in importance are the legends of Śiva including the immolation of Satī, destruction of Dakṣa's sacrifice, Śiva's marriage with Pārvatī, his sports on the Himālayas and ultimately his departure for mount Meru. The Purāṇa records one thousand eight names of Śiva.

Next to the legend of Śiva is the legend of Sun-god. The Purāṇa records one hundred and eight names of the solar deity, and illustrates his glory and origin. It refers to a Sūrya-kṣetra at Koṇārka and the holy place of Puri in Orissa.

But, in spite of the presence of multitude of gods, the trend is towards monotheism. The Purāṇa is a strong advocate of non sectarian religion where all gods stand on equal footing. It glorifies Ekāmra region sacred to Śiva and Puruṣottama kṣetra sacred to Viṣṇu. In the attempt to bring about integration of creeds in spite of their different forms, the Purāṇa follows liberal path, admitting no variation in the nature of essence that is present in all. To a sectarian, the three-eyed god Śiva may appear different from the four-armed Viṣṇu or the four-faced Brahmā, but in the ultimate review of this Purāṇa, there is no difference among Brahmā, Viṣṇu, Śiva or any other god, because one and the same energy inheres all.[2]

---

1. *Br. P.* 16. 57-58

   Bhadrāśve bhagavān Viṣṇur āste hayaśirā dvijāḥ /
   Vārāhaḥ Ketumāle tu bhārate Kūrmarūpadhṛk //
   Matsyarūpaśca Govindaḥ Kuruṣvāste sanātanaḥ /
   Viśvarūpeṇa sarvatra sarvaḥ sarveśvaro hariḥ //

2. Viṣṇu identifies himself with all gods :
   Br. P. 48. 4-6
   Śrībhagavān uvāca:

   Aham eva svayaṁ Brahmā ahaṁ Viṣṇuḥ Śivopyaham /
   Indrohaṁ Devarājaśca jagatsaṁyamano Yamaḥ //
   Pṛthvyādīni bhūtāni Tretāgnir hutabhuṅ nṛpa /
   Varuṇopām patiścāhaṁ Dharitrī ca mahīdharaḥ //

A unit of fourteen chapters (124-137) deals with some important aspects of philosophical nature. Though the ultimate end is the attainment of liberation, the means employed to that end consist in the knowledge of principles (*tattva-jñānam*) relating to Prakṛti and Puruṣa. The philosophy of this Purāṇa, as of other Purāṇas is generally derived from the concepts evolved and developed in the systems of Sāṁkhya and Yoga.

Yatkiñcid vāṅmayaṁ loke jagat sthāvara-jaṅgamam /
Carācaraṁ ca yad viśvaṁ madanyan nāsti kiñcana //

Br. P. 53. 14-15.

Ahaṁ Viṣṇurahain Brahmā Śakraścāpi dvijottama /
Ahaṁ Vaiśravaṇo rājā Yamaḥ Pretādhipas tathā //

Br. P. 53. 62-65.

Ahaṁ Śivas ca Somaś ca Kaśyapaś ca Prajāpatiḥ

Viṣṇu himself asks the Brahmin to raise a temple of Śiva in the Puruṣottama-kṣetra, for by that act he will be pleasing Viṣṇu himself, since the two (Viṣṇu and Śiva) are identical in essence though they are different in form.

Br. P. 53. 64-65

Śive saṁsthāpite vipra mama saṁsthāpanam bhavet
nāvayor antaraṁ kiñcid ekabhāvau dvidhākṛtau //
yo Rudraḥ sa svayaṁ Viṣṇur yo Viṣṇuḥ saḥ Maheśvaraḥ
ubhayor antaraṁ nāsti pavanākāśayor iva //

CHAPTER ONE

On the Origin of Devas and Asuras

1. After paying obeisance to Nārāyaṇa and also to Nara[1] the best among men and goddess Sarasvatī,[2] one should utter the Puranic lore.[3]

2. I make obeisance unto that eternal all-pervading, steadfast and pure entity named Puruṣottama from whom this entire illusory universe with all its extensive diversities is evolved, in whom it abides, in whom it gets ultimately dissolved[4] in the succeeding Kalpas and by meditating on whom, the sages attain eternal liberation without the tint of worldliness.

3. I make obeisance to Hari the delightful, spotless, omnipotent, attributeless, beyond the states of the manifest and unmanifest, devoid of worldliness, attainable by meditation alone, omnipresent and the destroyer of the cycle of birth and the unageing bestower of liberation, whom the learned at the time of samādhi meditate upon, who is pure space-like, abode of eternal bliss and the gracious lord, devoid of all dirt and attributes. He is devoid of manifoldness. He is beyond the manifest and unmanifest. He is the overlord, comprehensible through meditation alone. He is the cause of annihilation of worldly existence and unageing.

---

1. *Nara-Nārāyaṇa*:—Later epics and kāvyas speak of Nara as Arjuna and Nārāyaṇa as Kṛṣṇa. According to Mbh. Śānti Parva (Ch. 384) Nara and Narāyaṇa were the two incarnations of Mahāviṣṇu. According to another Tradition Nara and Nārāyaṇa were the two sages who did penance for thousands of years in the Badarikāśrama in the Himālayas. (P. Ency. p. 532).

2. *Sarasvatī*: The goddess of Speech and Learning (Brahma P. Ch. 43).

3. The verse is common to the Purāṇas. Originally it belonged to the Mahābhārata, since the term Jaya mentioned in the verse was applied to the Mahābhārata which originally consisted of eight thousand and eight hundred verses (P.E. under *Jaya*).

4. This is an old concept. But, later on, a single entity—Nārāyaṇa—was conceived as consisting of three forms: Brahmā, Viṣṇu and Śiva, representing the three qualities—Rajas, Sattva and Tamas respectively. The three are assigned separately the work of creation, existence and dissolution.

4-12. In the very holy, charming and extremely sacred Naimiṣa[1] forest, a great sacrifice lasting for twelve years was performed by the sages. The forest abounded in flowers of diverse kinds and trees such as Sāla, Karṇikāra,Panasa, Dhava, Khadira, Āmra, Jambū, Kapittha, Nyagrodha, Devadāru, Aśvattha, Pārijāta, Candana, Arjuna, Campaka and others. Many kinds of birds and beasts lived there. It abounded in Aguru, Pāṭala, Bakula, Sapta-Parṇa, Punnāga, Nāgakesara, Sāla, Tamāla, Nārikela and Arjuna. It was beautified by many trees, Campaka and others embellished by variety of water-reservoirs such as pools and holy lakes. It abounded in people of various castes—Brahmins, Kṣatriyas, Vaiśyas, Śūdras, people of all stages of life, students, householders, forest-dwellers and ascetics. It was richly endowed with birds of various sorts, cows and cattle wealth and storage of barley wheat, chick peas, pulses, beans, sesamum and sugarcane and other plants. It was adorned by stocks of paddy and other fresh vegetables. There in that forest the bright, sacred fire was kindled and the sages performed a sacrifice extending for twelve years. Thus the sages and other brahmins congregated there.

13-14. The brahmin guests were suitably welcomed and honoured by the hosts along with the duly seated priests. In the meanwhile there arrived Romaharṣaṇa,[2] the intelligent Sūta. On seeing him the excellent sages were extremely delighted and they honoured him in a fitting manner.

15. He too made obeisance to them and occupied a respectable seat. The brahmins conversed with Sūta for some time.

16. At the end of preliminary conversation, the sponsors of

---

1. *Naimiṣa or Naimiśa*, mod. Nimsar: It is situated on the left bank of Gomatī in the Sitapur district, U. P. The place is so called because the rim of the revolving wheel of Virtue was shattered here and virtue had to make a permanent abode in this region (*Vāyu* 2.7). Or the place is so called because here an army of Asuras was destroyed by Sage Gauramukha in a twinkling of eye (Varāha P.). According to Matsya, it was situated at the confluence of Gomatī and Gaṅgā. The place was sacred in Kṛta age, as Puṣkara in Tretā, Kurukṣetra in Dvāpara and Gaṅgā in Kali. Kāṭhaka Saṁhitā (10.6), Kauśitaki Brāhmaṇa (26.5), Chāndogya Upaniṣad (1.2.13) refer to it. The Rāmāyaṇa (7.91) states that Rāma performed Aśvamedha here.

2. *Romaharṣaṇa* or *Lomaharṣaṇa*: a famous disciple of Vyāsa to whom Vyāsa gave the collection of Purāṇas. Romaharṣaṇa had six disciples: Sumati, Agnivarcas, Mitrāyus, Śāṁśapāyana, Akṛtavraṇa and Sāvarṇi.

the sacrifice accompanied by the priests and other honoured guests who had congregated there wanted to clear their doubts by means of questions put to him.

The Sages said:

17. O excellent one, you are well-versed in Purāṇas, Āgamas and other holy texts together with traditional tales. You are aware of the origin and exploits of Devas and Daityas.

18. There is nothing unknown to you in the Vedas, Scriptures, Bhārata,[1] Purāṇa[2] and treatises on salvation. O highly intelligent one, you are omniscient.

19-21. Sūta, we desire to know how this entire visible world consisting of the mobile and immobile beings originated at the outset, along with Devas, Asuras, Gandharvas, Yakṣas, Rākṣasas and Serpents. Where did it get merged ? Where will it get dissolved ?

Lomaharṣaṇa said:

22-30. Obeisance to Viṣṇu, the universal Soul who is immutable, mysterious, of unchanging form and all-conquering. Obeisance to Hiraṇyagarbha[3], Hari and Śaṅkara Vāsudeva the protector who is the agent of creation, sustenance and destruction. Obeisance to Viṣṇu who has unitary and manifold forms. Obeisance to the deity who is gross as well as subtle. Obeisance to

---

The Vāyu P. (1.1.3) gives the derivation of his name as follows:

लोमानि हर्षयाञ्चक्रे श्रोतॄणां यत्सुभाषितैः ।
कर्मणा प्रथितस्तेन लोकेऽस्मिल्लोमहर्षणः ॥

1. *Bhārata*: The original name of the Mahābhārata was Jaya composed by Vyāsa. It consisted of eight thousand and eight hundred verses. Vaiśampāyana added fifteen thousand two hundred stanzas and the book was named Bhārata. When Sūta recited this book to the hermits in the Naimiṣa forest, the book had one lakh of stanzas. Hence, it was called Mahābhārata.

2. *Purāṇa*: Originally the word was used collectively for the sacred treatises which described Creation, Re-creation, Genealogies of Kings, Ages of Manus, History of rulers and distinguished persons. Later on, with the addition of more matter, it became an Encyclopaedia of General knowledge related to different subjects, divided and subdivided into Purāṇas and Upa-Purāṇas. For details see *Epics and Purāṇas of India*: Pusalkar and Majumdar.

3. *Hiraṇyagarbha*: Brahmā was born from the golden-egg formed out of the seed deposited in the waters—Manu 1.9. The word is often used in the Veda.

Viṣṇu who becomes manifest and unmanifest and who is the cause of liberation. Obeisance to Viṣṇu the Supreme Soul who is at the root of creation, maintenance and destruction of the universe and who is identical with the universe. I bow unto Acyuta, Puruṣottama who is the support of this great as well as small world (the macrocosm and microcosm). He is factually devoid of impurity. He has the form of perfect knowledge. He is stationed in the form of this Visual world in our illusory vision. I bow to Viṣṇu who consumes the universe, who is the lord of creation and sustenance, who is omniscient, lord of the universe, the birthless and deathless, immutable, and the primordial, subtle overlord of the universe. I bow to Brahmā and others. I bow to my lord preceptor, the son of Parāśara[1] and the knower of the essence of the import of all Śāstras and the Purāṇas. He is the master of the Vedas and Vedāṅgas.[2] After bowing down to my lord preceptor I shall recount the Purāṇa which is on a par with the Vedas.

31. I shall mention in the same manner as was mentioned by the lotus-born lord Brahmā[3] formerly on being asked by Dakṣa and other excellent sages.

32. Listen to the wonderful story that I narrate to you now and which is pregnant with meaning. It provides with auxiliary to those mentioned in the Vedas. I shall tell you the story that liberates people from sins.

33. He who listens to this story frequently, he who perpetually retains this in memory shall perpetuate his family and be honoured in the heavenly region.

---

1. *Parāśara*, father of Vyāsa from Satyavatī, the fisherman's daughter with whom he had an intercourse without marriage. This girl, later on, married Śantanu, king of Hastināpur.

2. *Vedāṅgas*: Certain classes of works regarded as auxiliary to the Vedas and designed to aid in the correct pronunciation and interpretation of the text and the right employment of mantras in ceremonials. The Vedāṅgas are six (1) *Śikṣā*—the science of proper articulation and pronunciation, (2) *Chandas*-the science of prosody, (3) Vyākaraṇa—grammar, (4) *Nirukta*—etymological explanation of difficult Vedic Words, (5) *Jyotiṣa*—astronomy and (6) Kalpa—ritual or ceremonial.

3 *Lotus-born Brahmā*: According to Puranic tradition, there grew up a lotus in the navel of Viṣṇu and in that lotus Brahmā took his form. Seated in the lotus, Brahmā performed penance. Thereafter he began the work of creation. He is called Padmāsana, Padmabhū etc. therefore.

34. Pradhāna is the eternal unmanifest cause which is of the nature of sat (existent) and asat (non-existent). Puruṣa, the lord, evolved the universe out of it.

35. O excellent sages, know that he is Brahmā of unmeasured refulgence. He is the creator of all living beings. He is Nārāyaṇa the greatest Being.

36. Cosmic Ego (Ahaṁkāra) was born of Mahat (great principle) : from Mahat, Bhūtas (Elements) were born. Varieties of living beings were born of the Elements. Thus is the eternal creation.

37. It is being glorified with details of all aspects in accordance with my intelligence and in the manner I have heard. Now listen to it. It shall enhance the reputation of all of you.

38-40. The glory of persons who had performed meritorious deeds and whose renown is permanent is proclaimed herein.

The Self-born lord who was desirous of creating varieties of subjects from the unmanifest Pradhāna created waters[1] alone at the outset. He instilled vigour in them. The waters are called Nāras (born of Nara—man); waters are the progeny of Nara.[2] At the outset, they were his place of resort. Hence he is remembered as Nārāyaṇa. A gold-wombed Egg took shape and floated on the waters.

41-42. Brahmā himself was born there. We have heard that he is self-born. The gold-coloured lord stayed there for a year and then split the Egg into two—heaven and Earth. In the middle of these two halves the Lord created firmament.

43-45. He held the Earth floating on the waters. He created ten quarters, as well as mind, speech, love, anger and pleasure.

Desirous of evolving creation befitting these, he created Prajā-

---

1. *Manu.* 1.8 *apa eva sasarjādau, tāsu vīryam avākṣipat.* "Waters are the first creation of the Self-existent. He laid seed in them.". The account of creation (sarga) as described here is formed in Manusmṛti Ch.I.

2. Cp. Manu 1.10.

आपो नारा इति प्रोक्ता आपो वै नरसूनवः ।
ता यदस्यायनं पूर्वं तेन नारायणः स्मृतः ॥

For the third Pāda, this Purāṇa reads:

अयनं तस्य ताः पूर्वं

patis[1] (Lords of subjects) viz. Marīci, Atri, Aṅgiras, Pulastya, Pulaha, Kratu and Vasiṣṭha. Thus the lord of great refulgence created seven mental sons.[2] In the Purāṇas these are known as the seven Brahmās.

46. Subsequent to the seven sons of Brahmā who were identical with Nārāyaṇa, Brahmā created Rudra out of his fury.

47. He created the divine lord Sanatkumāra who was the eldest of all his previous sons. O brahmins, the subjects and Rudras were born of these seven.

48-50. Skanda and Sanatkumāra stayed there condensing their brilliance. Seven great families of divine nature comprising the groups of Devas were born of seven Brahmās. They had progeny and they performed holy rites. The families were adorned by great sages. Brahmā created lightning, thunder, clouds, saffron-coloured rainbows, birds and Parjanya (lord of clouds) at the outset. He composed Ṛks, Yajus and Sāman for conducting sacrifices.

51. We have heard that he created Sādhyas and other Devas. Living beings high and low were born of his limbs.

52-53. Even when Prajāpati had created such an extensive horde of progeny, the created subjects did not multiply. Then he split his body into two halves. One half became a man and the other half a woman. The man begot of the woman different kinds of subjects.

54. With his grandeur he pervaded heaven and Earth and stored by Viṣṇu created Virāṭ (an immense being) and Virāṭ created Puruṣa.

55. Know that Manu was that Puruṣa. The Manvantara the ruling period of Manu is the second one of Manu, the mental son of Brahmā.

---

1. *Prajāpati-s*: lords of subjects. The word is as old as the Veda. Formerly, there were ten Prajāpatis. But as the number of subjects increased, eleven more were added to this number. Thus there were twentyone Prajāpatis whose functions were to facilitate creation. They were *Brahmā, Rudra, Manu, Dakṣa, Bhṛgu, Dharma, Tapa, Yama, Marīci, Aṅgiras, Atri, Pulastya, Pulaha, Kratu, Vasiṣṭha, Parameṣṭhi, Sūrya, Candra, Kardama, Krodha, and Vikrīta.*

2. *Seven Brahmās*—seven mental sons of Brahmā. Each Manvantara has different saptarṣis. The Saptarṣis of the present Vaivasvata Manvantara, consist of Marīci, Aṅgiras, Atri, Pulastya, Vasiṣṭha, Pulaha and Kratu.

56. That Vairāja (Son of Virāṭ) Puruṣa, lord of creation of the subjects, was the lord who created. The subjects created during Nārāyaṇa's creation as well as Manu's were not born of the womb.

57. On hearing this account of creation at the outset, a man becomes longlived, well-renowned and blessed with progeny. He will obtain his desired goal.

58. Āpava—that Puruṣa and Prajāpatī—was desirous of creating subjects. He obtained Śatarūpā,[1] an Ayonija lady as his wife.

59. With his grandeur, Āpava pervaded heaven and stood by. Then, O excellent sages, Śatarūpā was delivered of her progeny righteously.

60. She performed a severe penance for ten thousand years and obtained as her husband that Puruṣa of bright penance.

61. O brahmins, that Puruṣa is called Svāyambhuva Manu (Manu born of the selfborn lord). His Manvantara consisted of seventyone cycles of Yugas.

62-64. Śatarūpā bore to Vairāja Puruṣa the heroic sons Priyavrata and Uttānapāda. After the heroic sons (a daughter) Kāmyā was born. O excellent sages, Kāmyā (was the wife) of Kardama Prajāpati. The sons of Kāmyā were four viz. Samrāṭ, Kukṣi, Virāṭ and Prabhu. Prajāpati Atri adopted Uttānapāda as his son. Sūnṛtā bore four sons to Uttānapāda.

65. The charming daughter of Dharma is known as Sūnṛtā. She was born as a result of horse sacrifice. She was the illustrious mother of Dhruva.

66. Prajāpati Uttānapāda begot four sons of Sūnṛtā viz. Dhruva, Kīrtimān, Āyuṣmān and Vasu.

67. O brahmins, the highly blessed Dhruva, seeking very great fame, performed penance for three thousand divine years.

68. Prajāpati Brahmā being delighted gave him a stable abode, on par with his own in front of seven sages.

69. On observing his prestige and greatness flourishing, formerly Uśanas the preceptor of Devas and Asuras sang this Verse:

1. *Śatarūpā*—wife of Svāyambhuva Manu herein called Āpava. He took his sister Śatarūpā as his wife. The couple had two sons: Priyavrata and Uttānapāda and two daughters: Prasūti and Ākūti. Prasūti was married to Dakṣa Prajāpati and Ākūti to Ruci Prajāpati.

70. Wonderful is the power of his penance. Wonderful is his learning. Wonderful indeed is Dhruva[1] whom the seven sages have kept ahead of themselves.

71. Śambhu bore to Dhruva (two sons) viz. Śliṣṭi and Bhavya. Succhāyā bore five noble sons to Śliṣṭi.

72. They were Ripu, Purañjaya, Putra, Vṛkala and Vṛkatejas. Bṛhatī bore to Ripu the son Cākṣuṣa who had an all round splendour.

73. He begot Cākṣusa Manu of Puṣkariṇī, Vairiṇī the daughter of Araṇya the Prajāpati of great soul.

74. O leading sages, ten sons of great prowess were born to Manu and Naḍvalā the daughter of Prajāpati Vairāja.

75-76. The first nine were Kutsa, Puru, Śatadyumna, Tapasvin, Satyavāk, Kavi, Agniṣṭubh, Atirātra and Sudyumna. The tenth was Abhimanyu. These sons of great prowess were born of Naḍvalā. Āgneyī bore six sons of great lustre to Puru.

77. They were Aṅga, Sumanas, Khyāti, Kratu, Aṅgiras and Gaya. Sunīthā bore to Aṅga a single son Vena.

78. There was a great uproar due to the misdemeanour of Vena. For procreating progeny the sages churned his right hand.

79-81. A mighty king was born when his hand was churned. On seeing him the sages declared: "This king will make his subjects delighted. His refulgence is great. He will earn great renown." He was born equipped with a bow and a coat of mail. He was as lustrous as the burning fire: Pṛthu, the son of Vena protected this Earth. He was the oldest of Kṣatriyas. He was the first and foremost of those whose coronations were performed with a Rājasūya[2] sacrifice. He was the overlord of the Earth.

82-85. The intelligent Sūta and Magadha were born of being desirous of securing the means of subsistence for his subjects, the king (Pṛthu) milked this Earth in the form of a cow. O excellent sages. The king milked the cow alongwith Devas, sages, Pitṛs, Dānavas, Gandharvas, Apsaras, serpents, Puṇyajanas, creepers etc. On being milked by them the Earth gave

1. *Dhruva*—Svāyambhuva Manu, son of Brahmā, had two sons: Priyavrata and Uttānapāda. Uttānapāda had two wives: Suruci and Sunīti. Suruci gave birth to Uttama and Sunīti to Dhruva.

2. *Rājasūya sacrifice*—performed at the coronation of a king. MBh. II describes the Rājasūya sacrifice of king Yudhiṣṭhira in detail.

them as much milk as could fill up their vessels. They sustained their lives thereby. At the end of sacrifice, two righteous sons were born to Pṛthu viz Antardhi and Pātin.

86-87. Śikhaṇḍinī bore Havirdhāna to Antardhāna (i.e. Antardhi). Dhiṣaṇā, the daughter of Agni, bore six sons to Havirdhāna viz Prācīnabarhiṣ, Śukra, Gaya, Kṛṣṇa, Vraja and Ajina. Lord Prācīnabarhiṣ was a great Prajāpati.

88-91. After Havirdhāna, excellent sages, it was lord Prācīnabarhiṣ by whom the subjects moving about on the Earth were brought up and made to flourish. After concluding the rigorous penance on the shore (of the ocean), the king married Savarṇā the daughter of the ocean. Savarṇā, the daughter of the ocean, bore ten sons to Prācīnabarhiṣ. They were called Pracetas. They were well-versed in archery. Performing holy rites jointly they practiced a great penance for ten thousand years lying submerged under the waters of the ocean.

92-95. While the Pracetas were performing penance, the Earth was left unguarded. Hence the trees overgrew the Earth and enveloped it. Thereby, the destruction of subjects set in. The trees grew so dense that the wind was unable to blow. For ten thousand years the subjects were unable even to stir. All the Pracetas who were performing penance heard about it. They became furious and generated wind and fire through their mouths. The wind uprooted the trees and desiccated them. The terrible fire burned them. Thus the trees were destroyed.

96. On knowing that the trees were being destroyed and that only a few of them remained, Soma approached the Prajāpatis and said:

97. O kings, O son of Prācīnabarhiṣ, restrain your wrath. The Earth has been denuded of trees. May your fury and fire be subdued.

98-99. This girl of excellent complexion is the jewel of the forest. She had been held by me in my womb as I was aware of the future. This daughter of the forest is Māriṣā by name. O highly blessed ones, may she be your wife. May she raise the lunar race. For this purpose alone she has been created.

100. With half the splendour pertaining to you and with half of my splendour, the learned Prajāpati named Dakṣa will be born of her.

101. He is on par with Agni. He will make this Earth and the subjects flourish once again. He will develop this Earth, practically burned out by the fiery splendour pertaining to you.

102. Then, at the instance of Soma, the ascetics restrained their fury towards the trees and accepted Māriṣā as their lawfully wedded wife.

103. O brahmins, with a part of Soma, Dakṣa Prajāpati of great splendour was born of Māriṣā and the ten Pracetas.

104. After mentally creating the immobile and mobile beings, the bipeds and the quadrupeds, Dakṣa created women.

105. Lord Dakṣa gave ten of his daughters to Dharma, thirteen to Kaśyapa, the remaining (twentyseven) named after twentyseven constellations to king Soma.

106. Devas, birds, cows, serpents, Daityas, Dānavas, Gandharvas, Apsaras and other classes of people were born of them.

107. O leading brahmins, it was only after this that the procreation by means of sexual intercourse began. The subjects before are said to be born of mental conception, sight or touch.

The Sages said:

108. The origin of Devas, Dānavas, Gandharvas, serpents, Rākṣasas, as well as that of Dakṣa the great soul has been heard by us.

109-110. Indeed, Dakṣa of auspicious rites was born of the right thumb of Brahmā. His wife was born of the left thumb. How could Dakṣa of great penance be born of Pracetas ? O Sūta, please clarify our doubt. How did the grandson of Soma attain the status of his father-in-law ?

Lomaharṣaṇa said :

111. O brahmins, origin and annihilation do occur continuously among living beings. Sages and other learned people are not deluded in this respect.

112. Dakṣas and other beings are born in every Yuga. They are annihilated afterwards. A learned man does not become deluded thereby.

113. O excellent brahmins, formerly there was neither seniority nor juniorship (conditioned by time). Penance alone was the important factor. Power was the cause (of this consideration)

114. He who understands this side-creation of Dakṣa comprising the mobile and immobile beings, shall be blessed with progeny. He will live the full span of life. He is honoured in the heavenly world.

The Sages said:

115. O Lomaharṣaṇa recount in details the origin of Devas, Dānavas, Gandharvas, Rākṣasas and serpents.

Lomaharṣaṇa said:

116. Formerly, Prajāpati Dakṣa was directed by the self-born lord (who said) "create subjects." O brahmins now listen how he created them.

117. The Prajāpati created living beings mentally. He created sages, Gandharvas, Asuras, Yakṣas and Rākṣasas.

118-119. O brahmins, when his mental progeny did not multiply, the virtuous Prajāpati began to ponder over ways and means of increasing subjects. He became desirous of creating variety subjects by the process of sexual intercourse. He took Asikni the daughter of Prajāpati Vīraṇa as his wife. She was endowed with the power of penance. She, the great was capable of sustaining the worlds.

120-127. Prajāpati Dakṣa the great begot five thousand sons of Asikni the daughter of Vīraṇa. On seeing those highly blessed sons desirous of increasing the subjects, the celestial sage Nārada of sweet tongue spoke to them certain words which brought their destruction and invited a curse for himself (?). Formerly Sage Kaśyapa was afraid of Dakṣa's curse, hence he procreated the more excellent son (Nārada) in the daughter of Dakṣa. This Nārada was the son of Brahmā formerly. Like his father Brahmā, Dakṣa again created Nārada in his wife Asikni the daughter of Vīraṇa. Dakṣa's sons Haryaśvas were completely destroyed by Brahmā. Dakṣa of unmeasured exploits attempted to destroy Brahmā. Keeping the Brahmanical sages ahead he was requested by the latter not to be angry. Dakṣa then made a compromise with Brahmā. "May Nārada be born of my daughter as your son." Then Dakṣa gave his beloved daughter to Brahmā. Fearful of being cursed again (?) Sage Nārada was born of her.

The Sages said:

128. O lord, how were the sons of Prajāpati destroyed by Nārada the great sage ? We wish to hear all about it factually.

Lomaharṣaṇa said:

129. Haryaśvas, the extremely powerful sons of Dakṣa arrived (at a spot near the sea) desirous of making the subjects multiply: Nārada spoke to them.

130-131. "Alas, all of you are very puerile. You do not know the magnitude and extent of this Earth. Still, O sons of Pracetas you are desirous of creating subjects. But how will you create the subjects within it, above it and below it? On hearing his words they wondered in all directions.

132-134. They have not returned so far like rivers merging into the sea. When Haryaśvas vanished, lord Dakṣa, son of Pracetas procreated a thousand sons in the daughter of Vīraṇa. They were known as Śabalāśvas. They were also desirous of multiplying the subjects, Nārada spoke to them as he had spoken to Haryaśvas. They told one another.

135. The great sage said pertinently: let us trace out our brothers. When we have found them out and ascertained the extent of the Earth, we shall easily create the subjects."

136. They too went in all directions along the same path. Till today they have not returned like rivers flowing into oceans.

137. Ever since then, O brahmins, a brother who goes in search of a lost brother perishes himself. Thus a wise brother should not go in search of his lost brother.

138. On realising that they too had perished Prajāpati Dakṣa procreated sixty daughters in the daughters of Vīraṇa. This we have heard.

139. O brahmins Kaśyapa, lord Soma, Dharma and other sages took them as their wives.

140-141. He gave ten daughters to Dharma, thirteen to Kaśyapa, twentyseven to Soma, four to Ariṣṭanemi, two to Bahuputra, two to Aṅgiras and two to Kṛśāśva. Now listen to their names.

142-146. The ten wives of Dharma were Arundhatī, Vasu, Yamī, Lambā, Bālā, Marutvatī, Saṅkalpā, Muhūrtā, Sādhyā and Viśvā. O brahmins, understand the children born of these.

Viśvedevas were born of Viśvā. Sādhyā gave birth to Sādhyas, Marutvats were born of Marutvatī. Vasus were the sons of Vasu, Bhānus were the sons of Bhānu, Muhūrtas were born of Muhūrtā, Ghoṣa was the son of Lambā. Nāgavīthī was the daughter of Yamī; objects of the Earth were born of Arundhatī. Saṁkalpa, the soul of the universe was born of Saṅkalpā; Vṛṣala was born of Nāgavīthī the daughter of Yamī.

147. Dakṣa, the son of Pracetas, gave his daughter in marriage to Soma: All those are named after constellations. They are glorified in the Astral Science.

148. Those others who are known as Devas going ahead of luminaries are the eight Vasus. I shall mention them in detail.

149. Āpa, Dhruva, Soma, Dhava, (or Dhruva), Anila, Anala, Pratyūṣa and Prabhāsa are the names of Vasus.

150. Āpa's sons were Vaitaṇḍya, Śrama, Srānta and Muni. Dhruva's son was Kāla who reckons time in the world.

151. Soma's son was Varcas whereby people become refulgent. Draviṇa and Hutahavyavāha were the sons of Dhava. Manoharā's sons were Śiśira, Prāṇa and Ramaṇa.

152. Śivā was the wife of Anila. Her son was Manojava. Anila had two sons: Manojava and Avijñātagati.

153. Agni's son Kumāra was enveloped by splendour in the cluster of Śara reeds. His sons were Śākha, Viśākha and Naigameya.

154. He was the adopted son of Kṛttikās.[1] Hence he was called Kārttikeya. They say that the sage Devala was the son of Pratyūṣa.

155-156. Devala had two sons endowed with knowledge and forbearance. Bṛhaspati's sister Yogasiddhā was excellent lady who expounding the Brahman wandered over the entire world. She was detached at first, but later on she became the wife of Prabhāsa the eighth among the Vasus.

157. The highly blessed Prajāpati Viśvakarman was born

1. When Subrahmaṇya was born, Devas deputed six mothers to breast-feed him and they were called Kṛttikās. Certain Purāṇas hold that Subrahmaṇya had six faces and he was fed on six breasts at the same time. Six mothers were deputed to feed him, as he was born with six faces. Again according to certain Purāṇas it was Pārvatī who deputed the Kṛttikās. The child came to be known as Kārttikeya as it was fed by Kṛttikās.

of her. He was a carpenter of Devas and the architect of thousands of arts and crafts.

158. He was the maker of all ornaments and the most excellent among the artisans. It was he who made the aerial chariots for Devas.

159. Human beings too subsist on the works of art of that great architect.

Surabhi bore eleven Rudras to Kaśyapa.

160-162. That chaste lady sanctified by her penance (gave them birth) by the grace of Mahādeva.

They were Ajaikapāda, Ahirbudhnya, Tvaṣṭṛ, Rudra the powerful, Hara Bahurūpa, Tryambaka, Aparājita, Vṛṣākapi, Śambhu, Kapardī Raivata, Mṛgavyādha, Śarva and Kapālin O excellent brahmins, these are the eleven (?) well-known Rudras[1] lords of the universe.

163. A century of these Rudras of unmeasured strength has been mentioned in the Purāṇas. O leading sages, the entire universe consisting of the mobile and immobile beings is pervaded by them.

164-165. O leading brahmins, now listen to the names of the wives of Prajāpati Kaśyapa. They are Aditi, Diti, Danu, Ariṣṭā, Surasā, Khasā, Surabhi, Vinatā, Tāmrā, Krodhavaśā, Irā, Kadrū and Muni. O brahmins, know the children born of them.

166-169. In the previous Manvantara there were twelve magnificent and excellent Devas named Tuṣitas. When the Vaivasvata Manvantara was imminent they told one another thus—"During the Manvantara of Cākṣuṣa Manu of great fame, O Devas, all of you shall gather together for the welfare of the world. Come quickly ye all and enter the womb of Aditi. We shall be born then. It will be to our welfare and advantage" After saying thus they of prolific refulgence were born of Aditi and Kaśyapa in the Cākṣuṣa Manvantara.

170-171. Viṣṇu and Śakra were born again then. The following are the twelve Ādityas: Aryaman, Dhātṛ, Tvaṣṭṛ,

---

1. *Rudras* : According to this Purāṇa, eleven Rudras were born to Kaśyapa from Surabhi. Other Purāṇas give different origins and names of Rudras. The names of Rudras given there are the synonyms of lord Śiva.

Pūṣan, Vivasvan, Savitṛ, Mitra, Varuṇa, Aṁśa and Bhaga of great splendour alongwith Viṣṇu and Śakra.

172. In the Cākṣuṣa Manvantara they were known as Tuṣitas. In the Vaivasvata Manvantara they are called Āditya.

173. Brilliant children of unmeasured splendour were born of those ladies of holy rites who had been mentioned as the twenty-seven wives of Soma.

174-175. The wives of Ariṣṭanemi had sixteen children. The four Vidyuts were the sons of Bahuputra the wise sage. In the previous Cākṣuṣa Manvantara Ṛks were honoured by the brahmin sages. Devapraharaṇas are known as the children of Kṛśāśva, the celestial sage.

176. These are born again at the end of a thousand cycles of four Yugas, these are the groups of Devas. Thirty-three of them are born of Kāma.

177-178. O brahmins, annihilation and origin are said to befall them too. Just as the sun rises and sets in the firmament so also the groups of Devas in every Yuga.

We have heard that two sons were born to Diti.

179-180. They were Hiraṇyakaśipu and Hiraṇyākṣa. A daughter named Siṁhikā was also born to her. She became the wife of Vipracitti. Her sons of great strength are known as Saiṁhikeyas. Hiraṇyakaśipu had four sons of well reputed prowess.

181. They were Hrāda, Anuhrāda, Prahrāda and Saṁhrāda. Hrāda was the son of Hrada.

182. Hrada's sons were Māyāvī, Śiva and Kāla. Virocana was the son of Prahrāda, Bali was the son of Virocana.

183-184. O ascetics, Bali had hundred sons of whom Bāṇa was the eldest. (The most important of them are) Kumbha-Nābha, Gardabhākṣa, Dhṛtarāṣṭra, Sūrya, Candramas, Indra-tāpana, and Kukṣi. Bāṇa was the eldest and the strongest amongst them. He was a devotee of Śiva.

185. In a former Kalpa, Bāṇa propitiated lord Śiva and begged for this boon "I shall sport about at your side."

186-187. Hiraṇyākṣa had five sons. They were both scholars and warriors. They were—Bharbhara, Śakuni, Bhūta, Santapana, Mahānābha of great exploits and Kālanābha.

Danu had a hundred sons of energetic exploits. They were

ascetics of great prowess. I shall enumerate the most important among them.

188-192. They are Dvimūrdhā, Śaṅkukarṇa, Hayaśiras, Ayomukha, Śambara, Kapila, Vāmana, Mārīci, Maghavan, Ilvala, Śṛmaṇa, Vikṣobhaṇa, Ketu, Ketuvīrya, Śatahrada, Indrajit, Sarvajit, Vajranābha, Ekacakra, Mahābāhu, Tāraka of great strength, Vaiśvānara, Puloman, Vidrāvaṇa Mahāśiras, Svar-bhānu, Vṛṣaparva, Vipracitti of great virility. These sons of Danu were begotten by Kaśyapa.

193-194. Vipracitti was the chief among Dānavas of great strength. O excellent brahmins, it is not possible to enumerate their children because they are too numerous. The sons and grandsons were also too many to mention. Prabhā was the daughter of Svarbhānu, Śacī was the daughter of Puloman.

195. Upadānavī was the daughter of Hayaśiras, Śarmiṣṭhā was the daughter of Vṛṣaparvan, Puloman and Kālakā were the two daughters of Vaiśvānara.

196-198. They were the wives of Marīci. They had great strength and they bore many children. They had sixty thousand sons who delighted Dānavas. Marīci who performed a very great penance, procreated another fourteen hundred sons who stayed in the city of Hiraṇyapura. The Dānavas named Paulomas (Sons of Pulomā) and Kālakeyas (Sons of Kālakā) were very terrible. Vipracitti's sons were born of Siṁhikā. Due to the admixture of Daityas and Dānavas they became valorous and powerful.

199-201. Thirteen very powerful Saiṁhikeyas were known as Vaṁśya, Śalya, Nala, Bala, Vātāpi, Namuci, Ilvala, Sṛmaṇa, Añjika, Naraka, Kālanābha, Saramāna and the powerful Svarakalpa.

Mūṣaka and Huṇḍa were the sons of Hrada.

202. Mārīca the son of Sunda was born of Tāḍakā. These are the excellent Dānavas who made the race of Danu flourish.

203-204. Their sons and grandsons were hundreds and thousands. The Nivātakavacas were born in the family of Daitya Saṁhrāda who had purified his soul by observing penance. The highly blessed Vaidyutas are reputed to have been born to Tāmrā. They had three crores of sons and they resided in Maṇivatī.[1]

1. *Maṇivatī*—The capital of Vidyādharas, a group of semi-gods who wear garlands.

205-209. It was difficult for Devas to kill them. They were struck down by Arjuna (the Pāṇḍava.)

(Tāmrā's daughters were) Krauñcī, Śyenī, Bhāsī, Sugrīvī, Śuci and Gṛdhrī. Krauñcī gave birth to owls and crows, Śyenī to hawks and falcons, Bhāsī to Bhāsas (vultures, cocks), Gṛdhrī to Gṛdhras (vultures), Śuci to aquatic birds, Sugrīvī to horses, camels and donkeys. Thus listen to the race of Tāmrā.

Vinatā had two sons—Garuḍa and Aruṇa. Garuḍa is the most excellent among the flying birds. He is very terrible in his activities.

Surasā's children were a thousand serpents of unmeasured prowess and many heads. O brahmins, they move about in the firmament and they are noble souls. The sons of Kadrū were very strong and had unmeasured strength and prowess. They were one thousand in number.

210-213. The multiheaded Nāgas of mighty valour were born. They were under the control of Garuḍa. The most important of these were:

Śeṣa, Vāsuki, Takṣaka, Airāvata, Mahāpadma, Kambala, Aśvatara, Elāpatra, Śaṅkha, Karkoṭaka, Dhanañjaya, Mahānīla, Mahākarṇa, Dhṛtarāṣṭra, Balāhaka, Kuhara, Puṣpadaṁṣṭra, Durmukha, Sumukha, Śaṅkha, Śaṅkhapāla, Kapila, Vāmana, Nahuṣa, Śaṅkharoman, Maṇi and others.

214. Their sons and grandsons were in hundreds and thousands. There were fourteen thousand cruel snakes which live on air.

215. O brahmins, there is a group called Krodhavaśa. These have terrible fangs. The birds on land are infinite. They are the progeny of Earth.

216. Surabhi gave birth to cows and buffaloes, Irā gave birth to trees, creepers, plants and species of grass all round.

217-218. Khaśā gave birth to Yakṣas and Rākṣasas, Muni gave birth to Apsaras (celestial damsels); Ariṣṭā gave birth to Gandharvas of immense prowess and unmeasured energy. Thus these descendants of Kaśyapa consisting of mobile and immobile beings have been related. Their sons and grandsons are in hundreds and thousands.

219-223. O brahmins, this creation existed in the Svārociṣa Manvantara; what follows occurred in the Vaivasvata Manvantara. Brahmā commenced a big and extensive sacrifice pertaining to Varuṇa. Listen to the creation of subjects in the course of sacrifice whom Brahmā himself had created as his sons from his mind in the previous Kalpa.

O brahmins, then ensued the mutual animosity between Devas and Dānavas in which Diti lost all her sons. She propitiated Kaśyapa with great devotion; duly honoured and served by her, Kaśyapa was highly pleased. He permitted her to ask for a boon. She requested him for a son of unmeasured prowess who would be capable of killing Indra.

224-225. On being requested thus, Kaśyapa of great austerity granted her boon. After granting the boon Kaśyapa spoke to her—"Your son will kill Indra if you retain the foetus for a hundred autumns maintaining cleanliness and performing rites."

226. O excellent sages, "So shall it be" said that gentle lady with devotion (to her lord) of great austerity. Maintaining cleanliness she conceived.

227-228. After impregnating Diti Kaśyapa returned. He desired for an excellent group of Devas of unmeasured prowess. After withdrawing his invincible splendour that could not be destroyed even by the immortal beings he went to a mountain resolving to perform penance and holy rites.

229-231. The chestiser of Pāka[1] stood waiting for a loophole to gain entry within her. The unswerving Indra saw a loophole when the century of years nearly came to a close. Without washing her feet Diti went to bed and slept. Indra entered her belly. Armed with his thunderbolt he cut the foetus into seven parts. On being split by the thunderbolt the foetus groaned.

232-233. "Mā rodīḥ" (Do not cry) said Indra to the child. It split into seven parts. The infuriated Indra, the suppressor of enemies further cut each of these pieces into seven more pieces by means of his thunderbolt. O excellent brahmins, those children later on came to be known as Maruts.[2]

---

1. *Pākaśāsana*, Lord Indra who chastised the Asura Pāka.

2. *Maruts*—Diti bore a child in her womb. When Indra knew that the child when born would slay him, he entered the womb when Diti was asleep, with a desire to kill it there itself. The child began to cry but Indra said "Do

234. They became Maruts according to what Indra had said. These fortynine Devas became the associates of Indra, the wielder of thunderbolt.

235-238. O excellent brahmins, Hari desired for an excellent group of Devas of unmeasured prowess with these functioning as such. He allotted Prajāpatis for each multitude. Gradually, the kingdoms with Pṛthu at the head were organized. That Hari is the heroic Puruṣa, Kṛṣṇa, Viṣṇu, Prajāpati, Parjanya, Tapana and Ananta. The whole universe belongs to him. O excellent brahmins, there is no fear of recession unto him who knows perfectly this creation of living beings. Whence can be fear for the other world?

CHAPTER TWO

Origin and glory of Pṛthu

Lomaharṣaṇa said:

1. After crowning Pṛthu the son of Vena as the overlord, Brahmā began to allot realms to each deity separately.

2. He crowned Soma in the kingdom of birds, creepers, constellations, planets, sacrifices and austerities.

3. He crowned Varuṇa in the realm of waters. He made Vaiśravaṇa the lord of kings; Viṣṇu the lord of Ādityas and Pāvaka the lord of Vasus.[1]

---

not cry—mā ruda." Then Indra cut the child into fortynine pieces. They were born alive and they got the name Marut. When grown up they became helpers of Indra.

1. *Vasus*: a class of deities, eight in number: Āpa, or Aya, Dhruva, Soma, Dhara or Dhava, Anila, Anala, Pratyūṣa and Prabhāsa. Sometimes Aṁha is substituted for Āpa. Ādi Ch. 66, Verses 17, 18.

धरो ध्रुवश्च सोमश्च अंहश्चैवानिलोऽनलः ।
प्रत्यूषश्च प्रभासश्च वसवोऽष्टाविति स्मृताः ।।

Compare this Purāṇa, Ch. 1. Verse 149.

They were born to Dharmadeva of his wife Vasu, daughter of Dakṣa. Different Purāṇas give different names. This shows some of them had more than one appellation.

4. He made Dakṣa the lord of Prajāpatis, Indra the lord of Maruts, and Prahrāda of unmeasured prowess the lord of Daityas and Dānavas.

5-6. He crowned Yama the son of Vivasvat in the kingdom of Pitṛs. He made the trident-bearing Śiva the overlord of Yakṣas, Rākṣasas, kings, goblins and ghosts. He made Himavān the lord of mountains and the ocean the lord of rivers.

7. He made lord Citraratha the overlord of Gandharvas, Vāsuki the lord of Nāgas and Takṣaka the lord of Serpents.

8. He made Airāvata the king of elephants, Uccaiḥśravas the lord of horses and Garuḍa the lord of birds.

9. He made Śārdūla (tiger) the lord of animals and the bull the lord of cows. He crowned Plakṣa as the king of Vegetables and plenty.

10. After allotting realms like this, lord Brahmā established the guardians in each quarter.

11. In the eastern quarter he crowned Sudhanvan the son of Prajāpati Vairāja the guardian of quarters.

12. In the southern quarter he crowned Śaṅkhapāda the son of Prajāpati Kardama.

13. In the western quarter he crowned Ketumān the unswerving son of Rajas.

14. In the northern quarter he crowned Hiraṇyaroman the invincible son of Prajāpati Parjanya.

15. Till today the entire Earth consisting of its towns and continents is being virtuously administered by them with due deference to their respective jurisdiction.

16. In accordance with the injunctions laid down in the Vedas king Pṛthu was crowned[1] as the overlord in the course of Rājasūya Sacrifice.

17. Afterwards, when the Cākṣuṣa Manvantara of unmeasured splendour had passed off he allotted the realm on the Earth to Vaivasvata Manu.

18. I shall describe in detail the story of Vaivasvata Manu for your knowledge if you intend to hear. The story of this personage has been narrated in the Purāṇas.

---

1. Historians trace the origin of kingship to Pṛthu. The observance of consecration and the religious and political rites such as Rājasūya sacrifice support the view that the Hindu monarchial system is very old.

The sages said:

19-23. O Lomaharṣaṇa, please do describe the birth of Pṛthu in detail, how this earth was milked by that noble soul; how it was milked by Pitṛs, Devas, Sages, Daityas, Nāgas, Yakṣas, trees, mountains, ghosts, Gandharvas, excellent brahmins and Rākṣasas of immense strength. O sage of holy rites, it behoves you to recount the special vessels they took for milking. Please mention the calves that they had and the type of milk they received. Who milked the earth? Whatfor was the hand of Vena churned formerly by the infuriated sages? O dear one, relate the cause thereof.

Lomaharṣaṇa said :

24. Listen, I shall relate in detail the story of Pṛthu the son of Vena. O leading brahmins, listen with attention and zeal.

25. O brahmins, I shall never relate this to an unclean person, to a petty-minded one, to one who is not a disciple, to one who does not perform holy rites, to one who is ungrateful or to one who is antagonistic.

26. This story is conducive to heavenly pleasure, renown, longevity and wealth. It is on a par with the Vedas. Listen to this secret story in the manner it has been mentioned by the sages.

27. He who narrates this story of Pṛthu the son of Vena daily after bowing down to the brahmins shall not repent for his omissions and commissions.

28. Formerly, there lived a Prajāpati named Aṅga who was born in the family of Atri. He was as powerful as Atri and he guarded Dharma.

29. He had a son named Vena who was not interested in Dharma. Vena the patriarch was born of Sunīthā, the daughter of Yama.

30. Due to the fault of his maternal grandfather, Vena, the son of the daughter of Yama, turned his back on his virtuous duties and indulged in lust and covetousness.

31. That king broke the conventional barriers necessitated by Dharma. Transgressing the Vedic canons and codes he became engrossed in evil and sinful acts.

32. When he was Prajāpati, the subjects were deprived of an opportunity to study the Vedas or utter Vaṣaṭkāra Mantras. Neither sacrifices were performed nor Soma was drunk. Devas too could not drink Soma.

33. "No one should perform a sacrifice. No one should perform Homa"—was the cruel order promulgated by that monarch as his destruction was imminent.

34. "I am the person for whom the sacrifice should be made. I am the performer of sacrifices. I am the foremost among sattras. All sacrifices should be performed in my favour", he declared.

35. When he adopted an unbecoming and improper attitude and transgressed the traditional conventions, Marīci and other sages addressed him thus.

36-37. "O Vena, do not commit a sinful deed. For many years we have taken up this vow of sacrifice. This is the eternal norm. O king, you are born of Atri. You are undoubtedly a Prajāpati. You have entered into a solemn agreement thus "I will protect the subjects"[1]

38. The wicked Vena conversant solely with what was harmful ridiculed the instructions of great sages and acted contrarily.

Vena said:

39. Who else is he the creator of Dharma ? Whose behest am I to pay heed to ? In this Earth who can equal me in learning, strength, austerity and truthfulness ?

40. I am the source of origin of all living beings and of holy rites in particular. You are confounded and deluded. You are of unsound mind (and hence) do not understand me.

41. If I wish I can burn this Earth or float it in the waters. I can blockade and torment the earth as well as heaven.

42-43. When they could not dissuade him from his arrogant deluded pose, the sages got infuriated. Even as the mighty king was throbbing with rage the sages caught hold of him. In their fury they churned his left thigh.

44. As the king's thigh was being churned a short-statured dark-complexioned being came up.

45. O excellent brahmins, utterly frightened he stood there with his palms joined in reverence. On seeing him excessively bewildered the sage Atri asked him to sit.

46. O foremost among the eloquent, he became the founder of Niṣādas. He created Dhīvaras (fishermen) from the sins of Vena.

---

1. The statement shows that kingship was conditioned by certain responsibilities. See the *Coronation Oath* in the Aitareya Brāhmaṇa. For details Jayaswal's *Hindu Polity*.

47. The Tuṣāras[1] and Tunduras[2] who have their abodes on the Vindhya[3] mountains and who indulge in sinful deeds, O brahmins, have emanated from the thigh of Vena.

48. Thereafter, the noble sages who were still in tension, caught hold of his right hand and churned it like the Araṇi (the wood for generating fire by attrition).

49-50. Pṛthu was born of that hand. He blazed like fire. His body dazzled with fiery brilliance. He held a bow that banged with a loud report and some divine arrows too. The name of the bow was Ajagava; for his protection he wore a coat of mail of great lustre.

51. When he was born, the living beings all around were very much delighted and they flocked there. O highly blessed one, Vena went to heaven.

52. O brahmins, Vena the tiger among men was saved from hell named 'Pum'[4] by that noble and virtuous son who was born of his hand.

53. The oceans and rivers took jewels (to present him with) and waters for his ablution and approached him reverently.

54-55. Lord Brahmā came there accompanied by Devas and Aṅgirasas. The living beings too both mobile and immobile came there and sprinkled water over Pṛthu. The subjects were delighted by that mighty monarch.

56. Pṛthu, that valorous son of Vena of great splendour, was duly crowned as the sovereign monarch by those who were experts in holy rites.

57. The subjects who were alienated by his father were reconciled to him. Due to affection his title 'Rājā'[5] became meaningful.

---

1. *Tuṣāras*—Tochari tribe on the north of Hindu Kush mountains. In the Harivaṁśa they are classed along with Śakas, Dāradas, Pahlavas and considered to be Mlecchas and Dasyus (115). But they are ranked with wild tribes, originating from king Vena's sins and located in the Vindhya region. They are said to have been repressed by king Sagara.

2. *Tunduras*: Classed with Tuṣāras and located in the Vindhya region.

3. *Vindhya mountain*: One of the seven chief mountain chains which separates South India from North India.

4. Put, a hell to which the childless are condemned. 'Putra' 'a son' is so called because he protects his ancestors from this hell.

5. *Rājā* from rañj, so called because he delighted his subjects.

58. As he marched against the oceans, waters stood stunned and solidified. Mountains gave way. Never did his banner-post break down.

59. The earth yielded rich harvest without being ploughed. Cooked food cropped up at the very thought: cows yielded milk in abundance. There was honey in every leafy cup.

60. Meanwhile during the course of splendid sacrifice of Brahmā the intelligent Sūta was born of Sūti on the Sautya day.

61. In the very same sacrifice Māgadha too was born. They were called there by the sages for eulogising Pṛthu.

62. The sages told Sūta[1] and Māgadha.[2] May this king be eulogised. This job befits you and this king deserves it also.

63-64. Then Sūta and Magadha addressed those sages—"It is Devas and sages that we propitiate by performing sacred rites. O brahmins, we do not know the name, fame, traits or exploits of this brilliant king whereby we would eulogise him."

65-66. They were persuaded to eulogise Pṛthu by means of what would happen in future. O excellent sages, all those activities which Pṛthu of great strength pursued later on in the three worlds were proclaimed by them by way of blessings and benedictions. Ever since that day in all the three worlds benedictions are offered by Sūtas, Māgadhas and Bards.

67. Delighted by their eulogy Pṛthu, the lord of subjects, granted the Anūpa[3] land to Sūta and Magadha to Māgadha.

68-69. On seeing him the subjects were extremely pleased. The

---

1. *Sūta* was a royal herald or bard, whose business was to proclaim the heroic deeds of the king and his ancestors and who had therefore to know by heart the portions of the epic poems and ancient ballads. The most celebrated Sūta was Lomaharṣaṇa who was a pupil of Vyāsa.

2. *Māgadha*—One who used to adulate the king. He is called Māgadha because he belonged to Magadha.

3. Anūpa—"A country situated near water" or "a marshy country." The name was applied to tracts near the seacoast, generally in combination "Sāgarānūpa" in Bengal; in or near the Pāṇḍya Kingdom in the south, in the north and west of the peninsula of Kathiawar and on the western coast generally. But the name was more specially applied to a tract on the west coast which constituted a kingdom in the Pāṇḍava's time. The only country which rests on the Vindhyas and borders on the sea is the tract on the east of the Gulf of Cambay, north of Narmadā river. For details see Mār. P. fn. p. 344, Pargiter's edition.

learned men said—"This king will offer all of you the means of subsistence". They requested Pṛthu, the noble son of Vena saying—"At the instance of great sages offer us the means of our subsistence."

70. Thus approached in a body by the subjects the mighty king was moved by a desire to do what was conducive to the welfare of subjects. Seizing his bow and arrow he pursued the Earth.

71. Afraid of him the earth took the form of a cow and fled. As she fled, Pṛthu chased her with bow and arrows.

72. After passing through the world, Brahmaloka etc. due to the fear of Pṛthu she saw Pṛthu with bow held ready for discharge (standing before her).

73. He was of unerring aim. He was brightly illumined by the sharp blazing arrows. He was a great Yogin of noble soul. He was invisible even to the immortals.

74-75. Unable to obtain a way of escape she resorted to him. Herself worthy of being honoured by the three worlds she joined her palms in reverence and said to Pṛthu :—"You don't seem to see sin in killing a woman. O king, how will you sustain your subjects without me ?

76-80. O king, the worlds are stationed in me. The universe is supported by me. O king, with my destruction the subjects will perish. Understand it. If you desire to do what is conducive to the welfare of your subjects you will not kill me. O Protector of Earth listen to these words of mine. Begun with proper means all activities become fruitful. Find out some means whereby you will be able to sustain subjects. O king, Even if you kill me you will not be able to nurture your subjects. I shall be favourable to you, O highly intelligent one, restrain your wrath. They say that women even in the lower species of animals, should not be killed.[1] Seeing with your open eyes, O protector of Earth, it does not behove you to eschew virtue."

81. On hearing these and many other statements the noble-minded king, of virtuous soul, controlled his anger and spoke to the Earth:

---

1. Dharmaśāstras prohibit the slaying of Brāhmaṇas and women.

Pṛthu said:

82-87. If one were to kill many animals or a single animal for the sake of a person whether it be himself or any other, one may incur sin thereby. If many were to obtain happiness, when one inauspicious person is killed there cannot be any major or minor sin in slaying that inauspicious person; O gentle lady. As for me, O earth it is in the interest of subjects that I will be killing you, should you, at my instance not be prepared to do what is conducive to the welfare of the universe. If you turn your face against my bebest I will kill you with my arrow and proclaiming myself I will sustain the subjects myself. Hence, O foremost one among the righteous persons, pay heed to my behests and enliven the subjects. Indeed, you are capable of sustaining them. Submit to me and be my daughter. Then I shall withdraw this arrow that is frightful in its appearance and that is now ready to kill you.

The Earth said:

88-89. O heroic one, undoubtedly I shall do all these things. Bind my calf so that I can discharge milk with my affection kindled. O foremost one among those who uphold virtue, keep me levelled up everywhere so that the milk that flows down shall spread everywhere.

Lomaharṣaṇa said:

90. Then with the tip of his bow the son of Vena, Pṛthu swept aside hundreds and thousands of mountains. Therefore, the height of the mountains increased.

91. In the previous creation when the surface of the Earth was uneven there was no demarcation of villages and cities.

92. There were no cultivated plants, no breeding of cattle, no agricultural occupation nor was there any bazar or shopping centre. There was no problem of truth and falsehood. There was neither greed nor indecent rivalry and competition.

93. It was only after the advent of Vaivasvata Manvantara, ever since the days of Vena (and his descendants), that all these began to appear.

94. O brahmins, wherever the land was level the subjects began to colonise.

95. Then the diet of subjects consisted of fruits and roots. They were faced with great difficulties, as we have heard.

96-97. Pṛthu made lord Svāyambhuva Manu the calf. He the tiger among men, then milked the Earth in his own hand. Pṛthu the valorous son of Vena milked the vegetable kingdom. Even to this day the subjects subsist on those food grains and edibles.

98-99. O excellent brahmins, the sages, Devas Pitṛs, reptiles, Daityas, Yakṣas, Puṇyajanas, Gandharvas, mountains, trees—all these milked the Earth. The milk, calf, milkman and vessel were separate for each of them.

100. O brahmins, to the sages the calf was Soma, the milkman was Bṛhaspati; their milk was penance and the Vedic metres were their vessels.

101. To Devas—the vessel was gold, the calf was Indra, the milk was Ojaskara (that which enhances prowess) and the milkman was Sun-god himself.

102. To Pitṛs—the vessel was silver; the calf was Yama; the milkman was Antaka and their milk was nectar.

103. To Nāgas—the calf was Takṣaka ; the vessel was Alābu (gourd); the milkman was Airāvata; their milk was poison.

104. To Asuras—the milkman was Madhu; the milk was Maya; the calf was Virocana and the vessel was iron.

105. To Yakṣas—the vessel was unbaked mudpot; the calf was lord Vaiśravaṇa; the milkman was Rajata-nābha and the milk was Antardhāna.

106. To Rākṣasas—the calf was Sumāli, the milk was blood, the milkman was Rajatanābha and the vessel was skull.

107. To Gandharvas—the calf was Citraratha, the vessel was lotus; the milk-man Suruci and the milk was sweet scent.

108. To mountains—the vessel was rock; the milk was jewels and medicinal herbs; the calf was Himavān and the milk-man was the great mountain Meru.[1]

1. *Meru.* At the churning of the ocean the milkman was the mountain Meru. Compare *Kumārasambhava—Merau sati dogdhari dohadakṣe.*

According to the Purāṇas, Meru forms the central point of Jambūdvīpa. It has been equated with the high land of Tartary north of the Himālays (MW). According to S. M. Ali (*The Geography of the Purāṇas*), Meru can be identified with the Pamir plateau.

109. To trees—the calf was Plakṣa; the milkman was the Sāla tree in full bloom; the vessel was the leaf of Palāsa tree and the milk was the skill for re-plantation of rice after it was cut or burned.

110. And then the Earth is Dhātrī (the supporter), Vidhātrī (maker), Pāvanī (purifier), Vasundharā, holder of riches. It is the source of origin of all beings mobile and immobile. It is the support of all.

111. It yields everything that everyone desires. It grows all plants. It extends to the oceans. It is well known as Medinī.

112. The (fat) of the asuras Madhu and Kaiṭabha spread throughout the Earth. Hence Earth is called Medini by the exponents of Truth.

113. O brahmins, the Earth enjoyed the honour of being the daughter of king Pṛthu, the son of Vena. Hence, the Earth is called Pṛthvī.

114. The Earth divided and reformed by Pṛthu flourished with mines and plants. It abounded in towns and cities.

115. Pṛthu, the son of Vena, wielded a great prowess. He was the most excellent among kings. Undoubtedly he was worthy of being honoured by all beings.

116. Pṛthu indeed is worthy of being honoured by the highly blessed brahmins who have mastered the Vedas and Vedāṅgas because he is eternal with Brahmā as the source of his origin.[1]

117. Pṛthu the first king, the valorous son of Vena should be honoured by highly blessed kings who desire stable kingship (on the earth).

118. The primordial king who grants subsistence to the world, the well renowned Pṛthu should be honoured by valorous warriors who are desirous of attaining victory in the battle-field.

119. The warrior who goes to war after glorifying king Pṛthu returns unscathed from the terrific scene and attains fame.

120. Pṛthu alone should be honoured by the Vaiśyas who seek for wealth and who take up trade and such-like activities. Pṛthu grants the means of subsistence. For he is renowned for that.

---

1. Pṛthu, the first king, has been equated with Brahmā. The comparison suggests that he is divine. In fact, he is human but becomes divine when he is consecrated. He is invested with kingly responsibilities which he has to shoulder. He attains divinity by his acts secular or ceremonial and not otherwise.

121. Pṛthu should be honoured by Śūdras who serve the three castes seeking for their welfare.

122. Thus different calves, milkmen, milk and vessels have been mentioned by me. What more shall I describe now?

CHAPTER THREE

MANVANTARAS[1]

The sages said:

1-2. O Lomaharṣaṇa, O highly intelligent one, describe in detail the Manvantaras along with their previous creations. O Sūta, we wish to hear factually, how mnay Manus were there and how long the Manvantaras lasted.

Lomaharṣaṇa said:

3. O brahmins, they cannot be described in detail even in hundreds of years. O brahmins, listen to the brief description of the Manvantaras.

4-7. There were six Manus in the past viz. Svāyambhuva, Svārociṣa, Uttama, Tāmasa, Raivata and Cākṣuṣa, O brahmins, Vaivasvata is the present Manu. There will be seven Manus in future:—Viz. Sāvarṇi, Raibhya, Raucya, and four Merusāvarṇis. Thus the Manus of the past, present and future, are fourteen in number. I shall now mention sages, Devas and their sons too.

8. The following seven were the sons of Brahmā:—Marīci, Atri, Aṅgiras, Pulaha, Kratu, Pulastya and Vasiṣṭha.

9-10. O brahmins, there are seven sages in the northern quarter. Ten sons of great prowess were born of Svāyambhuva Manu:—Agnīdhra, Agnibāhu, Medhya, Medhātithi, Vasu, Jyotiṣmān, Dyutimān and Havya. O brahmins, thus the first Manvantara has been cited.

---

1. A manvantara contains seventyone cycles of Mahāyugas which are equal to 12,000 years of gods. The Purāṇas mention fourteen Manvantaras which derive their names from fourteen successive mythical progenitors and sovereigns of the earth. There are seventyone Caturyugas in each Manvantara. At the end of 71 such Caturyugas (71 × 4) a Manu completes his life-span.

11-15. Aurva the son of Vasiṣṭha, Stamba, Kaśyapa, Prāṇa, Bṛhaspati, Datta, Atri, and Cyavana—O brahmins, these great sages have been acclaimed by Vāyu as sages of great holy rites. Devas in the Svārociṣa Manvantara are known as Tuṣitas. O brahmins the following were the noble sons of Svārociṣa Manu:—Havighna, Sukṛti, Jyotiṣ, Āpomūrti, Pratīta, Nabhasya, Nabha and Ūrja. Thus, the kings of great virility and exploits have been glorified. O brahmins, thus the second Manvantara has been mentioned by me.

16-19. O excellent brahmins, I shall mention the third Manvantara now. Vasiṣṭha had seven sons. They are known as Vāsiṣṭhas. Hiraṇyagarbha's sons were extremely refulgent. O excellent sages ! understand these ten sons of Manu as I mention them to you.

They are:—Iṣa, Ūrja, Tanūrja, Madhu, Mādhava, Śuci, Śukra, Saha, Nabhasya and Nabhas. Devas in this Manvantara are Bhānus. The third Manvantara has been cited thus.

20-23. Now, I shall mention the fourth Manvantara. O brahmins, the seven sages therein are:—Kavya, Pṛthu, Agni, Jahnu, Dhātā, Kapivān and Akapivān. O excellent brahmins, their sons and grandsons are glorified as noble brahmins in the Purāṇas. In the Manvantara of Tāmasa Manu, the groups of Devas are Satyas. These have been glorified as the ten sons of Tāmasa Manu:— Dyuti, Tapasya, Sutapas, Tapobhūta,Sanātana, Taporati, Akalmāṣa, Tanvi, Dhanvi and Parantapa. This is the fourth Manvantara O excellent sages:

24-28. In the fifth Manvantara the seven sages are Devabāhu, Yadudhra, Vedaśiras, Hiraṇyaroman, Parjanya,Ūrdhvabāhu son of Soma, and Satyanetra son of Atri. Devas are Abhuktarajas. The Prakṛtis are Pariplava and Raibhya. The sons of Raivata are Dhṛtimān, Avyaya, Yukta, Tattvadarśin, Nirutsuka, Araṇya, Prakāśa, Nirmoha, Satyavāk and Kṛti. This is the fifth Manvantara.

29-33. I shall mention the sixth Manvantara now. O excellent brahmins, understand that there are seven great sages: Bhṛgu, Nabha, Vivasvān, Sudhāma, Virajas, Arināman and Sahiṣṇu. O brahmins, the following are Devas in Cākṣuṣa Manvantara. The heaven-dwellers are not different from sages. There are five groups of Devas named Lekhas. O excellent sages, the Nāḍvaleyas of great prowess and noble souls are the sons of sage Aṅgiras. The ten sons of Cākṣuṣa Manu, Ruru and others are well known. The sixth Manvantara has been mentioned thus. I shall narrate seventh Manvantara now.

34-41. Atri, Vasiṣṭha, Kaśyapa the great sage, Gautama Bharadvāja, Viśvāmitra and Jamadagni the son of Ṛcīka of noble soul are seven sages in the heaven now. The following are Devas in the present Vaivasvata Manvantara—viz. Sādhyas, Rudras, Viśvedevas, Vasus, Maruts, Ādityas and Aśvins born of Vivasvat. Ikṣvāku and others are the ten sons of Vaivasvat. O brahmins, the sons and grandsons of these great sages of great prowess mentioned herein are present in all quarters. In all Manvantaras the seven groups of seven are well reputed. They are present in the world for establishing virtue and protecting the world. When a Manvantara passes off, four groups of seven proceed to heaven after completing their duties and reach Brahmaloka free from ailments. Then others endowed with penance fill up their places. O brahmins, these (Manus and others) of past and present rule in this order.

42-46. The following are known as the great sages of future. They will be present in the Manvantara of Sāvarṇi: Rāma, Vyāsa and Ātreya. They are brilliant and well known. Bharadvāja, Droṇa's son Aśvatthāmā of great lustre, Gautama who never grows old, Śaradvat son of Gautama, Kauśika, Gālava, and Aurva son of Kaśyapa will be born as the sons of Sāvarṇa Manu, O excellent sages. O leading brahmins, Vairin, Adhvarīvan, Śamana, (?) Dhṛtimān, Vasu, Ariṣṭa, Adhṛṣṭa, Vāji and Sumati—these seven will be noble heroes.

47. By repeating their names after getting up early in the morning, one attains happiness as well as fame and will also become long-lived.

48. These seven Manvantaras have been mentioned. Now, listen to the succinct description of the future Manvantaras.

49-53. O brahmins, the Sāvarṇa Manus are five. Understand them. One of them is the son of Vivasvat. Four are the sons of Prajāpati Parameṣṭhin, O brahmins, who attained golden complexion like the mountain Meru. They are the grandsons of Dakṣa and the sons of Priyā, the daughter of Dakṣa. They will become kings endowed with strict austerity on the ridge of Meru.

They are of great prowess. The son of Prajāpati Ruci is known as Raucyamanu. He is Ruci's son begot of the gentle lady Bhūti. Hence, he is named Bhautya. These are the future Manus in this Kalpa. O excellent brahmins, the whole earth including cities and seven continents will be protected by them for the period of a thousand cycles of four ages.

54-56. Annihilation occurs continuously in these Manvantaras due to the penance of Prajāpati. Seventyone sets of four Yugas, Kṛta, Tretā, Dvāpara and Kali constitute what is called Manvantara. These fourteen Manus who have been glorified enhance reputation. They are mentioned as very powerful in the Vedas and Purāṇas. O brahmins, they are Prajāpatis whose glorification is conducive to the achievement of wealth and blessedness.

57. At the end of Manvantaras there is annihilation and at the conclusion of the process of annihilation creation takes place. It is impossible to mention their ultimate end even in the course of hundreds of years.

58-60. O brahmins, it is impossible to mention the ultimate end of creation or destruction of subjects.O excellent brahmins, destructions in the course of Manvantaras are mentioned in the Vedas. At that time, Devas and seven sages stay on with their parts still retained since they are endowed with penance, knowledge and celibacy. When a thousand cycles of four Yugas are completed the Kalpa comes to an end. Then the living beings are burned by the rays of the sun.

61-64. Keeping Brahmā at their head, along with Ādityas, the brahmins enter Lord Hari, Nārāyaṇa the most excellent among gods. He is the creator of all creatures. Again and again at the end of every Kalpa they enter him. The lord is unmanifest and permanent. This entire universe belongs to him. O leading sages, now I shall recount the creation of Vaivasvata Manu, the current one of great lustre. Here, in the context of the description of races, the family where lord Hari, the supreme Ātman, was born is being mentioned. The lord was born in the family of Vṛṣṇis.

CHAPTER FOUR

Evolution of Vivasvat Āditya

Lomaharṣaṇa said:

1. O excellent brahmins, Vivasvān was born of Dākṣāyaṇī and Kaśyapa. The gentle lady, the daughter of Tvaṣṭṛ named Saṁjñā was the wife of Vivasvān.

2. That beautiful lady was well known in the three worlds as Sureśvarī (goddess of Devas). She was the wife of lord Mārtaṇḍa of great soul.

3. Saṁjñā had been endowed with fair complexion, beauty and freshness of youthful bloom. She was not satisfied with the complexion of her husband. She was endowed with penance that had made her brilliant and dazzling.

4. Since, Āditya's limbs had been burnt by the refulgence of his disc, Āditya's complexion did not appear to be very attractive.

5. Āditya is called Mārtaṇḍa for the following reason:—Once unknowingly Kāśyapa had uttered out of his filial affection "I hope he is not dead even as he lay in the womb."

6. The refulgence of Vivasvān increased day by day whereby the son of Kaśyapa scorched the three worlds too much.

7. O brahmins, Āditya the foremost among those who scorched the earth begot three children of Saṁjñā, a daughter and two Prajāpatis.

8. At the outset, Vaivasvata Manu, the Prajāpati known as Śrāddhadeva was born. Yama and Yamunā were born as twins.

9. On seeing the dark-coloured Vivasvān, Saṁjñā could not bear it. Therefore, she created her own shadow known as Savarṇā.

10-11. That illusory Saṁjñā arising out of her shadow bowed to Saṁjñā. O excellent brahmins, with her palms joined in reverence she said—"O lady of pure smiles tell me. What shall I do for you. O fair-complexioned lady, I abide by your directives. Command me."

Saṁjñā said:

12. "Welfare unto thee, I shall go to my father's abode. Thou wilt unhesitatingly stay behind in my house.

13. These two sons of mine and this daughter of beautiful slender waist should be nurtured by thee. O splendid lady, never should this secret be divulged to our lord."

Savarṇā said:

14. "O gentle lady, not until I am caught hold of by my tresses, never till I am threatened with a curse, will I divulge the secret. O gentle lady, obeisance to Thee. You shall go comfortably assured thus".

Lomaharṣaṇa said:

15-17. Having commended Savarṇā and having been assured by her saying. "So, it shall be" that lady in her pitiable state approached (her father) Tvaṣṭṛ and stood by him bashfully. That splendid lady standing thus abashed near her father was rebuked by him. Again and again she was directed by him, saying "Go back to your husband". Assuming the form of a mare and thereby concealing her beauty that blameless lady went to the northern Kurus and began to graze grass.

18-19. Taking the second Saṁjñā to be the real Saṁjñā, Āditya begot of her a son equal to himself in every respect. O brahmins, since he was on a par with his elder brother Manu, he too became Manu by name. He is called Sāvarṇa (son of Savarṇā) too.

20-21. The second son who was born of her was known as Śanaiścara. Samjñā, like an ordinary woman of Earth, loved her own sons more. She was not equally disposed to the elder ones. Manu forgave this weakness on her part but Yama did not.

22. Out of anger and childishness or may be due to the inevitability of what was destined to happen, Yama, the intrinsically careless son of Vivasvat lifted up his leg (as though to kick her) and threatened Saṁjñā.

23. The mother of Savarṇa, who became extremely distressed cursed him wrathfully—"May this foot of yours fall down".

24. Extremely frightened and distressed due to the curse, and growing suspicious by the utterances of Saṁjñā, Yama intimated everything to his father with palms joined in reverence.

25-27. "May this curse be averted" said he to his father, O

brahmins. "A mother should be impartially affectionate to all her sons. O Vivasvān, she wants to remove us and she desires to become the sole beneficiary. Of course the foot was lifted up by me to her but it did not touch her, maybe due to my puerile whim, maybe due to my extreme desire, maybe due to my delusion—whatever that maybe—it behoves you to forgive me. O lord of worlds, O most excellent one among those who scorch, I have been cursed by my mother. O lord of rays, may my foot never fall off, I beg you favour".

Vivasvān said:

28. In this matter, O son, there will undoubtedly be a great reason wherefore fury has stirred you who are conversant with righteousness and who (invariably) speak the truth.

29. It is impossible to falsify the words of your mother. Worms will take the flesh from your foot and it will fall off to the ground.

30. The words of your mother will be rendered truthful but you will be saved by avoiding the worse effects of the curse.

31. Āditya spoke to Saṁjñā:—"How is it that more affection is shown to one when all sons are on a par with one another?"

32. Evading (a straight reply) she did not tell (the truth) to Vivasvat. He entered into self-meditation and found out the truth by his Yogic power.

33-35. O excellent sages, the lord was ready to curse her to destruction but she mentioned the truth to Vivasvān in the manner it had transpired before. On hearing the same, Vivasvat was infuriated and rushed to Tvaṣṭṛ. On seeing Vivasvat, Tvaṣṭṛ honoured him suitably. As the sun was about to scorch him in anger, he appeased him quietly.

Tvaṣṭṛ said:

36-38. Affected by excessive refulgence this complexion of yours is not alluring. It was because she could not brook it. She is now grazing grass in the meadow in a forest. O lord of rays, by adopting Yogic power you will presently see your wife of auspicious conduct who is worthy of praise and who is endowed with Yogic powers. O lord ! O suppressor of foes, if my suggestion is approved by you I shall turn your complexion favourable to you. I shall make it alluring.

39. When Vivasvat agreed to the proposal Tvaṣṭṛ mounted him on the lathe, whetted him and made his complexion sparkling.

40. Then his form became more dazzling due to the well knit refulgence. It was very alluring and he appeared very splendid.

41. Adopting his Yogic power be met his wife who had assumed the form of a mare. She could not be thwarted by any living being due to her observance of holy rites and her own brilliance.

42-43. The lord assumed the form of a horse and approached her as she grazed about fearlessly in the form of a mare. It was in her mouth that he had his sexual intercourse, as she began fidgeting due to her suspicion that he might be a person other than her own husband. She let out the semen of Vivasvat through her nostrils.

44-49. Two sons were born of her thus. They were Aśvins who later became excellent physicians. They were known as Nāsatya and Dasra. They were thc sons of the eighth Prajāpati.

Bhāskara revealed his alluring form to Saṁjñā. O excellent sages, on seeing her husband in the attractive form she became delighted.

Yama was extremely distressed due to his activity. He delighted his subjects by his righteous conduct. He was known as Dharmarāja. Due to his righteous activities he became extremely brilliant and attained the lordship of Pitṛs and status of the guardian of a quarter, O ascetics, Manu the son of Sāvarṇa is the future Prajāpati in the Sāvarṇika Manvantara. Even today he is performing penance on the top of Meru.

50-54. His brother Śanaiścara attained the status of a planet. With that refulgence (of Āditya) Tvaṣṭṛ evolved the discus of Viṣṇu for destroying the Asuras. The weapon is never thwarted in a battle. The youngest daughter Yamī became the famous excellent river Yamunā who sanctifies the world. The brother is called Sāvarṇa Manu. The second son, the brother of Manu, became Śanaiścara, the planet saturn, honoured in the world. He who listens to this narrative on the origin of Devas and retains the same in his memory will attain great fame. Even when involved in adversities he will be liberated therefrom.

CHAPTER FIVE

Review of the Solar Race

Lomaharṣaṇa said:

1-2. Vaivasvata Manu had nine sons, all equal to him in every respect. They were Ikṣvāku, Nabhaga, Dhṛṣṭa, Śaryāti, Nariṣyanta, Prāṁśu, Riṣṭa, Karūṣa and Pṛṣadhra. O excellent sages, these were the nine sons.

3-7. O brahmins, before the birth of these sons, Prajāpati Manu of great intellect had been desirous of begetting sons and so performed the sacrifice with Mitra and Varuṇa as deities. In the course of that sacrifice, O excellent brahmins, Manu poured libation in the part pertaining to Mitra and Varuṇa. It is said in the Vedas that Ilā was born therefrom. She was clad in divine garments and bedecked in divine ornaments. She had a divine physical form. Manu the holder of the sceptre called her Ilā, and said—"O gentle lady, follow me. "Ilā spoke these words in reply to Prajāpati who was desirous of a son and who was righteous.

Ilā said:

8. "O foremost among the eloquent, I am born in the portion pertaining to Mitra and Varuṇa. I shall go to them. Do not violate my Dharma."

9. After saying this to lord Manu and approaching Mitra and Varuṇa, Ilā the lady of beautiful hips spoke to Mitra and Varuṇa with palms joined in reverence.

10. "O Devas, I am born in the portion pertaining to you. What shall I do unto you. I had been asked by Manu to follow him."

11. O excellent brahmins, Mitra and Varuṇa spoke thus to the chaste lady Ilā who was devoted to piety and who had spoken the truth.

12-16. "O fair-complexioned lady of beautiful hips, we are delighted by your piety, self-control, humility and truthfulness. O highly blessed lady, you will become famous as our daughter. You alone will turn out to be the son of Manu perpetuating his line. You will become famous in the three worlds well known as Sudyumna, favourite of the universe, practising piety and making the race of Manu flourish".

After hearing this, she returned. While she was returning from the presence of her father, Budha availed himself of the opportunity and invited her for sexual dalliance. O brahmins, Purūravas was born to her by her union with Budha, son of Soma.

17. After giving birth to Purūravas Ilā became Sudyumna. He got three sons who were extremely virtuous.

18-23. O brahmins, they were Utkala, Gaya and Vinatāśva. O brahmins, the Utkala land was given to Utkala[1], Vinatāśva had his land in the western quarter, and O leading sages, Gaya had the land Gayā[2] in the eastern region where Manu suppressed the challenging foes. He divided the Earth into ten provinces to be ruled over by them. Among them the eldest son obtained the Middle Country. In view of his being a daughter as well, Sudyumna did not get this realm, but at the instance of Sage Vasiṣṭha he got a foothold in Pratiṣṭhāna[3].

Dhṛṣṇu, Ambarīṣa and Daṇḍaka got equal shares. The excellent Daṇḍaka forest was named after Daṇḍaka. Merely on entering this forest a man becomes liberated from his sins. O brahmins, after begetting sons Aila Sudyumna went to heaven.

O excellent brahmins, the kingdom of the righteous king Sudyumna was fairly established. After attaining the kingdom, the king of great fame gave it to Purūravas. O excellent sages, he was a son of Manu with the characteristics of a woman and a man. He ruled over the kingdom as Ilā as well Sudyumna. He was well renowned.

24. The Śakas were the sons of Nariṣyanta. Ambarīṣa the most excellent of kings, was the son of Nabhaga, O brahmins.

---

1. *Utkala* (Oḍra)—modern Orissa.
2. *Gayā*—A renowned place of pilgrimage sacred to the Pitṛs.
3. *Pratiṣṭhāna*—A sacred place in Prayāga now called Jhusi. Once this place was ruled over by king Yayāti.

25. Dhārṣṭakas became very proud of their might to fight in battles. The residents of Kārūṣa[1] the land of Karūṣa were Kṣatriyas irrepressible in war.

26. The sons of Nabhaga and Dhṛṣṭa were originally Kṣatriyas who later on became Vaiśyas.[2] Aṁśu had an only son who is known as Prajāpati.

27-31. Nariṣyanta's son was king Yama who held the staff of chastisement. Śaryāti had twins as children. The son was known as Ānarta. The daughter was known as Sukanyā who became the wife of Cyavana. Raivata was the son of Raiva (?). His eldest son Kakudmī was very righteous. He ruled in the city of Kuśasthalī.[3] Accompanied by his daughter he approached Brahmā and listened to Gandharva music for the duration of a Muhūrta of the Lord. O brahmins, actually it comprised of many Yugas of the mortals. He returned to his city which was peopled by the Yādavas.

32. It had been converted into a city named Dvāravatī. It looked very beautiful with many gateways. It was protected by the Bhojas, Vṛṣṇis and Andhakas whose leader was Vāsudeva.

33-34. O excellent brahmins, Raivata realized the true nature of existence. He gave his daughter Revatī of good holy rites to Balarāma in marriage and himself went to the peak of Mount Meru. He stayed there and performed penance. Balarāma the righteous, sported about in the company of Revatī and was very happy.

The sages said:

35-36. O highly intelligent one, how is it that even after the lapse of many Yugas, old age did not afflict Revatī or Raivata Kakudmin? How was the line of Śaryāti perpetuated on earth after he had gone to Meru. We wish to hear everything precisely.

Lomaharṣaṇa said:

37-41. O excellent sages, O sinless ones, neither old age nor hunger nor thirst nor death nor the circle of seasons has any

---

1. Kārūṣa was a hilly country south of Kāśī and Vatsa between Cedi and Magadha. It comprised the hilly country of which Rewa is the centre from about the river Ken on the west as far as the confines of Behar on the east.

2. This shows that the system of caste was not rigid in those days.

3. *Kuśasthalī*—Dvāravatī—Mod. Dvārakā.

adverse influence in the Brahmaloka at any time. When Raivata Kakudmin departed for the heavenly world, O brahmins, the city of Kuśasthalī was attacked and destroyed by Puṇyajanas[1] and Rākṣasas. That righteous noble king had a hundred brothers. On being attacked and massacred by the Rākṣasas they fled in all directions. O excellent brahmins, after fleeing in all directions they established their extensively large line in different places. O excellent sages, their Kṣatriya groups are well-reputed as Śaryātas. They were endowed with good qualities and became famous in all quarters. They had entered dense forests all round. They were endowed with great prowess.

42-46. The two sons of Nabhaga and Riṣṭa were originally Vaiśyas who later became brahmins. The Kārūṣas (the Kṣatriya sons of Karūṣa) were irrepressible in battles. O excellent brahmins, Pṛṣadhra inflicted violent injuries on the cow of his preceptor and due to the curse of his preceptor he attained the state of a Śūdra. Thus, O excellent sages, the nine sons of Vaivasvata Manu have been recounted. O brahmins, it was when Manu sneezed that his son Ikṣvāku was born. Ikṣvāku had a hundred sons who distributed monetary gifts in plenty. Vikukṣi was the eldest among them and he was endowed with great valour. He was a great lord exceptionally conversant with religious virtues. He became the lord of Ayodhyā[2] He had five hundred sons. The eldest among them was Śakuni.

47-50. They were very powerful and the sole protectors of the Northern region. O excellent brahmins, there were other administrations in the Southern region numbering fifty-eight. Śaśāda was the leader of all these. On the Aṣṭaka day Ikṣvāku commanded Vikukṣi—"O powerful one, kill some rabbits and bring their flesh for performing Śrāddha."[3]

---

1. *Puṇyajanas*—According to Viṣṇu Purāṇa, Raivata, King of Kuśasthalī, born of the race of Śaryāti, went to see Brahmā. Taking advantage of his absence from the place, Puṇyajana took control over Kuśasthalī. Afraid of the demon the hundred brothers of Raivata left the country. After that Śaryāti dynasty merged with that of Haihaya.

2. *Ayodhyā*—A city in North India which enjoyed great importance and reputation for many years as the capital of kings of solar race. Till the time of Śrī Rāma this city maintained pomp and glory, and after that gradually it fell in decay.

3. *Śrāddha*—The offering given to Pitṛs. According to the Purāṇas,

O brahmins, after planning to perform the Śrāddha rite but before executing it he ate part of the meat of the rabbit which was meant for the Śrāddha. Hence, he was called Śaśāda. At the instance of Vasiṣṭha he was exiled by Ikṣvāku.

51. O brahmins, when Ikṣvāku passed away Śaśāda became the king. Śaśāda's heir and successor was a powerful king named Kakutstha.

52. Kakutstha's son was Anenas and Pṛthu was his son. Vīrāśva was Pṛthu's son and Ārdra was born of him.

53. O brahmins, Yuvanāśva was Ārdra's son and his son was Śrāvasta. Srāvasta was the king by whom Śrāvastī[1] was built.

54. Bṛhadaśva was the successor of King Śrāvasta; his son Kuvalāśva was a very righteous monarch.

55-56. It was he who obtained the title Dhundhumāra, the slayer of Dhundhu.

The Sages said:

O highly intelligent one, we wish to hear about the manner whereby Dhundhu was slain. We wish to hear it precisely how Kuvalāśva came to be known as Dhundhumāra.

Lomaharṣaṇa said:

57. Kuvalāśva had a hundred sons. All of them were good bowmen, powerful, clever in learning and unassailable.

58. All of them were righteous. All performed sacrifices wherein they distributed plenty of money as gifts. Bṛhadaśva crowned his son Kuvalāśva in the kingdom.

Śrāddha is a very important ceremony. *MW* offers the following remarks about Śrāddha. "Śrāddha is a ceremony in honour and for the benefit of dead relations observed with great strictness at various fixed periods and on occasions of rejoicing as well as mourning by the surviving relatives. These ceremonies are performed by the daily offering of water and on stated occasions by offering Piṇḍas or balls of rice and meals to three paternal and three maternal forefathers, i.e. to father, grandfather and great grandfather".

1. *Śrāvasti*—Name of a city situated north of the Ganges and founded by king Śrāvasta of Ikṣvāku dynasty. It was the ancient capital of Kosal where the rich merchant Anāthapiṇḍika built for Buddha a residence in the Jetavana monastery which became his favourite retreat during the rainy season. Other authorities derive the name from Sage Sāvatta who resided there; it has been identified by General Cunningham with the modern city Sahet Mahet, 58 miles north of Ayodhyā.

59. After transferring the royal glory to his son he entered the forest. Uttaṅka, the brahminical sage, stopped him as he was about to leave.

Uttaṅka said:

60-71. It is your duty to protect your subjects O king. I am unable to perform a carefree penance; very near my hermitage there is a flat sandy waste land of desert. The sea (nearby) is filled with sand. It is known by the name of Uddālaka. There is a great Asura Dhundhu who remains hidden under the ground beneath the sand. His body is huge. He is very powerful. He is indestructible even by Devas. He is the son of Asura Madhu. He is lying down there performing a severe penance for the destruction of the entire world. At the end of a year when he heaves a deep sigh the whole Earth shakes. A great column of dust is raised by the air he lets out when he sighs. His huge body today conceals the path of the sun. The Earth-quake lasts for a week. The column of dust is accompanied by flames, burning coal and smoke. He is extremely terrible. Hence, O dear one, I am unable even to stay in my hermitage. With a desire to do what is beneficial so the worlds, slay that huge monster. May the worlds heave a sigh of relief after he has been assassinated by you. O lord of the Earth, indeed, you alone are competent to kill him. O king, in the previous Yuga, a boon had been granted unto you by Viṣṇu. Due to this boon granted to you, you will enhance the refulgence and splendour of the person who slays that terrible great Asura of inordinate power. Indeed, this Dhundhu of great splendour cannot be slain, O king, by a person of mean splendour even after a long time, nay, not even in the course of hundreds of Yugas. His virility is immense; inaccessible even to Devas.

On being requested thus, by the noble Uttaṅka, the saintly king gave him his son Kuvalāśva for the work of killing Dhundhu.

Bṛhadaśva said:

72-73. "O saintly lord, I have already laid down my arms. Here is my son, O excellent brahmin, he will undoubtedly slay Dhundhu."

After directing his son for slaying Dhundhu, the saintly king went to the mountain and adopted holy rites.

Lomaharṣaṇa said:

74. O brahmins, accompanied by his hundred sons and sage Uttaṅka, Kuvalāśva proceeded ahead for slaying Dhundhu.

75. At the behest of Uttaṅka and with a desire for achieving the welfare of the worlds, lord Viṣṇu permeated him with his own splendour.

76. When that invincible king proceeded ahead a loud sound arose in heaven—"This glorious and invincible king will become the slayer of Dhundhu".

77. They showered him all round with divine scents and garlands. The celestial drums were sounded loudly.

78. Accompanied by his sons, that powerful king, the most excellent among the victorious, went to the sea and dug up the inexhaustible sandy deposit.

79-81. O brahmins, Dhundhu was ferretted out by his sons who dug the entire western portion. Even as he lay concealed by the sands he appeared to whirl up furiously all the worlds by the fire of his mouth. O leading sages, like the ocean at the rise of the moon he let out jets of water coming up in waves and foams. All the hundred sons of the king excepting three were killed by that demon.

82. Then that brilliant king of immense splendour who had resolved to kill Dhundhu approached the powerful Asura.

83-84. The king, a great Yogin, drank up the speedy current of water let out by the monster and quenched the fire with the very same water. After slaying the aquatic Asura of huge body by means of his inordinate strength the king fulfilled his mission and met Uttaṅka sage.

85. Uttaṅka granted boons unto the noble king. He granted him inexhaustible wealth and non occurrence of defeat at the hands of his enemies.

86. He granted him a perpetual interest in righteousness and everlasting stay in the celestial world. To those sons who were slain by the Asura he granted permanent abodes in heaven.

87. The eldest of those who remained is called Dṛḍhāśva and the junior princes were called Candrāśva and Kapilāśva.

88. Haryaśva is known as the son of Dṛḍhāśva, son of Dhundhumāra. Haryaśva's son was Nikumbha who was ever devoted to Kṣatriya duties.

89. O brahmins, Saṁhatāśva son of Nikumbha was an expert in warfare. Akṛśāśva and Kṛśāśva were the sons of Saṁhatāśva.

90. His daughter Haimavatī became famous as Dṛṣadvatī. Her son Prasenajit was renowned in the three worlds.

91. Prasenajit married the chaste lady Gaurī by name. Cursed by her husband she became the river Bāhudā.[1]

92. His son Yuvanāśva was a lord of kings. Māndhātā was Yuvanāśva's son and he conquered the three worlds.

93. His wife Caitrarathī was the daughter of Śaśabindu. She was called Bindumatī also. She was a chaste lady and in the whole world she was unrivalled in beauty.

94. That chaste lady was the eldest sister of ten thousand brothers. O brahmins, Māndhātā procreated in her two sons.

95. They were Purukutsa who was conversant with holy rites and Mucukunda who became the king. Purukutsa's son Trasadasyu became a monarch.

96-97. Sambhūta, his son, was born of queen Narmadā. Sambhūta's successor was Sudhanvan, Sudhanvan's son was Tridhanvan, suppressor of enemies. The scholarly Trayyāruṇa was the son of king Tridhanvan. His son Satyavrata was a mighty prince.

98-99. He was wicked. He put in obstacles when the Mantras were chanted in the course of a marriage. He abducted the wedded wives of other persons. Whether it was due to his childishness or lust, or delusion, or fool-hardiness or fickle-mindedness, he abducted lustfully the daughters of many citizens.

100. Calling out furiously "O disgraceful one" many times, Trayyāruṇa banished him on account of his sinful deeds.

101-102. Thus exiled he said to his father. "Where shall I go ?" He asked him many times.

The father replied—"Go and stay among the Cāṇḍālas. O defiler of my family, I do not seek such a son as you." Thus commanded he went out of the city at the instance of his father.

---

1. *Bāhudā*: From the numerous references to this river, in the Purāṇas, it appears to have been a considerable river between the Gomatī and Gaṅgā in or near the territory of Ayodhyā, having its sources well up in the Himālayas. The only river which satisfies these conditions is the modern Rāmagaṅgā which joins the Ganges on the left, near Kanauj.

103-109. Vasiṣṭha the holy sage did not restrain him. O brahmins, the heroic Satyavrata, banished by his father stayed near the slums of the Cāṇḍālas. His father went away to the forest. O brahmins, on account of that sin, Indra did not rain in that land for twelve years.

Sage Viśvāmitra of great penance kept his wife in that land and performed an elaborate penance beyond the sea. His wife tied her middle son round her neck and went about offering him for sale in exchange of a hundred cows for maintaining the other sons. O brahmins, seeing the son of the great sage tied round the neck for sale, the righteous son of the king released him. Satyavrata the mighty prince sustained him for pleasing Viśvāmitra and to get his sympathy. Since he was tied round the neck he was called Gālava. The intelligent sage of severe penance was thus relieved by that heroic monarch.

CHAPTER SIX

Kings of the Solar Race

Lomaharṣaṇa said:

1. Lord Satyavrata, abiding by the rules of graceful behaviour maintained the wife of Viśvāmitra, out of sympathy and as a result of his own vow.

2. He killed wild buffaloes, boars and deer and tied up the pieces of their meat to a tree near Viśvāmitra's hermitage.

3-6. He adopted the holy rite of Upāṁśu Vrata (maintaining silence) and took to initiation (for a penance) lasting for twelve years. He stayed there at the instance of his father. When the king went to the forest it was sage Vasiṣṭha who administered the city of Ayodhyā, and the whole kingdom. He looked after the affairs of the harem as well in view of his relationship as the preceptor and the family-priest of the monarch. O sinless ones, whether it was due to his childishness or to the unavoidability of the future events, Satyavrata maintained a perpetual grudge against Vasiṣṭha. For, when he was banished, in spite of his being a favourite son, by his father, sage Vasiṣṭha had not tried to intercede.

7-8. The Mantras chanted at the celebration of a marriage become effective when the seventh step is taken.[1] Hence Satyavrata killed the bridegrooms at the seventh step. But O brahmins, Satyavrata cherished anger against Vasiṣṭha thinking in his mind—"Although Vasiṣṭha knows Dharma he does not save me."

9-10. It was on ethical grounds that Vasiṣṭha the saintly lord, did not intervene on behalf of Satyavrata. This silent behaviour was not understood by Satyavrata. The noble father too was dissatisfied with him. Therefore, Indra did not shower rain for twelve years.

11-16. But now he took upon himself the vow of a great holy rite which is very difficult to maintain on the Earth. O brahmins, he maintained it thinking that expiation for his sin would be done thereby and the family saved. Vasiṣṭha the saintly lord did not restrain his father when he was being banished because the sage thought that his father might crown his son.

The powerful Satyavrata maintained the vow for twelve years.

Once when there was no meat anywhere, the prince saw Kāmadhenu[2] cow of sage Vasiṣṭha.[3] O excellent sages, the king who followed the convention of the land where he stayed killed that cow. He had been so hungry and utterly exhausted. Due to his anger against Vasiṣṭha and delusion (he did not hesitate in this heinous crime). He ate the meat of cow and fed the sons of Viśvāmitra therewith. On knowing about it, Vasiṣṭha became furious.

Vasiṣṭha said:

17-19. O ruthless one, undoubtedly I shall fix this peg of sin even if the previous two pegs are not effective. Now your sin is threefold, dissatisfying your father, abducting another man's

1. *Saptapadī* a rite of walking seven steps round the sacred fire at the conclusion of the marriage ceremony.

2. *Kāmadhenu*: A mythical cow of Vasiṣṭha which satisfied all desires.

3. *Vasiṣṭha or Vaśiṣṭha*: Son of Varuṇa, a celebrated sage, the family priest of the solar race of kings and author of several Vedic hymns, particularly of the seventh Maṇḍala of the Ṛgveda. He was the typical representative of the Brahmanic dignity and power. The efforts of Viśvāmitra to rise to his level form the subject of many legends.

wife and slaying of the cow belonging to your preceptor. Seeing thus his three pegs of sin, the sage of great penance called him Triśaṅku.[1] Hence he is known as Triśaṅku.

20. Since he maintained his wife, sage Viśvāmitra was pleased and he granted him boons.

21. When the prince was asked to choose a boon as he pleased he said "I shall like to go to heaven in this physical form".

22-23. When the drought of twelve years[2] had passed off, the sage Viśvāmitra crowned him in the ancestral kingdom and performed a sacrifice on his behalf. This sage of great penance made him ascend heaven in his physical form even as the gods and Vasiṣṭha looked on.

24. His wife Satyarathā born of the family of Kaikeya[3] bore him a sinless son, Hariścandra.

25. That king is known (both as Hariścandra and Traiśaṅkava. He is wellknown as an emperor and the performer of Rājasūya sacrifice.

26. Hariścandra's son was the king named Rohita. Harīta was Rohita's son and his son is known as Cañcu.

27. O excellent sage, Vijaya was the son of Cañcu. He was the conqueror of the entire Earth. hence, he was called Vijaya.

28. Ruruka was his son; and he was an expert on Royal wealth and virtue. Vṛka was the son of Ruruka and Bāhu was born of Vṛka.

29-30. The kings Haihayas and Tālajaṅghas ousted him from power. His pregnant wife took shelter in the hermitage of Aurva. Even in that righteous Yuga he was not very pious. Sagara the son of Bāhu was born alongwith the poison.

31-34. He went to the hermitage of Aurva and was well protected by Bhārgava. From Bhārgava the king Sagara obtained the miraculous weapon belonging to Agni. He conquered Earth

1. *Triśaṅku*: Satyavrata, son of king Trayyāruṇa. He was called Triśaṅku because he had committed three sins: (i) he had invited the wrath of his father by going astray, (ii) he abducted other men's wives; (iii) he had consumed the cow's flesh.

2. *Drought of twelve years*: There are several references to such droughts in the Puranic lore.

3. *Kaikeya*: the King of Kekaya deśa. The country and the tribe derived their names from him. The dynasty belonged to the solar race.

after killing Haihayas and Tālajaṅghas[1]. That unerring king the knower of real Dharma suppressed the religious rituals of Śakas,[2] Pahlavas[3], Kṣatriyas and the Pāradas,[4] O excellent sages.

The sages said :

How was he born alongwith the poison in the forest? Why did that unerring king furiously suppress the traditional religious rites of Śakas and others as well as those of Kṣatriyas of mighty prowess? O highly intelligent one, narrate this to us in detail.

Lomaharṣaṇa said:

35-36. Bāhu was indulging in vice. Hence, he was entirely deprived of his kingdom, O excellent brahmins, by Haihayas and Tālajaṅghas alongwith Śakas. The five groups of kings viz Śakas, Yavanas,[5] Pāradas, Kambojas[6] and Pahlavas exhibited

---

1. *Haihayas and Tālajaṅghas*: The Haihaya race comprised the following tribes, Vītihotras (or Vītahavyas), Śaryātas, Bhojas, Avantis, Tuṇḍikeras (or Kuṇḍikeras), Tālajaṅghas, Bharatas, Sujātyas, Yādavas, Śūrasenas, Ānartas and Cedies.

2. *Śakas* were originally Kṣatriyas, but they were demoted as Śūdras as they incurred the displeasure and anger of Brahmins.

Śakas and Yādavas had helped the Haihaya kings. Paraśurāma, Sagara and Bharata defeated them in war and drove them off from the country.

Mbh (Udyoga Parva Ch. 19) mentions that king Sudakṣiṇa of Kambojas approached Duryodhana with an Akṣauhiṇī, along with the Yavanas to take part in the Bhārata war.

3. *Pahlavas*: Pahlavi people or ancient Persians who lived in the Punjab. King Sagara defeated their confederation, abrogated their laws, degraded them and made them wear beards.

4. *Pāradas*: They are mentioned with hill tribes, to have dwelt in the Western portion of the Himālayas. Manu (x. 43-44) states they were Kṣatriyas but were degraded because they did not observe sacred rites. They were ordered by king Sagara to wear long hair and they became Mlecchas and Dasyus.

5. *Yavanas*: They were originally Kṣatriyas, but became Śūdras by the curse of Brāhmaṇas. According to Mbh (Ādi P. Ch. 85) the Yavana race originated from Turvasu, son of Yayāti. Mbh (Udyoga P. Ch. 19) mentions that king Sudakṣiṇa of Kamboja joined Duryodhana and fought on his side. His army consisted of Kambojas, Yavanas and other tribes. Paṇini derives the word Yavana from yu—to mix and not to mix, i.e. those who could be associated with in certain matters such as alliance in war but not in other matters such as alliance by marriage, since they were degraded people.

6. *Kambojas* lived in the extreme north of India beyond Indus and were

their valour on behalf of Haihayas.

37. Deprived of his kingdom king Bāhu went to the forest followed by his wife. In his unbearable misery he put an end to his life.

38. His pregnant wife hailing from the family of Yadus followed him. O sinless ones, previously poison had been administered to her by her co-wife.

39. This co-wife arranged the funeral pyre of their common husband in the forest and ascended it. O brahmins, Aurva, the descendant of Bhṛgu, protected her sympathetically.

40. The child in the womb came out along with the poison at the hermitage and thus the mighty king Sagara was born.

41. Aurva performed the post-natal and other rites for the child. He taught him Vedas and Śāstras. Thereafter, he taught him the mode of wielding miraculous weapons.

42-43. He taught him the miraculous weapons of fire, O highly blessed ones, which were unbearable even to the immortals. Endowed with great strength enhanced by the power of miraculous missiles the king, ere long, killed the Haihayas in battle like the infuriated Rudra destroying the Vasus. Foremost among the renowned persons he earned further reputation in the world.

44. Thereafter, he resolved to exterminate Śakas, Yavanas, Kambojas, Pāradas and Pahlavas.

45. Being slaughtered by that heroic noble Sagara they sought shelter in Vasiṣṭha after submitting to that learned sage.

46. Vasiṣṭha the extremely brilliant sage offered them freedom from fear on certain conditions. He then restrained Sagara.

47. On hearing the words of his preceptor and being faithful to his promise Sagara suppressed their traditional rituals and changed their guise.

48. He released Śakas after shaving half of their heads. He completely shaved off the heads of Yavanas and Kambojas.

---

classed with Dāradas, Yavanas, Śakas and Chīnas. The country was famous for its large fleet, and breed of horses. Lessen places Kambojas south of Kashgar and east of modern Kafiristan. They were Aryans by speech. They were of Kṣatriya caste and became degraded through the extinction of sacred rites. They were called Mlecchas as they followed evil customs. They were degraded by King Sagara who ordered them to shave their heads like Yavanas.

49. The Pāradas were made to keep their tresses untied and the Pahlavas were asked to grow moustaches and beards. They were deprived of Vedic studies and the chanting of Vaṣaṭkāra Manras by that noble king.

50-51. O excellent brahmins, all these Kṣatriyas—viz. "Śakas, Yavanas, Kambojas, Pāradas, Kālasarpas,[1] Māhiṣakas,[2] Daryas,[3] Colas[4] and Keralas were deprived of their traditional religious practices by king Sagara of noble soul at the instance of Vasiṣṭha.

52. After conquering this Earth, that virtuous and victorious king took initiation for the horsesacrifice and released the sacrificial horse to wonder at will.[5]

53. His horse that was roaming about near the South-Eastern sea on the shore was stolen and taken underground.

54-55. Thereupon, the king got that place dug up through his sons. When the great ocean was being dug up they came upon the primordial Puruṣa, lord Hari, Prajāpati Kṛṣṇa and Lord Viṣṇu who was sleeping in the guise of Kapila.[6]

56. O excellent sages, they were burned by the fiery splendour that came out of his eyes as he woke up. But four of them escaped.

57. They were Barhiketu, Suketu, king Dharmaratha and the valorous Pañcanada. These were the kings who maintained the line.

---

1. *Kālasarpas*—not identifiable.

2. *Māhiṣakas*—the same as the Māhiṣmakas of Māhiṣmatī—an ancient city which was situated on Narmadā river at a place where the Vindhyas and Ṛkṣa mountains contact the valley. The town is identifiable with Oṅkāra Māndhātā in Madhya Pradesh.

3. *Daryas*—the reading is defective.

4. *Colas*—people living in the Cola country in the South. The Cola country extended along the Coromandal coastal plain from Tirupati to Pudukottai where it abutted on the Pāṇḍya territory. Its core was the middle Kāverī basin with Karur and Tiruchirpalli as its main centres.

5. *The horse-sacrifice*. A particular horse was let loose and allowed to wander at will for a year. If another king, out of jealousy or malice captured the horse, he had to fight with the army which protected the horse. The fight lasted till he was forced to submit. A hundred such sacrifices entitled the sacrificer to displace Indra from the Dominion of heaven. The horse was sometimes not immolated, but kept bound during the ceremony.

6. *Kapila*: An ancient sage, identified with Viṣṇu and considered as the founder of Sāṁkhya system.

58-59. Lord Hari, Nārāyaṇa granted him the boon that Ikṣvāku's race would be everlasting and they would have unreceding fame. The lord said that the ocean will be known as his son and his residence in the heavenly world would be everlasting. Taking Arghya unto him the ocean saluted the monarch.

60. Hence, the ocean earned the title Sāgara. Sagara got back the sacrificial horse from the ocean.

61. That king of great fame performed a hundred horse sacrifices. We have already heard that he had sixty thousand sons.

The sages said:

62. O Sūtaja, how were the mighty valorous sixty thousand sons of Sagara born ? By what process or holy rite were they born ?

Lomaharṣaṇa said:

63-64. Sagara had two wives. They had their sins burnt by penance. The elder wife was the daughter of Vidarbha named Keśinī. The younger one was Mahatī the daughter of Ariṣṭanemi. She was extremely righteous and unrivalled in beauty in the world.

65-72. Aurva granted them a boon, understand it, O excellent brahmins. (He said)—"one of you endowed with penance may accept sixty thousand sons. Let the other accept one son who will perpetuate the race. You can choose as you please". One of them, accordingly accepted sixty thousand sons and the other accepted one son who would uphold the race. The sage said—"So be it". Keśinī bore a son Asamañjasa to Sagara. That son of great bustle became the king by the name of Pañcajana. The other lady gave birth to a gourd full of seeds. So we hear. There, sixty thousand foetuses, each of the size of a gaṅgelly seed, grew up. As time passed they grew bigger comfortably. The nurses deposited those foetuses in pots filled with ghee. They gave each of them nourishing food. In the course of ten months they grew up in due order. These princes delighted Sagara in due course. O brahmins, thus he had sixty thousand sons. The sons of the king were born out of the gourd, like big foetus. The divine splendour of Nārāyaṇa had permeated the bodies of those noble persons.

73. The only son (of the other lady) named Pañcajana became the king. Pañcajana's son was Aṁśumān. He was very valorous.

74-77. Dilīpa was his son. He became renowned as Khaṭvāṅga. He obtained only a Muhūrta-long span of life. He came down from heaven and conceived of the three worlds by means of his intellect and intrinsic strength. O sinless ones, Dilīpa's successor was lord Bhagīratha. He was the person who made the sacred river Gaṅgā descend (from heaven). He took it to the ocean and made it his daughter. Hence, Gaṅgā is called Bhāgīrathī by the chroniclers. Bhagīratha's son was renowned by the name Śruta.

78. Nabhaga was Śruta's son. He was extremely virtuous. Ambarīṣa was the son of Nabhaga and the father of Sindhudvīpa.

79. Ayutajit was the valorous successor of Sindhudvīpa. Ayutajit's son was Ṛtuparṇa of great fame.

80. He was conversant with the divine Mantra called Akṣahṛdaya. That mighty king was a friend of Nala. Ṛtuparṇa's son was Ārtaparṇi. He had earned great fame.

81. Sudās was his son. That king became the friend of Indra. King Saudāsa was the son of Sudās.

82. King Mitrasaha became well known as Kalmāṣapāda. Kalmāṣapāda's son was known as Sarvakarma.

83. Sarvakarma's son was the famous Anaraṇya. Nighna was the son of Anaraṇya. Nighna had two sons.

84. They were Anamitra and Raghu. They were the most excellent of all good kings. Anamitra's son was Duliduha who was a scholarly king.

85-87. Dilīpa was his son. He was the great-grand-father of Rāma. Dilīpa's son Raghu was the mighty king of Ayodhyā. Aja was born as the son of Raghu. To him was born Daśaratha. Rāma was born to Daśaratha. Rāma's son was Kuśa.

88. Atithi was born of Kuśa. He was a righteous king of great fame. The valorous son Niṣadha was born of Atithi.

89. Nala was the son of Niṣadha; Nabha was the son of Nala. Nabha's son was Puṇḍarīka and his son was Kṣemadhanvan.

90. The valorous Devānīka was the son of Kṣemadhanvan. The son of Devānīka Ahīnagu was a great lord.

91. Ahīnagu's successor was Sudhanvan. Sudhanvan's son was king Śala.

92. Śala's son was a righteous soul, Ukya. Vajranābha was his son and Nala was the son of that noble monarch.

93. O excellent sages, only two Nalas are known in the Purāṇas. One was Vīrasena's son and the other a leading scion of the Ikṣvāku race.

94. The kings born in the family of Ikṣvāku have been glorified in accordance with their importance. Such were the kings of the solar race who were highly brilliant and brave.

95. He who reads this creation of Āditya, Vivasvān, lord Śrāddhadeva, the bestower of nourishment to the people shall be blessed with progeny. He will attain the world of Vivasvān.

CHAPTER SEVEN

Birth of Soma

1. O Brahmins, the father of Soma, the saintly lord Atri was the mind-born son of Brahmā who was desirous of creating subjects.

2. Formerly, Atri performed a great penance for three thousand divine years. So we have heard.

3. His semen attaining the state of Soma juice rose up. Water exuded from his eyes in ten directions and illuminated the ten quarters.

4. The ten delighted goddesses of the quarters conceived that foetus. They held it collectively but they were unable to do so any longer.

5. When the ten quarters were unable to uphold the foetus, it fell down to the Earth along with them.

6. On seeing Soma fallen to the earth, Brahmā, the grandfather of the worlds, made him ride in a chariot for the welfare of the worlds.

7. O excellent sages, when the son of Atri the noble sage fell down, Devas, the sons of Brahmā, and others eulogised him.

8. The splendour of the refulgent Soma who was being eulogised, was spread all round for the nourishment of the worlds.

9. The Soma of excessive fame, circumambulated the ocean-girt Earth twentyone times by means of that inportant chariot.

10. His splendour that exuded reached the Earth and turned into the medicinal herbs whereby the universe is sustained.

11. Lord Soma acquired refulgence through the eulogies and holy rites. The highly blessed lord performed penance for hundred thousand billion years.

12. Thereafter, O excellent sages, Brahmā the foremost among those who know the Brahman offered him kingdom of seeds, medicinal herbs, brahmins and waters.

13. After acquiring that extensive realm, Soma the most excellent of those who possess gentleness performed the Rājasūya sacrifice with hundreds and thousands of gold pieces as sacrificial gifts.

14. O brahmins, we have heard that Soma distributed the three worlds as gifts to those important brahminical sages who had assembled there for sacrifice.

15. The Ṛtvik was Hiraṇyagarbha Brahmā, Atri and Bhṛgu Adhvaryus. Hari together with many sages was the participant.

16. Nine goddesses who served him—Sinivālī, Kuhū, Dyuti, Puṣṭi, Prabhā, Vasu, Kīrti, Dhṛti, Lakṣmī.

17. After the Avabhṛtha[1] ablution the overlord Moon who was unexcited and who was worshipped by Devas and sages shone excessively illuminating the ten quarters.

18. After attaining this rare prosperity coveted even by the sages, his intellect, O dear ones, whirled. In his impudence tactlessness too clouded his intellect.

19. Slighting the son of Aṅgiras, Soma who was deluded by the arrogance of excessive prosperity, suddenly abducted the wife of Bṛhaspati.

20. Although repeatedly requested by Devas and celestial sages he did not hand over Tārā back to Aṅgiras.

---

1. *Avabhṛthasnāna* : ablution of the sacrificer and the sacrificial vessels after a sacrifice.

21-22. Uśanas then attacked Aṅgiras from the rear. Taking his bow Ajagava Rudra did the same. A massive miraculous missile Brahmaśiras was discharged by that noble deity aiming at Devas. Thereby their fame was destroyed.

23. Thereupon, the battle between Devas and Asuras ensued. It became known as Tārakāmaya battle. The battle raged furiously causing destruction of the worlds.

24. O brahmins, Devas and Tuṣitas who remained alive sought shelter in the eternal and primordial god Brahmā.

25. Then Brahmā himself restrained Rudra and Uśanas and handed over Tārā back to Aṅgiras.

26. On seeing her pregnant, Bṛhaspati was furious and said—"By no means should the foetus be retained by you in your vaginal passage that belongs to me."

27. She went to a forest of Iṣīkā reeds and expelled the foetus. Immediately after the birth that lordly child seized the bodies of Devas.

28. Thereupon, the excellent Devas became suspicious and said to Tārā "Tell us the truth; who is the father of this child Soma or Bṛhaspati ?"

29. When she did not answer them on being asked by Devas, Kumāra the foremost among the slayers of Dasyus, began to curse her.

30. Thereupon, Bıahmā restrained him and asked Tārā to clarify the doubt "O Tārā, tell us the truth whose son is this ?"

31-32. With her palms joined in reverence she told Brahmā that he was the son of Soma. Then Prajāpati Soma kissed him on the head and named the son Budha. Budha stands in the firmament diametrically opposite to Bṛhaspati.

33. In a princess he begot a son. His son was Purūravas of great brilliance, the son born to Ilā.

34. That noble king begot of Urvaśī seven sons. Thus the birth of Soma that increases fame has been recounted to you.

35-36. O excellent sages, now understand his line. Listening to the story of Soma is conducive to attaining wealth, longevity and health. It is holy. It is the means of attaining whatever is thought of. On hearing it one is released from all sins.

CHAPTER EIGHT

Kings of the Lunar Race

Lomaharṣaṇa said:

1. O excellent sages, Budha's son Purūravas was learned and brilliant. He was liberal and he performed sacrifices distributing gifts extensively.

2. The king was an expounder of Brahman. When attacked by the enemy in battle he was irrepressible. He performed Agnihotra and other sacrifices.

3. He was truthful in speech and pious in mind. He indulged in sexual intercourse very secretly. He was perpetually unrivalled in renown.

4. The entire Vedic lore was present in him due to his penance. The famous celestial damsel Urvaśī set aside prestige and wooed him.

5-6. O brahmins, the king spent periods of ten, five, five, six, seven and eight years staying with Urvaśī in the charming garden Caitraratha, on the banks of Gaṅgā, in Alakā[1], in Viśālā and in the excellent park Nandana.

7. He stayed in the Northern Kurus which abounded in charming fruit trees, in the foothills of Gandhamādana[2] and in the top of the Meru.

---

1. *Alakā*: the capital of Kubera, situated on a peak of the Himālayas inhabited also by Śiva.

2. *Gandhamādana*: S. M. Ali (*the Geography of the Purāṇas*, pp. 58, 59) remarks: the Gandhamādana is the range the location of which is highly controversial. There is a confusion in the Purāṇas about the ranges which immediately surround or flank Meru. The Viṣṇu Purāṇa states Meru is confined between the mountains Nila and Niṣadha (on the North and South). The Gandhamādana is also mentioned in some Purāṇas. It is also spoken of as one of the Southern Buttresses of Meru (*Matsya*), as one of the filament mountains on the west, as a range of boundary mountain on the south, and a Varṣa mountain of Ketumāla (*Vāyu*). The Bhāgavata gives different names to different parts of Gandhamādana. For instance, the buttress is called Merumandara, the filament mountain the Haṁsa, Gandhamādana is restricted to the eastern range. But according to S. M. Ali, Gandhamādana means the northern ridge of the Hindukush arch with its northern extension the Khwaja Mohammad range, the Hindukush consists of two parallel ranges which come closer to each other at the apex of the arch, south of the Pamirs (Meru). These ridges are well-defined in Afghanistan, less so in Kashmir and reappear again

8. In these excellent and important sylvan regions usually frequented by Devas, the king dallied in the company of Urvaśī[1] with great joy.

9. He sported about in extremely holy lands praised by sages. He administered his kingdom from Prayāga.[2]

10. The royal son of Ilā, the most excellent among men, wielded power. He earned fame at Pratiṣṭhāna on the northern bank of Gaṅgā.

11-12. The seven sons of Aila Purūravas were on a par with the sons of Devas. Those noble princes born in celestial ragions were Āyu, Amāvasu, Viśvāyu, Śrutāyu, Dṛḍhāyu, Vanāyu, Bahvāyu. These were the sons of Urvaśī.

13. Amāvasu's successor was Bhīma, an imperial king. The glorious Kañcanaprabha was the king who succeeded Bhīma.

14. Kañcana's successor was the mighty and learned Suhotra. Jahnu was the son of Suhotra. He was born of the womb of Keśinī.

15-21. He performed a great sacrifice of long duration. Greedily seeking a husband Gaṅgā wooed him as her husband. Since he dissented, Gaṅgā flooded his sacrificial hall. O excellent brahmins, on seeing his sacrificial hall thus flooded the infuriated son of Suhotra, king Jahnu[3] cursed her. He proclaimed—"See, I shall drink up your waters and make your effort futile. O Gaṅgā, ere long reap the fruit of your arrogance." Thereafter, on seeing Gaṅgā drunk up by the saintly king the sages brought her back. Thereafter, she came to be known Jāhnavī the daughter of Jahnu. Jahnu married Kāverī the daughter of Yuvanāśva. Due to the curse of Yuvanāśva Gaṅgā

---

on the east. The Purāṇas called the northern ridge Gandhamādana. The contradictory statements in the Purāṇas that Gandhamādana is in the south, east or west are reconciled if we keep in mind the correct alignment of the northern range of Hindukush. This range touches the Pamirs in the south and falls away from it towards southwest and southeast.

1. *Urvaśī*: A heavenly nymph. For details P.E.

2. *Prayāga*—a holy city in Uttara Pradeśa, situated at the meeting-point of Gaṅgā and Yamunā.

3. *Jahnu*—A sage. There is a legend that once Gaṅgā which flowed through the earth submerged the hermitage of Jahnu who became angry at her haughtiness and drank up the river. But at the entreaty of Bhagīratha he pushed Gaṅgā through his ear. Since that event Gaṅgā got the name Jāhnavī.

flowed into two halves flanking Kāverī the most excellent of rivers, the uncensured wife of Jahnu. Jahnu begot his beloved and righteous son Sunandā, of Kāverī. Ajaka was his son.

22. Ajaka's successor, king Balākāśva was a habitual hunter. Kuśa was his son.

23-27. Kuśa had four sons of divine brilliance: Kuśika, Kuśanābha, Kuśāmba and Mūrtimān. This king Kuśika was ousted from power by the Pahlavas and he roamed in the forest. Resolving "I shall obtain a lordly son equal to Indra" he performed a penance. Indra in his fear approached him and understood his purpose. When full thousand years had passed, Indra met him. On realising that he was competent to procreate a son, after seeing the sage of severe penance the thousand-eyed Indra agreed to become his son.

Most excellent of Devas Lord Indra resolved to become his son. King Gādhi was Maghavan himself born as the son of Kuśika.

28. Paurukutsānī (Daughter of Purukutsa) was his wife and Gādhi was born of her. Gādhi's daughter was the blessed splendid lady Satyavatī.

29. Lord Gādhi gave her in marriage to Ṛcīka the son of Kāvya. Her husband the descendant of Bhṛgu, the delighter of the members of the family of Bhṛgu, was pleased with her.

30. He prepared two Carus for securing sons for her and Gādhi too. Ṛcīka the descendant of Bhṛgu called her and said:

31-32. One part of Caru should be used by you, and the other part should be used by your mother. A brilliant son, the leader of Kṣatriyas will be born to her. He will not be conquered by the Kṣatriyas in the world. He will slay the leading Kṣatriyas. O auspicious lady, this Caru will secure for you a calm and courageous son who will be the most excellent brahmin with austerity as his asset."

33-36. After saying this to his wife, Ṛcīka the scion of the family of Bhṛgu, perpetually devoted to penance, entered the forest. At that time in the context of his pilgrimage to holy places the king Gādhi came to the hermitage of Ṛcīka accompanied by his wife in order to see his daughter. Carefully handling the Carus, Satyavatī approached her mother and told her about their efficacy. As they looked alike, the mother in her ignorance gave to her daughter her own Caru and swallowed the daughter's Caru instead of her own.

37-40. Then Satyavatī conceived a foetus that was destined to destroy the Kṣatriyas. Her body became bright and resplendent. She assumed a fearful look. Ṛcīka saw her and understood the fact by his Yogic power. The most excellent brahmin said to his fair-complexioned wife—"By changing the Carus, O gentle lady, you have been deceived by your mother. An extremely fearful son of ruthless activities will be born to you. You will have a brother, an ascetic who will realise the Brahman.

41-47. The entire Vedic lore had been instilled (into the Caru) by me with my penance."

Thus warned by her husband, the highly blessed Satyavatī propitiated her husband—"Let not a base brahmin like this be born as a son unto me begotten by you."

When requested thus, the sage said—"O gentle lady, this is not my desire. I did not imagine that it should be thus. But the son is destined to be ruthless in activities on account of his father and mother."

Thus addressed, Satyavatī said: "O sage, if you wish you can create even worlds. What then about a mere son ? It behoves you to grant me a straightforward son of subdued nature. O my lord, well may such a grandson be born to us if this cannot be altered otherwise, O excellent brahmin."

Then, he blessed her through the power of his penance. He said "O gentle lady of fair complexion, whether it be the son or grandson I don't feel any difference. Everything shall take place in accordance with what you desire."

48. Thereafter, Satyavrata gave birth to a son named Jamadagni. He was tranquil and devoted to penance. (As a descendant of Bhṛgu) he was also known as Bhārgava.

49-54. It was due to the change of Caru pertaining to Indra and Viṣṇu given by Bhṛgu. Jamadagni was born due to the sacrifice performed in the half pertaining to Viṣṇu. The holy-natured Satyavatī devoted to truthful virtue flowed as a great river named Kauśikī[1].

1. Kauśikī—the hermitage of sage Viśvāmitra stood on its bank. It has been identified with Gomatī (P.E.) The modern name of this river is Kosi which flows through Bihar.

There was a king in the family of Ikṣvāku named Reṇu. His blessed daughter was Kāmali known also as Reṇukā. The son of Ṛcīka endowed with penance and learning begot the terrible Jāmadagnya Rāma of Kāmali, daughter of Reṇu. He was an excellent master of the science of archery as well as all lores. He shone like the blazing fire. Thus Jamadagni the most excellent among the knowers of Brahman was born as the extremely famous son of Satyavatī due to the potency of penance of Ṛcīka son of Aurva. (The middle son was Śunaḥśepha and the youngest was Śunaḥpuccha.

55-60. Gādhi, the son of Kuśika begot Viśvāmitra as his son and successor. He was subdued in mind due to his penance and learning. Viśvāmitra the righteous soul attained equality with the brahminical sage (Vasiṣṭha) and later became a brahminical sage. He is remembered by the name Viśvaratha too. Due to the grace of Bhṛgu he was born of Kauśika and perpetuated the race of Kauśika. Devarāta and others are known as the sons of Viśvāmitra. They are famous in the three worlds. Their names are Devarāta, Kati, Hiraṇyākṣa, Reṇu, Reṇukā, Saṁkṛti, Gālava, Mudgala, Madhucchandas, Jaya, Devala, Aṣṭaka, Kacchapa, and Hariya, The Kātyāyanas are the descendants of Kati. Hiraṇyākṣa, Ṛeṇu and Reṇuka were born of Śālavatī.

61-63. The spiritual lines of the noble Kauśikas are famous. They are: Prāṇins, Babhrus, Dhyānajapyas, Pārthivas, Devarātas, Śālaṅkāyanas, Bāṣkalas, Lohitas, Yamadūtas, Kārūṣakas, Sauśravas, Kauśikas, Saindhavāynas, Devalas, Reṇus, Marṣaṇas from Yājñavalkya, Audumbaras, Ambubhiṣṇāvas, Tārakāyaṇas, Cuñculas, Śālavatyas, Hiraṇyākṣas, Sāṁkṛtyas, Gālavas, Nārāyaṇis. The Kauśikas are numerous and their lines are merged with many other sages. O excellent sages, in this race there is that admixture of brahmins and Kṣatriyas[1] as evidenced by that of the descendants of Puru and the brahminical sage Kauśika.

64. Śunaḥśepha is known as the eldest of the sons of Viśvāmitra. That excellent sage changes his spiritual line from that of Bhārgava to that of Kauśika.

65-68. Śunaḥśepha, the son of Viśvāmitra was employed as the sacrificial animal in the sacrifice of Hariścandra. Śunaḥśepha

1. This shows that the caste was not rigid during this period.

was handed over to Viśvāmitra by Devas. Since he was handed over by Devas he came to be known as Devarāta. Seven sons beginning with Devarāta were born to Viśvāmitra. Aṣṭaka, the son of Viśvāmitra, was born of Dṛṣadvatī. Aṣṭaka's son was Lauhī. Thus the group of descendants of Jahnu has been mentioned by me. Henceforth, I shall mention the family of Āyu the noble soul.

CHAPTER NINE

Genealogy of Ancient Kṣatriyas

Lomaharṣaṇa said:

1-2. Āyu had five sons who were mighty heroes born of the daughter of Svarbhānu named Prabhā. They became kings. Nahuṣa was the eldest among them. Vṛddhaśarmā came next. The rest—Rambha, Raji and Anenas became famous in the three worlds.

3. Raji begot five hundred sons. This group of Kṣatriya princes is known as Rājeya. They generated fear even in the mind of Indra.

4. When a battle between Devas and Asuras, destined to be tremendously terrible, was imminent, both went to Brahmā and spoke to him:

Devas and Asuras said :

5. O lord of living beings, who will be victorious in the battle between us ? We wish to hear precisely.

Brahmā said:

6-7. There is no doubt that only those will conquer the three worlds, on whose behalf lord Raji takes up arms and fights in the battle. Where there is Raji there is courage; where there is courage there is glory. Where there is glory and courage there is righteousness and victory.

8. Thus advised by Lord Brahmā Devas and Asuras became

delighted. Desirous of victory and hopeful of winning him over they approached Raji the leader of the people.

9. Indeed, king Raji born of Prabhā, and the grandson of Svarbhānu, was excessively resplendent. He was destined to perpetuate the lunar race.

10. Delighted in their minds, Devas and Asuras said to Raji—"Please take up your excellent bow for our victory".

11. Thereupon, conversant with the purpose of Devas and Asuras, Raji said thus, with an eye on his own interest and revealing his glory.

Raji said:

12. "O Indra, I shall fight in the battle if after conquering the asuras through my valour I can duly become Indra.

13. At the outset O brahmins, Devas who were delighted in their minds assented to the proposal. "O king, this desire of your can be realised as you wish".

14. On hearing the words of Devas king Raji asked the leaders of Asuras too, in the same manner as he had asked Devas.

15. The Asuras full of arrogance and realising their own interest, proudly spoke to the monarch thus.

Asuras said:

16-21. "Our Indra is Prahrāda on whose behalf we fight and conquer. O excellent king, you join us shining with glory in this battle."

Even as the king was about to say "so be it" he was urged by Devas, "You will certainly become Indra after conquering Asuras". The king who was thus urged, killed those Asuras who could not be slain by the thunderbolt-armed Indra. After killing all Asuras lord Raji of great glory and self-control redeemed the lost glory of Devas. Then, in the company of Devas, Indra said to Raji of great valour—"I am Rajiputra (son of Raji), O dear one, you are Indra of all Devas. I, Indra, am your son, I shall attain fame through your activities.

On hearing these words of Indra Raji was deceived by his Māyā.

22-25. The delighted king said to Indra—"So be it."

When that saintly king passed away Raji's sons seized their legacy, the kingdom of heaven from Indra. The five hundred sons attacked the abode of Indra, the heavenly world Triviṣṭapa.[1]

When they became excessively deluded, passionately mad, irreligious and batters of the brahmins, their power and valour were destroyed. Then Indra regained his prosperity and the excellent abode after killing the sons of Raji who were slaves of lust and wrath.

26. He who listens to this narrative of dethronement and re-establishment of Indra and he who retains it in memory will never fall to wretchedness.

Lomaharṣaṇa said:

27. Rambha was issueless. I shall mention the line of Anenas. King Pratikṣatra of great fame was the son of Anenas.

28. Pratikṣatra's son Sṛñjaya was very famous. Jaya was Sṛñjaya's son and Vijaya was his son.

29. Kṛti was the son of Vijaya and his son was Haryatvata. Haryatvata's son Sahadeva was a valorous king.

30. Sahadeva's son the pious Nadīna was a famous king. Nadīna's son was Jayatsena and Jayatsena's son was Saṁkṛti.

31. Saṁkṛti's son was Kṣatravṛddha. He was righteous-souled and he earned great fame. The line of Anenas has been recounted. Now hear Kṣatravṛddha's lineage.

32. Kṣatravṛaddha's son was Śunahotra of great fame Śunahotra had three successors who were extremely righteous.

33-34. They were Kāśya, Śalla and Gṛtsamada. Gṛtsamada's son was Śunaka. Śaunakas (sons of Śunaka) were brahmins, Kṣatriyas, Vaiśyas and Śūdras. Ārṣṭiṣeṇa was the son of Śalla and his son was Kaśyapa.

35-37. Kaśyapa's son was Dīrghatapas who ruled over Kāśi. Dhanvan was the son of Dīrghatapas and Dhanvantari was his son. At the conclusion of a great penance when the king had become old, lord Dhanvantari was born. He was the great ruler of Kāśi and was an expert physician. He could cure all ailments.

38. He learnt medical science from sage Bharadvāja He divided therepeutic processes into eight sections and taught them to his disciples.

1. *Triviṣṭapa*—Abode of Indra.

39. Dhanvantari's son was Ketumān. The heroic Bnīmaratha was the son of Ketumān.

40. Bhīmaratha's son was Divodāsa. Divodāsa was a righteous monarch who became the ruler of Vārāṇasī.

41-42. At this time, O brahmins, a Rākṣasa named Kṣemaka attacked Vārāṇasī and rendered it desolate. It had been cursed by Nikumbha that it would remain void and desolate for a thousand years.

43. As soon as it had been cursed king Divodāsa founded a beautiful city at the extremity of his realm on the banks of Gomatī.

44-48. Formerly, Vārāṇasī belonged to Bhadraśreṇya. It was after killing one hundred sons of Bhadraśreṇya who were excellent bowmen, that king Divodāsa occupied the territory. By that powerful king the realm of Bhadraśreṇya was seized. Bhadraśreṇya had a son Durdama who later became famous. As he was a child, Divodāsa let him alone out of mercy. Then the king seized the hereditary realm of Haihaya.

The legacy of his forefathers that had been forcefully taken away by Divodāsa was retaken by Durdama the son of Bhadraśreṇya. O blessed ones, thus revenge was taken by that king of good spiritual splendour.

49. The heroic Pratardana was born of Dṛṣadvatī and Divodāsa. That son even as a boy mightly beat back the enemy.

50. Pratardana had two sons: Vatsa and Bharga. Vatsa's son was Śatrujit and his son was Ṛtadhvaja.

51. His son was Alarka. He was favourably disposed to the brahmins and truthful in speech. A verse has been sung by the veterans about Alarka the saintly monarch.

52. He was a handsome youth. He ruled for sixtysix thousand years. He upheld his family by his mighty prowess.

53. By the grace of Lopāmudrā he attained the maximum longevity. Endowed with youth and beauty he ruled over a very extensive kingdom.

54. When the period of curse came to an end the mighty king killed the Rākṣasa Kṣemaka and re-occupied the beautiful city of Vārāṇasī.

55. Sannati's successor was a righteous king Sunītha. Sunītha's successor Kṣema gained good fame and glory.

56. Kṣema's son was Ketumān and Suketu was his son. We know from traditional records that Dharmaketu was the son of Suketu.

57. Dharmaketu's successor was the mighty warrior Satyaketu. Satyaketu's son was king Vibhu.

58. Ānarta was Vibhu's son and Sukumāra was his son. Sukumāra's son Dhṛṣṭaketu was extremely virtuous.

59. The successor of Dhṛṣṭaketu was king Veṇuhotra. Veṇuhotra's son was king Bharga.

60. Vatsabhūmi was the son of Vatsa and Bhargabhūmi the son of Bharga. These were the descendants of Aṅgiras the scions of the family of Bhṛgu.

61. They were brahmins, Kṣatriyas and Vaiśyas, thousands in number and endowed with brilliance. These Kāśyapas (rulers of Kāśi) have been recounted. Understand the descendants of Nahuṣa.

CHAPTER TEN

The Narrative of Yayāti

Lomaharṣaṇa said:

1. Nahuṣa had six successors who possessed the refulgence of Indra and Viṣṇu. They were born of Virajā the daughter of Pitṛs.

2. They were—Yati, Yayāti, Śaryāti, Āyāti, Yāti and Suyāti. Among them it was Yayāti who became the king.

3. Yati was the eldest. Yayāti was junior to him. The extremely virtuous Yati married Gomatī the daughter of Kakutstha but he became a sage. He realised Brahman and attained absolution.

4-8. Yayāti, the eldest of the remaining five conquered the Earth. He married Devayānī the daughter of Uśanas and Śarmiṣṭhā the Asura lady the daughter of Vṛṣaparvan.

Devayāni gave birth to Yadu and Turvasu. Śarmiṣṭhā the daughter of Vṛṣaparvan gave birth to Druhyu, Anu and Purū.

Indra who was pleased with him gave him an extremely resplendent divine chariot. It had all its parts made of gold. Excellent divine white horses as fast as the mind were fitted to it. He conducted his activities by means of this chariot. With this fine chariot the invincible Yayāti conquered the Earth in six days and defeated Devas and Asuras in battle.

9-17. That chariot belonged to the kings of Kuru race. From Janamejaya the descendant of Kuru, whose other name was Saṁvartavasu it was handed over to Emperor Parikṣita the scion of the family of Kuru. The chariot vanished due to the curse of sage Garga. King Janamejaya spoke harsh words to Garga and violently injured Garga's son who was then a mere boy. Hence, he incurred the sin of brahmin slaughter. Emitting the bad odour of rusting iron the saintly king roamed about here and there. He was shunned by the citizens and the country-folk. He did not attain pleasure of peace of mind by any means. He was extremely miserable. He failed to get consolation from any quarter. The king then sought refuge in Śaunaka the leading brahmin. O excellent brahmins, in order to sanctify him, Śaunaka performed a horse sacrifice on behalf of king Janamejaya. When he had completed the concluding ablution of Avabhṛtha the stinking odour of rusting iron was expelled. The divine chariot was in the possession of Cedi ruler having been handed over to him by Indra who was pleased with him. From him Bṛhadratha acquired it. From him it came into the possession of king Bṛhadratha (Jarāsandha). After killing Jarāsandha, Bhīma redeemed that excellent chariot. Out of love the scion of the family of Kuru, Bhīma gave it to Vasudeva.

18. After conquering the Earth extending to the oceans and containing seven continents Yayāti, the son of Nahuṣa, divided his kingdom among his sons.

19-21. Yayāti crowned his eldest son Yadu in the Eastern quarter; Purū in the middle land; Turvasu in the South-Eastern quarter. The entire Earth with its cities and seven continents is being ruled till today by them with due deference to their respective jurisdiction. O excellent sages, I shall recount their progeny later on.

22. The king was ageing. He set aside his bows and arrows.

He entrusted the entire administration to his kinsmen including the five leading men, his sons.

23. Having deposited his arms, the king roamed over the Earth. King Yayāti was extremely delighted.

24-25. After distributing the kingdom thus, Yayāti said to Yadu—"Dear son, accept my old age. Becoming youthful once again by your handsome features and depositing my old age with you, I shall travel round the Earth on another mission. Do accept my old age".

Yadu said:

26. O king, Alms have been promised to a brahmin by me. I have not yet handed them over to him. Without fulfilling it I shall not take up your old age.

27. There are many defects in senility caused by drink and diet. Hence, O king, I am not enthusiastic over accepting your old age.

28. O king you have many sons whom you love more than me. O knower of virtues, choose another son to take up your senility.

29. Thus repulsed by Yadu the king became furious. Yayāti, the most excellent among the eloquent said thus, rebuking his son.

Yayāti said:

30. "What other stage of life will you have? What virtue or righteousness is left for you, O wicked one, after slighting me since I am your preceptor".

31. Saying thus, O brahmins, in his anger he cursed his son thus—"O deluded one, your subjects will be undoubtedly deprived of their kingdom.

32. O excellent brahmins, Yayāti was repulsed by three of his other sons too, the king repeated the same to Druhyu, Turvasu and Anu.

33. The infuriated Yayāti, the unconquerable monarch cursed them also. O excellent brahmins, everything about him has been precisely mentioned by me.

34. After cursing the four sons elder to Purū thus, O brahmins, the king addressed the very same words to Purū also.

35. "O Purū, if you agree, I shall become youthful once again with your handsome features and shall roam about the Earth after depositing my old age with you."

36. That valorous Purū took over the senility of his father. With the handsome features of Purū, Yayāti roamed about the Earth.

37. Seeking the ultimate satiety of lustful dalliance the lord, the most excellent of kings indulged in amorous sports in the garden Caitraratha in the company of Viśvācī.

38. When he became utterly dissatisfied and disgusted with lustful orgies and enjoyment of pleasures the king took back his senility from Purū.

39-46. In this connection, O excellent sages, the following verses were sung by Yayāti—"He who withdraws within himself all lustful passions like the tortoise that draws its limbs within itself is indeed a person who has attained yoga[1]

Never does lust and lechery subside by indulging in the enjoyment of sexual pleasures. Just as the fire blazes all the more with the ghee poured in, so also it increases at every indulgence. If one were to possess all grains of rice and barley on the Earth, if one were to possess all gold, if all were to become the master of all animals on the Earth or if one were to indulge in sexual union with all women one will find that it is not enough to quench thirst. That being so one should not be deluded by these things. When one does not have any sinful feeling towards any living being, mentally, physically and verbally one is likely to attain Brahman. When one is not afraid of others, when none is afraid of him or when one does not like or dislike others too much, one attains Brahman. Happiness befalls that person who eschews greed and covetousness which are impossible to be eschewed by the wicked, which do not become old even when one becomes old and decrepit and which is an oilment that comes to an end only when the vital airs die out. When one becomes old, one's hair grow old; when one becomes old, one's teeth become old; but the hope and greed for wealth and life never grow old when one grows old. The happiness that one is supposed to derive from

1. The tortoise simile is very popular with the yogins. A yogi withdraws his lustful passions within himself just as the tortoise withdraws its limbs within itself.

indulgence in sexual pleasure, the great happiness that one may have in heaven—these two do not deserve even a sixteenth part of happiness one is sure to have when greed is destroyed."

47-51. After saying this that saintly king entered the forest accompanied by his wife. He performed a great penance of long duration. That king of great fame performed penance on the peak Bhṛgutuṅga.[1] At the conclusion of penance he performed holy rite of refraining from taking food and cast off his mortal body. Accompanied by his wife he attained heaven. O excellent sages, there were born five excellent saintly kings in his family. The entire Earth is pervaded by them as if by the rays of the sun. O excellent sages, the man who listens to the story of Yayāti continuously shall become endowed with progeny, longevity and renown. Now listen, I shall recount the family of Yadu honoured by kings. It was in this that Nārāyaṇa, Hari was born as the uplifter of the family of Vṛṣṇis.

CHAPTER ELEVEN

Dynasty of Yayāti

The brahmins said:

1. O Śveta, we would like to hear precisely the line of successors of Purū, Druhyu, Anu, Yadu and Turvasu, separately.

Lomaharṣaṇa said:

2. O leading sages, listen at the outset of the race of Purū even as I relate it in detail and in due order.

3. Suvīra was the son of Purū: Manasyu was his son. The king Abhayada was the son of Manasyu.

4. King Sudhanvan was the son of Abhayada, Sudhanvan's son wss Subāhu, Raudrāśva was his son.

1. *Bhṛgutuṅga*—A place made sacred by the performance of tapas by Bhṛgu. Ṛcīka had lived there with his wife and children. It has been located either in the Himālayas or in the Vindhyas (MW).

5-8. Raudrāśva had ten sons and ten daughters. The sons were—Daśārṇeyu, Kṛkaṇeyu, Kakṣeyu, Sthaṇḍileyu, Sannateyu, Ṛceyu, Jaleyu, Sthaleyu, Dhaneyu, and Vaneyu. The daughters were Bhadrā, Śūdrā, Madrā, Śaladā, Maladā, Khaladā, Naladā, Surasā, Gocapalā and Strīratnakūṭā. Sage Prabhākara of the family of Atri was their husband.

9-14. When the sun was eclipsed by Rāhu and he seemed to be falling down from the firmament to the Earth, the whole world was enveloped in darkness. Then it was his sage who caused light. At this utterance of the sage, 'Hail to Thee', the sun who was about to fall did not fall to the Earth from the firmament. This sage of great penance founded the excellent spiritual lines after Atri. In sacrifices Devas offered him the same power as were bestowed on Atri. He begot of Bhadra a son named Soma. In all he had ten sons of great merit who were engaged in severe penance. O brahmins, they established their spiritual lines. They were masters of the Vedas. They were known as Svastyātreyas. They were devoid of three types of worldly wealth, viz. gold, cattle and land.

Kakṣeyu had three sons of great might and heroism.

15. They were Sabhānara, Cākṣuṣa and Paramanyu, Sabhānara's son was the learned king Kālānala.

16. Kālānala's son Sṛñjaya was conversant with virtue. The heroic king Purañjaya was the son of Sṛñjaya.

17. O excellent sages, Janamejaya was the son of Purañjaya, Mahāśāla was the son of pious king, Janamejaya.

18. He was recognized by Devas and his fame was established all over the Earth. The son of Mahāśāla named Mahāmanas was virtuous.

19. Mahāmanas was a born hero; he was honoured by Devas too. O brahmins, Mahāmanas begot two sons.

20-23. They were Uśīnara who was conversant with Dharma and Titikṣu who was very mighty.

Uśīnara had five wives, daughters of king Vṛṣa as a result of great penance. They were Nṛgā, Kṛmi, Navā, Darvā and Dṛṣadvatī. Uśinara begot of them five sons who perpetuated his line. Nṛga was born of Nṛgā, Kṛmi of Kṛmi; Nava of Navā and Suvrata of Darvā, Śibi of Dṛṣadvatī.

24-29. O brahmins, the realm of Śibi is known as the Śibis,

that of Nṛga as the Yaudheyas; that of Nava as the Navarāṣṭra, the city of Kṛmila belonged to Kṛmi. The realm of Ambaṣṭhas belonged to Suvrata.

Understand the sons of Śibi. The four sons of Śibi are known as the Śibis. They were—Vṛṣadarbha, Suvīra, Kaikeya and Madraka. Their realms were very flourishing by the names of Vṛṣadarbhas, Suvīras, Kaikeyas and Madrakas.

O brahmins, Titikṣu became a king in the Eastern region. He had many sons. Uṣadratha of great vigour was prominent among them. His son was Phena. Sutapas was born of Phena. Bali was the son of Sutapas. His quiver was golden. He was a great Yogin and a king.

30-36. He procreated five sons who continued his lineage on the Earth. Aṅga was born at the outset. Then were born Vaṅga, Suhma, Puṇḍra and Kaliṅga. The Kṣatriya descendants of Bali are known as Bāleya Kṣatras. There were brahminical descendants of Bali too. They too established their family on the earth.

O brahmins, a boon had been granted to Bali by Brahmā who was pleased with him. Thereby he acquired the following attributes:

He was a great Yogin. His span of life extended to that of a Kalpa. He was unequalled in strength. He had a deep insight in the principles and topics of Dharma. He was unconquerable in battle. He held an important position in the matter of deciding what Dharma was. He had a clear vision of three worlds. He was accorded prominence at the sacrifice of Prasava (?). When this was said to him by the lord, viz "you will establish the four castes duly" he attained mental peace. O brahmins, after a great deal of time, he went to the heavenly abode.

The realms of the five descendants are—Aṅgas, Vaṅgas, Suhmakas, Kaliṅgas and Puṇḍrakas.

Now the descendants of Aṅga are related.

37. Aṅga's son was Dadhivāhana, the leader of kings. Dadhivāhana's son was king Diviratha.

38. The son of Diviratha was Svargaratha who was equal in valour to Indra. His son was Citraratha.

39. While he performed a sacrifice on the Kālañjara[1] moun-

1. Kālañjara (a mountain). It is one of the twenty mountains spread on the four sides of mount Mahāmeru.

tain the Soma juice was drunk by Svargaratha along with Indra.

40. Citraratha's son was Daśaratha. He became famous by the name Lomapāda and Śāntā was his daughter.[1]

41. By the grace of Ṛṣyaśṛṅga a heroic son of great fame was born to Daśaratha who commanded the four divisions of the army and made the family flourish. His name was Caturaṅga.

42. Caturaṅga's son was known by the name Pṛthulākṣa. The king of great fame Campa was the son of Pṛthulākṣa.

43. Campa's city was Campā which was formerly known as Mālinī. By the grace of Pūrṇabhadra, his son Haryaṅga was born.

44. Then Ṛṣyaśṛṅga made the excellent vehicle, the elephant of Indra descend to the Earth by means of Mantras.

45. King Bhadraratha was the son of Haryaṅga. King Bṛhatkarman was the son of Bhadraratha.

46-48. Bṛhaddarbha was his son and Bṛhanmanas was born to him. The leading king Bṛhanmanas begot Jayadratha. King Dṛḍharatha was born to him. Dṛḍharatha's successor was Janamejaya the conqueror of the universe. His son was Vikarṇa. Vaikarṇa was his son. He had a hundred sons who made the family of the Aṅgas flourish.

49. Thus, all the kings born of the family of Aṅga have been glorified by me. They were noble souls pledged to truthfulness. They were mighty warriors and they procreated children.

50. O brahmins, O excellent sages, listen. I shall mention the family of king Ṛceyu the son of Raudrāśva.

51-53. Ṛceyu's son was king Matināra who ruled over the whole Earth. Matināra had three extremely virtuous sons—Vasurodha, Pratiratha and the righteous Subāhu. All of them were conversant with the Vedas, truthful in speech and favourable to the brahmins. O excellent sages, his daughter Ilā was an expounder of the Brahman. Taṁsu married her.

54-55. Taṁsu's valorous son was the pious king Dharmanetra. He was an expounder of Brahman and an assailer of foes. His wife was Upadānavī, who bore four splendid sons to him viz Duṣyanta, Suṣmanta, Pravīra and Anagha.

1. There is some confusion here. Śāntā was the daughter of king Daśaratha. Lomapāda had adopted her as his daughter. She was married to sage Ṛṣyaśṛṅga. Lompāda was not identical with Daśaratha.

56-61. Duṣyanta's valorous heir was Bharata. His original name was Sarvadamana. He had the strength of ten thousand elephants. The son of Duṣyanta, the great soul was a great Emperor. Bharata was born of Śakuntalā and this country is named Bhārata after him. The sons of king Bharata perished through the fury of Mātṛs (Mothers). This story had been told by me previously. Thereupon, the great brahminical sage Bharadvāja the son of Bṛhaspati, the descendant of Aṅgiras performed great sacrifices. Due to the effort of Bharadvāja, a son was born to Bharata who was so named because the birth of the previous sons had been futile. After the birth of Vitatha, Bharata had passed away. After crowning Vitatha, Bharadvāja returned to his hermitage.

62-64. Vitatha begot five sons—viz. Suhotra, Suhotṛ, Gaya, Garga and Kapila.

Suhotra had two sons, Kāśika of great might and king Gṛtsamati. Gṛtsamati had Brahmin, Kṣatriya and Vaiśya sons. Kāśika had two sons viz Kāśeya and Dīrghatapas.

65. The learned scholar Dhanvantari was the son of Dīrghatapas. Dhanvantari's son Ketumān is well known.

66-67. The scholarly Bhīmaratha was the son of Ketumān. The son of Bhīmaratha became the ruler of Vārāṇasī. He was well known as Divodāsa and he destroyed all Kṣatriya kings. The heroic king Pratardana was the son of Divodāsa.

68. Pratardana had two sons, viz Vatsa and Bhārgava. Alarka was the son of king Sanmatimān. He too was a king.

69-70. The king seized the hereditary property of Haihaya. The ancestral property forcibly seized by Divodāsa was taken back by irrepressible son of Bhadraśreṇya, the noble Durdama. He had been formerly let off mercifully by Divodāsa thinking that he was a mere boy.

71-72. The king Aṣṭaratha was the son of Bhīmaratha. O brahmins, that boy was struck by this Kṣatriya son desirous of putting a stop to the enmity, O excellent sages.

Alarka, king of Kāśi, was truthful in speech and favourable to the brahmins.

73. This scion and the uplifter of the family of Kāśi kings was a youth endowed with handsome features who ruled for sixty-six (thousand) years.

74-75. It was to the grace of Lopāmudrā that he attained the maximum span of life. O excellent sages, towards the end of his life the king killed the Rākṣasa Kṣemaka and re-established the beautiful city of Vārāṇasī. Alarka's successor was king Kṣemaka.

76. Kṣemaka's son was Varṣaketu. King Vibhu was his successor.

77. Anarta was the son of Vibhu and Sukumāra was his son. Sukumāra's son was the mighty warrior Satyaketu.

78. This son of great refulgence became an extremely virtuous king. Vatsabhūmi was the son of Vatsa and Bhargabhūmi was born of Bhārgava.

79. These descendants of Aṅgiras were born in the family of Bhṛgu. O excellent sages, they were brahmins, Kṣatriyas, Vaiśyas and Śūdras.

80-87. There is another line of kings viz. Ajamīḍha. O excellent brahmins, may it be listened to. Bṛhat was the son of Suhotra. Bṛhat had three sons viz. Ajamīḍha, Dvimīḍha and the powerful Purumīḍha. Ajamīḍha had three wives endowed with fame viz.—Nīlī, Keśinī and Dhūminī. All of them were excellent ladies. The valorous Jahnu was born of Keśinī and Ajamīḍha. He performed a sacrifice of long duration called Sarva Medhāmakha. Eager to have him as her husband Gaṅgā approached him like a humble lady. As he declined the proposal Gaṅgā flooded his sacrificial hall. O brahmins, on seeing the sacrificial chamber thus flooded all round king Jahnu became infuriated. He said to Gaṅgā—"O Gaṅgā, ere long, reap the fruits of this arrogance of thine. I shall condense your water flourishing in the three worlds and drink it up."

On seeing Gaṅgā drunk up, the highly blessed great sages of noble souls bought her back as Jāhnavī his daughter.

Jahnu married Kāverī, daughter of Yuvanāśva. Later on, due to the curse of Gaṅgā half of her body was turned into a river.

88-91. The valorous beloved son of Jahnu was Ajaka. Ajaka's successor was king Balākāśva who was fond of hunting. Kuśika was his son. This king was murdered by wild foresters along with the Pahlavas. Kuśika performed a penance resolving to himself—"I shall obtain a lordly son equal to Indra." Indra approached him out of fear and understood his purpose. Indra himself became the son of Kuśika. He was king Gādhi. Viśvāmitra was the son of Gādhi and Aṣṭaka was born of Viśvāmitra.

[1](O brahmins, Viśvabādhi, Śvajit and Satyavatī (also) were born. Jamadagni was born of Satyavatī and Ṛcīka. Devarāta and others were the sons of Viśvāmitra. They became famous in three worlds. O brahmins, listen to their names. They were Devarāta, Kati, Hiraṇyākṣa and Reṇu. The descendants of Kati were Kātyāyanas. Hiraṇyākṣa was born of Śālavatī. Reṇukā was the daughter of Reṇu. The spiritual lines of noble Kauśikas are known as Sāṁkṛtyas, Gālavas, Maudgalyas, Paṇins, Babhrus, Dhyānajapyas, Pārthivas, Devarātas, Śālaṅkāyanas, Sauśravas, Lohitas, Yamadūtas, Kārīṣis, and Saindhavāyanas. O brahmins, there and other descendants of Kuśika are well known in the world. Many descendants of Kuśika are those who could have marriage alliances with other sages. O excellent sages, in this family there is thus the admixture of brahmins and Kṣatriyas due to the connection of Paurava and the brahminical sage Kauśika. Sunaḥśepha was the eldest of the sons of Viśvāmitra. That leading sage was originally a Bhārgava (descendant of Bhṛgu). Later on, he attained the state of being a descendant of Kuśika. Devarāta and others were also the sons of Viśvāmitra. Dṛṣadvatī's son Aṣṭaka was born of Viśvāmitra).

92-97. Aṣṭaka's son was Lauhi. Thus descendants of Jahnu have been mentioned by me. May another line pertaining to Ajamīḍha be heard, O excellent sages. Suśānti was born of Nīlinī and Ajamīḍha. Purujāti was the son of Suśānti. Bāhyāśva was born of Purujāti. Bāhyāśva had five sons comparable to the immortals. They were—Mudgala, Sṛñjaya, king Bṛhadaśva, Yavīnara the valorous and Kṛmilāśva the fifth one. These five kings are known as Pañcālas because they were competent to protect the five realms. Their five realms were flourishing. Hence they got the designation Pañcālas. Mudgala's successor of very great fame was Maudgalya. Indrasenā bore Vadhnyaśva to him.

*(His son Satyadhṛti was a master of archery. On seeing a celestial lady in front of him, his semen got discharged among some reeds of Śara. Twins were born of it. Out of sympathy

*The text puts these verses within brackets without number.

Śantanu who had gone ahunting took them up and brought them up. The boy was known as Kṛpa, the girl Gautamī was known as Kṛpī. These are said to be Śāradvatas. These are known as Gautamas too. Henceforth, I shall mention the line of succession of Divodāsa. Divodāsa's successor was king Mitrayu (who became a) brahminical sage. Mitrayu's son was Soma. Therefore they are known as Maitreyas. These too though born of Kṣatriya family entered the spiritual line of Bhṛgu)[1]

98. Pañcajana was the son of Sṛñjaya. King Somadatta was the son of Pañcajana.

99-101. Sahadeva of great fame was the successor of Somadatta. Sahadeva's son Somaka was well known. Ajamīḍha of great power was the son of Gṛtsamatī. When the family declined in prosperity Ajamīḍha's son Somaka was born. Jantu was the son of Somaka. His hundred sons shone brilliantly. The youngest of them Lord Pṛṣata was the father of Drupada. These noble Somakas are known as Ajamīḍhas.

102-105. Dhūminī the crowned queen of Ajamīḍha longed for a son. O excellent sages, she was highly blessed, chaste and noble. Desiring a son she performed holy rites. For ten thousand years she performed a difficult penance. She conducted sacrifices duly. The pious lady ate very little. O excellent sages, she lay down only on the Kuśa of Agnihotra. Ajamīḍha had sexual union with the gentle lady Dhūminī and procreated Ṛkṣa who was smoke-coloured and handsome in appearance.

106. Saṁvaraṇa was born of Ṛkṣa and Kuru was born of Saṁvaraṇa. He shifted his capital from Prayāga and founded Kurukṣetra.

107. That spot is holy, beautiful and frequented by pious persons. His family is extensive and his descendants are known as Kauravas.

108. Kuru had four sons—Sudhanvan, Sudhanu, Parīkṣit and the most excellent Arimejaya.

109. The righteous Janamejaya was the successor of Parīkṣit. Śrutasena, Agrasena and Bhīmasena (succeeded him).

*(The intelligent Suhotra was the successor of Sudhanvan. His son was king Cyavana who was an expert on virtue and

1. The text puts these verses within brackets without number.

wealth. Kṛtayajña was born of Cyavana. This knower of Dharma performed sacrifices and begot the heroic Caidyoparivara as his son. He was a well known king who became a friend of Indra. He was known as Vasu too and he could traverse the skies.

Girikā bore to Caidyoparivara seven manly sons. They were Bṛhadratha who was a mighty warrior and king of Magadha; Pratyagratha, Kratha whom they call Maṇivāhana, Sakala, Juhu, Matsya and Kāli the seventh. Bṛhadratha's successor Kuśāgra was well known. Kuśāgra's scholarly and valorous son was Ṛṣabha. Now, I shall mention the family of Juhu. It is endowed with all good qualities. Juhu begot a son Suratha who became a king.

110. All these were highly blessed, valorous and mighty. The intelligent Suratha was the son of Janamejaya.

111. The valorous Vidūratha was born as the son of Suratha. Ṛkṣa of great might was the successor of Vidūratha.

112. His second son was born through the favour of Bharadvāja and he became well known by that name. In this lunar race there were two Ṛkṣas and two Parikṣits.

113. O brahmins, there were three Bhīmasenas and two Janamejayas. Bhīmasena was the son of second Ṛkṣa.

114. Pratīpa was born of Bhīmasena. Three mighty sons were born to Pratīpa. They were Śantanu, Devāpi and Bāhlika.

115. O excellent brahmins, Śantanu was a king of this race. Now listen to the race of Bāhlika the saintly king.

116. Somadatta of great fame was the son of Bāhlika. Three sons were born of Somadatta. They were Bhūri, Bhūriśravas and Śala.

117. Sage Devāpi became the preceptor of Devas. Cyavana's son Kṛtaka was a chum of this noble sage.

118. Śantanu the foremost among the descendants of Kuru became a king. I shall mention the family of Śantanu well known in the three worlds.

119. That lord begot of Gaṅgā a son named Devavrata. He became famous by the name of Bhīṣma. He was the grandfather of the Pāṇḍavas.

120. Kālī bore the son Vicitravīrya to Śantanu. He was a righteous soul devoid of sins.

121. Kṛṣṇa Dvaipāyana generated Dhṛtarāṣṭra, Pāṇḍu and Vidura in the wives of Vicitravīrya.

122. Hundred sons were begotten of Gāndhārī by Dhṛtarāṣṭra. Among them Duryodhana was most excellent. He became the lord of all.

123. Arjuna was the son of Pāṇḍu and his son was Abhimanyu. Parīkṣit was the son of Abhimanyu.

124. Pārīkṣita (Abhimanyu) begot two sons of Kāśī, viz. the king Candrāpīḍa and Sūryāpīḍa the knowers of Brahman.

125. Candrāpīḍa begot hundred sons who were excellent bowmen. They are known as the Kṣatriya descendants of Janamejaya.

126. The mighty Satyakarṇa was the eldest among them. In the city of Hastināpura he performed a sacrifice in which much wealth was distributed as gift.

127. Satyakarṇa's successor was the valorous Śvetakarṇa. That righteous king was issueless and he entered a penance-grove.

128. His beautiful wife Mālinī, daughter of Subāhu, (otherwise known as) Grahamālinī, and a descendant of Yadu became pregnant in the forest.

129. When the conception had taken place, king Śvetakarṇa continued his journey as he had done previously.

130. On seeing her beloved husband going, the chaste lady Mālinī the lotus-eyed daughter of Subāhu followed him to the forest.

131. On the way the youthful maiden gave birth to a tender son. Leaving the son there she followed the king to the forest.

132. The highly blessed chaste lady did the same thing as Draupadī the chaste lady had done before[1]. The tender, tiny boy began to cry amidst the mountain bushes.

133-136. Taking pity on that noble boy, clouds appeared in the sky. The two sons of Śraviṣṭhā, Paippalādi and Kauśika saw him. They took pity on him, took him up and washed him with water. His sides drenched in blood were scraped on the rock. When his sides were carefully scraped the boy became dark-complexioned like a goat. Hence, the two brahmins named him

1. Draupadī had followed Yudhiṣṭhira to the forest.

Ajapārśva. The boy was brought up by the two brahmins in the chamber of Romaka.

137. The wife of Romaka adopted him as her son and brought him up. The boy became the son of Romaki and the two brahmins became her attendants.

138. Such is the race of Purū. The family of the Pāṇḍavas was established there. Their sons and grandsons had their spans of life simultaneously.

139-140. In this context the following verse had been sung by Yayāti the son of Nahuṣa. That intelligent king was highly pleased when old age was transferred to his son. This Earth may be devoid of sun, moon and planets. But the Earth will never be devoid of descendants of Purū.

141. This well known dynasty of Purū has been mentioned to you by me. I shall now mention the dynasties of Turvasu, Druhyu, Anu and Yadu.

142. Vahni was the son of Turvasu. Gobhānu was his son. The unconquerable king Traiśānu was the son of Gobhānu.

143-144. Karandhama was the son of Traiśānu and his son was Marutta. Another Marutta, the son of Avikṣita has already been mentioned by me. This king had been issueless. He performed sacrifice where much wealth was gifted in charity. A daughter named Saṁyatā was born to the king.

145. She was given to the noble Saṁvarta as gift. She obtained a pious son Duṣyanta, descendant of Purū.

146. Thus, O excellent brahmins, the race of Turvasu merged into the family of Purū as a result of the curse of Yayāti in the context of transferring his old age.

147-148. Duṣyanta's successor was king Karūroma. Āhrīda was born of Karūroma. He had four sons. They were called:— Pāṇḍya, Kerala, Kola and king Cola. Their flourishing realms are Pāṇḍyas, Colas and Keralas.

O king ! Babhrusetu was Druhyu's son.

149-151. Aṅgārasetu was his son. He is called the lord of winds. This mighty king was killed with difficulty in the course of battle with Yauvanāśva. A tremendous battle ensued that lasted for ten months. The king Gandhāra was the successor of Aṅgārasetu. The great country of Gandhāra was named after him. The horses hailing from Gandhāra are the most excellent of all horses.

152. Dharma was the son of Anu. Dhṛta was his son. Śatadruha was born of Dhṛta. Pracetas was his son.

153-154. Sucetas was the son of Pracetas His sons have been mentioned by me.

Yadu had five sons comparable to the sons of Devas. They were Sahasrada, Payoda, Kroṣṭā, Nīla and Añjika. Sahasrada had three virtuous sons.

155. They were Haihaya, Haya and king Veṇuhaya. The son of Haihaya was Dharmanetra.

156. Kārta was the son of Dharmanetra. His son was Sāhañja. The city Sāhañjanī was founded by Sāhañja.

157. The valorous Bhadraśreṇya was the son of Mahiṣmān. The successor of Bhadraśreṇya was named Durdama.

158. The son of Durdama was Kanaka. The forebears of Kanaka were well known in the world.

159. They were Kṛtavīrya, Kṛtaujas, Kṛtakarman and Kṛtāgni. Arjuna was born of Kṛtavīrya.

160. Endowed with a thousand hands he became the lord of the Earth consisting of seven continents. All alone, he conquered the Earth with a chariot that had the brilliance of the sun.

161. Performing a penance that was extremely difficult to be performed, for the period of ten thousand years Kārtavīrya propitiated Datta the son of Atri.

162-164. Datta granted him four boons of inordinate glamour:—(1) the full complement of a thousand arms. (2) the ability to retain knowledge even in sinful atmosphere (3) After conquering the Earth with fierce ruthlessness, acquiring an ability to reconcile and propitiate the subjects through righteousness, and (4) having won in many battles and having killed thousands of enemies in battle, death at the hands of one superior to him in battle.

165. O brahmins, he acquired a thousand arms only when he was engaged in fighting. They manifested themselves as if by the power of Yoga in the case of a Master of Yogic feats.

166. This entire earth consisting of seven continents and

oceans, towns and cities was conquered by him by a ruthless and fierce process.

167. O excellent sages, it is heard that seven hundred sacrifices were duly performed by him in the seven continents.

168-169. O excellent sages, hundreds and thousands of gold pieces were distributed as gifts; in each of these there were golden sacrificial altars. All of them were made splendid by Devas, Gandharvas and celestial maidens stationed in their aerial chariots and fully bedecked in ornaments.

170. In his sacrifice Nārada the musician, son of Varīdāsa, sang this laudatory song. Nārada was wonder-struck by his grandeur.

Nārada said :

171. Other kings will certainly never emulate Kārttavīrya in performing sacrifices, offering charitable gifts, practising austerities, possessing valour or learning.

172. That Yogin was seen moving about in the seven continents in his chariot, wielding his leathern shield, sword and bow.

173. Due to the power of that great king who protected the subjects righteously there was neither grief nor bewildered flutter among the subjects. No money or valuable article was lost by them.

174. He became an emperor endowed with the enjoyment of all jewels. He alone was the guardian of the cattle. He alone was the guardian of fields.

175-181. That Arjuna who could create showers because he was a Yogin was the lord of clouds. With his thousand arms the skin whereof had become hardened because the bowstring had frequently struck it, he shone like the sun in Autumn with his thousand rays. That brilliant king defeated Nāgas, sons of Karkoṭaka and established them in his city Māhiṣmatī[1]. That lotus-eyed king playfully restrained the onward rush of the ocean with his arms during the rainy season and made it flow back. The river Narmadā abounding in crocodiles was rolled up by him

1. *Māhiṣmatī*—identified with the modern Maheśvara on Narmadā, but this seems to be untenable, for Maheśvara lies within the ancient Avanti. Probably the city can be identified with Oṁkāra Māndhātā or such some place near there.

when he sported in its waters. With its thousand waves moving to and fro it appeared as though the river approached him hesitatingly. When the great ocean was agitated by his thousand arms, the mighty Asuras residing in the netherworlds hid themselves in fright. With his thousand arms the king agitated the ocean scattering the great waves into sprays, making the fishes and huge whales move about in flutter and flurry, causing the gusts of wind split the foams and stirring up the eddies.

182-185. Thus, he agitated the ocean like the Mandara mountain that had been churned formerly by Devas and Asuras and that stirred up the milk ocean.

Great serpents were frightened by stirring up the ocean. They were suspicious that Garuḍa was about to swoop down on them. In their fear they jumped up. On seeing the terrible excellent king they bowed down with their hoods motionless. They appeared like the stumps of plantain trees swayed by the wind in the evening. By the exercise of his bowstrings he bound the haughty king of Laṅkā (Rāvaṇa)[1] after making him faint with five arrows. He defeated his army in the battle of Laṅkā. Capturing and bringing him under his control forcibly he imprisoned him in his city of Māhiṣmatī.

186. On hearing that his grandson Rāvaṇa had been imprisoned by Sahasrārjuna, sage Pulastya went to Māhīṣmatī and met Sahasrārjuna.

187-193. On being requested by Pulastya he released Rāvaṇa the grandson of Pulastya.

The loud twanging report of his bowstring made on his thousand arms resembled that of the thunderbolt of the throbbing cloud at the close of Yugas.

---

1. Rāvaṇa—grandson of Pulastya and son of Viśravas. He had two brothers Kumbhakarṇa and Vibhīṣaṇa and a sister Śūrpaṇakhā. He had also a step-brother, Kubera who being the eldest among brothers became the king of Laṅkā. But Rāvaṇa drove him out and himself became a king. Well-versed in the Vedas and the performer of penance and sacrifices Rāvaṇa was called a Rākṣasa because he and his mighty team of warriors protected the country's coast. The Vālmīki Rāmāyaṇa, which contains the oldest record of his activities derives the term Rākṣasa from rakṣ to protect. Because of his immoral activities the term lost its original meaning and came to be used in derogatory sense.

Indeed, the vain and vigour of Bhārgava was very wonderful since he cut off the thousand arms of that king, the arms that resembled the golden cluster of palm trees.

Once, thirsty fire-god begged of him for enough material to quench his thirst. Accordingly the heroic Sahasrārjuna granted the fire-god his request for alms, the seven continents, cities, villages, cowherd colonies—nay the whole of his realm. Due to the power of Sahasrārjuna all these blazed along with the eagerness of fire-god to burn more. He burned the mountains and forests of Kārttavīrya. Though accompanied by the firegod he was extremely frightened when he burned the vacant but beautiful hermitage of Vasiṣṭha the son of Varuṇa. Formerly, Varuṇa had begot this brilliant excellent son who became a seer.

194-201. That sage Vasiṣṭha became famous as Āpava. The saintly lord Āpava cursed Arjuna—"A great misdeed has been perpetrated by you, O Haihaya, in not having spared this forest of mine. A powerful man will kill you. The mighty and valorous son of Jamadagni named Rāma will chop off your thousand arms. The powerful resplendent brahmin the descendant of Bhṛgu will thrash you and kill you."

No doubt, the king had secured the boon whereby the subjects obtained prosperity and did not come to grief. (No doubt) he suppressed his foes. The prosperity of his subjects could be retained only as long as he protected them righteously.

But, due to the curse of the sage, he acted unrighteously and had to court death. In fact, O brahmins, a boon to that effect (i.e. death at the hands of his superior alone) had been chosen by himself. The noble king had a hundred sons, but only five of them survived. These were heroic, mighty and righteous. They were trained in the right use of missiles. They were famous. They were Śūrasena, Śūra, Vṛṣaṇa, Madhupadhvaja and Jayadhvaja.

This Jayadhvaja was a king of Avanti. Kārttavīrya's sons were mighty and vigorous.

202. Jayadhvaja's son was Tālajaṅgha of great might. He had a hundred sons who became well known as Tālajaṅghas.

203-204. O excellent sages ! many groups of valorous kings are well known among the noble descendants of Haihaya. They were—the Vītihotras, Suvratas, Bhojas, Avantis, Tauṇḍikeras,

Tālajaṅghas, Bharatas and Sujātas. They had not been recounted in detail because they are too numerous.

205. O brahmins, Vṛṣa and others were the descendants of Yadu (Because of Yadu they are called Yādavas). They were meritorious in their activities. Vṛṣa was the founder of a separate line. Madhu was his son.

206. Madhu had a hundred sons. Vṛṣaṇa was the perpetuator of the line. Because of Vṛṣaṇa they are called Vṛṣṇis. Because of Madhu they are known as Mādhavas.

207-209. The Haihayas are called Yādavas after Yadu.

He who daily repeats the story of Kārttavīrya will never incur the loss of wealth. He will regain what is lost.

O excellent brahmins, the lines of the five sons of Yayāti have been glorified thus. They were heroes (wellknown all over the world. O excellent sages, just as the five elements sustain the mobile and immobile beings, they support the worlds.

210-213. On hearing the five lines of kings a king will become an expert on virtue and wealth. He will have self-control. He will have five sons. He will get five rare and excellent things in the world—longevity, fame, sons, prowess and prosperity by retaining five groups in memory. Even as I relate, O excellent sages, listen to the line of kings descending from Kroṣṭṛ who perpetuated the line of Yadu, who performed sacrifices and who was meritorious in his activities. One is liberated from all sins on listening to the line of Kroṣṭṛ since in his family was born god Viṣṇu himself. He uplifted the family of Vṛṣṇi.

CHAPTER TWELVE

Birth of Kṛṣṇa

Lomaharṣaṇa said:

1. Kroṣṭṛ had two wives—Gāndhārī and Mādrī. Gāndhārī gave birth to Anamitra of great might.

2. Mādrī gave birth to Yudhājit and Devamīḍhuṣa. Thus the flourishing family of Vṛṣṇis came to be threefold.

3. Mādrī had two (more) sons : the splendid Vṛṣṇi and Andhaka. Vṛṣṇi had two sons—Śvaphalka and Citraka.

4. O excellent sages, there is no fear from sickness, no fear of drought in the place where Śvaphalka the righteous soul is present.

5. O excellent sages, once, Indra the chastiser of Pāka did not shower rain in the realm of the king of Kāśi, for three years.

6. He therefore brought the excessively honoured Śvaphalka there (to his kingdom). Due to the arrival of Śvaphalka, Indra showered rain.

7-8. Śvaphalka married the daughter of the king of Kāśī, named Gāndinī. She was so called because she gave every day a cow to a brahmin. Akrūra a liberal donor, a performer of sacrifices, a learned hero and one fond of receiving guests, was born of Śvaphalka. He distributed wealth as gift to the Brahmins.

9-10. Other sons too were born viz.—Upamadgu, Madgu, Medura, Arimejaya, Avikṣita, Akṣepa Śatrughna, Arimardana, Dharmadhṛk, Yatidharma, Dharmokṣa, Andhakaru, Āvāha and Prativāha. Varāṅganā a beautiful daughter was also born to him.

11. O excellent brahmins, Prasena and Upadeva of divine splendour were born to Ugrasenā, a woman of beautiful limbs, by Akrūra.

12-17. Citraka begot these sons—viz. Pṛthu, Vipṛthu, Aśvagrīva, Aśvabāhu, Svapārśvaka, Gaveṣaṇa, Ariṣṭanemi, Aśva, Sudharmā, Dharmabhṛt, Subāhu, and Bahubāhu, and two daughters Śraviṣṭhā and Śravaṇā. He begot of Asiknī the heroic son Śūra, Devamīḍhuṣa. Ten courageous sons were born of the crowned queen Bhojyā. At the outset was born the mighty Vasudeva (otherwise known as) Ānakadundubhi (so called because) when he was born drums were beaten in heaven and the loud report of Ānaka drums arose in the skies. At that time heavy shower of flowers fell on the abode of Śūra. In the whole of this mortal world there was none equal to him in handsome features. He was foremost among men and he had the splendour of the moon.

18-24. The other nine sons were born:—Devabhāga, Devaśravas, Anādhṛṣṭi, Kanavaka, Vatsavān, Gṛñjama, Śyāma, Śamīka and Gaṇḍūṣa. He had five excellent ladies as daughters—

Pṛthukīrti, Pṛthā, Śrutadevā, Śrutaśravā and Rājādhidevī. These five were mothers of mighty heroes. Jagṛhu was born as the son of Śrutadevā and the king of Avanti. King Śiśupāla was born of Śrutaśravā and the king of Cedī. Formerly, he had been Hiraṇyakaśipu the king of Daityas. Dantavakra of great might, the heroic overlord of Karūṣas was born of Pṛthukīrti as the son of Vṛddhaśarman. Kunti adopted Pṛthā as his daughter. Pāṇḍu married her. King Yudhiṣṭhira conversant with virtuous conduct was born of Kunti through the blessings of Dharma; Bhīmasena was born through the blessings of Vāyu and Arjuna was born through the blessings of Indra. Arjuna was a hero who had valour and exploit equal to that of Indra. In the whole world he had none to face him in a chariot-battle. Śini was born of Anamitra the youngest of the sons of Vṛṣṇi.

25. Satyaka was the son of Śini and Yuyudhāna was the son of Satyaka. Uddhava was the blessed son of Devabhāga.

26-28. They call the excellent Devaśravas the most excellent among the learned men. Anādhṛṣṭi begot of Aśmaki, Śatrughna a son who repulsed foes and earned fame.

Śrutadevā too gave birth to a son. The son of Śrutadevā is well known as Naiṣādi (a son of Niṣāda-hill tribe). O excellent sages, he was Ekalavya who was brought up by the Niṣādas (huntsmen).

Vasudeva the valorous son of Śūra gave his broom-born heroic son Kauśika to Vatsāvan who had no issue. He gave the son (as in a religious act) along with water libations.

29-31. To Gaṇḍūṣa who had no son, Viṣvaksena gave his sons Cārudeṣṇa, Sudeṣṇa and Pañcāla who had characteristic-marks of a warrior. He was a warrior who never remained without a battle. O excellent brahmins, this mighty warrior was the youngest son of Rukmiṇī. When Cārudeṣṇa went on his compaigns thousands of crows closely followed him thinking—"Today we will enjoy the delicious flesh of those who are killed by Cārudeṣṇa".

32. Tantrija and Tantripāla were the two sons of Kanavaka. Vīru and Aśvahanu were the two heroic sons of Gṛñjama.

33-34. Śamīka was the son of Śyāma. Śamīka ruled over a kingdom. He felt depressed being a mere Bhoja. Hence he performed a Rājasūya sacrifice. Ajātaśatru the destroyer of enemies was born to him. Henceforth, I shall describe the heroic sons of Vasudeva.

35. Thus the race of Vṛṣṇi is threefold. It is mighty and it has many branches. One who retains this extensive race in memory is never afflicted by any calamity.

36-38. Vasudeva had fourteen excellent women as his wives. The first five were: a descendant of Purū named Rohiṇī, Madirā, Vaiśākhī, Bhadrā and Sunāmnī. The second set of seven ladies comprised Sahadevā, Śāntidevā, Śrīdevī, Devarakṣitā, Vṛkadevī, Upadevī and Devakī. The thirteenth and the fourteenth were Sutanu and Yādavī. These two had at first been maid servants.

39. The descendant of Purū named Rohiṇī was the daughter of Bāhlika. O excellent sages, she was the eldest and most favourite wife of Ānakadundubhi.

40-41. Rohiṇī had eight sons and a daughter. The eldest son was Rāma. The others were Śāraṇa, Śaṭha, Durdama, Damana, Śubhra, Piṇḍāraka and Uśīnara. The daughter was named Citrā. O excellent sages, this Citrā afterwards became famous as Subhadrā.

42. The renowned Śauri (Kṛṣṇa) was born of Devakī and Vasudeva. The beloved son Niśaṭha of Rāma was born of Revatī.

43. Abhimanyu, the skilled chariot-fighter was born of Subhadrā and Arjuna Satyaketu was born of the daughter of king of Kāśī and Akrūra.

44. Understand individually by their names the sons of great valour who were born to Vasudeva in his highly blessed seven wives.

45-50. Bhoja and Vijaya were the two sons of Śāntideva. Vṛkadeva and Gada were the two sons of Sunāmā. Vṛkadevī gave birth to the noble son Agāvaha. The daughter of the king of Trigarta and wife of Śiśirāyaṇi was inquisitive to ascertain his manliness. No semen was discharged. In his twelfth year he had the colour of a black pig. Falsely accused, Gārgya was urged by anger. He seized a cowherd lass and began to indulge in sexual intercourse. That cowherd lass was a heavenly nymph in disguise. She conceived the foetus of Gārgya. It was unerring and very difficult to bear. It was through the behest of the trident-bearing lord Śiva that the heavenly nymph, the wife of Gārgya, in human form had done this. A heroic son of great might named Kālayavana was born of her.

51-57. O excellent sages, the boy grew up in the harem of a Yavana who had no son. He grew into a youth of leonine frame. The upper half of his body was shapely muscular and cylindrical. Hence, he came to be called Kālayavana.

The king (Yavana) was in the habit of fighting. He asked the excellent brahmin Nārada who mentioned the Vṛṣṇis and Andhakas as the persons whom he should fight. He marched against Mathurā with an Akṣauhiṇī of soldiers. He sent a messenger to the Vṛṣṇis and Andhakas. Keeping the highly intelligent Kṛṣṇa as their leader the Vṛṣṇis and the Andhakas met together and took counsel as they were afraid of the Yavana king. They decided to run away. Out of deference to the Pināka-bearing lord Śiva they abandoned Mathurā and resolved to colonise Kuśasthalī, Dvāravatī.

CHAPTER THIRTEEN

The Family of Vṛṣṇis

Lomaharṣaṇa said:

1. Kroṣṭṛ had a son of great fame named Vṛjinīvān. Svāhi the most excellent of sacrificers was the son of Vṛjinivān.

2-3. King Uṣadgu the most excellent of eloquent ones was the son of Svāhi. Desirous of progeny, a very excellent son, he performed several sacrifices wherein much wealth was gifted to the sacrificing priests. Citraratha endowed with many holy rites was born as his son.

4. Heroic Śaśabindu was the son of Citraratha. He performed sacrifices wherein much wealth was distributed as the sacrificial fee. He followed the holy conduct of life lived by saintly kings.

5. King Pṛthuśravas of extensive fame was the son of Śaśabindu. Those who are conversant with the Purāṇas praise Antara as the deserving son of Pṛthuśravas.

6-7. Suyajña was the son of Antara. Uṣat was the son of Suyajña. He performed all sorts of sacrifices. He had great reverence for Religion. Śineyu the scorcher of enemies was the son of Uṣat. King Maruta his son was a saintly king.

8-9. Marut obtained Kambalabarhis as his eldest son. Although he was against holy rites due to wrath, he performed many such rites desiring to obtain a son for his son Kambalabarhis. After a hundred still born children the son Rukmakavaca was born.

10. After killing a hundred bowmen protected with coats of mail by means of sharp arrows in the battle, Rukmakavaca attained excellent glory.

11-13. Parajit, the slayer of inimical heroes, was born of Rukmakavaca. Parajit had five valiant sons. viz.—Rukmeṣu, Pṛthurukma, Jyāmagha, Pālita and Hari. The father gave Pālita and Hari to Videhas. With the support of Pṛthurukma, Rukmeṣu became a king. Externed by both of them, king Jyāmagha stayed in a hermitage.

14-16. The tranquil king was advised by the brahmins (to conquer new territories). Taking up his bow and waving his flag in his chariot the king went to another land on the banks of Narmadā. Single-handed he conquered the cities of Mekhalā[1] and Mṛttikāvatī.[2] After conquering the mountain Ṛkṣavān[3] he stayed in Śūktimatī.[4] Jyāmagha's wife Śaibyā was a powerful chaste woman. Hence, though he had no son in her he did not marry another woman.

1. *Mekhalā* (*Mekalā*). Mekhalā was a country which had attained Puranic fame in ancient India. The inhabitants of this place were called Mekhalas. They were Kṣatriyas (warriors) formerly. But they became persons of low caste when they showed jealousy towards the Brahmins.

2. *Mṛttikāvatī,* a place of habitation in ancient Bhārata. Bhojas, as a Yādava tribe, dwelt in Kṛṣṇa's kingdom in Su-rāṣṭra and Bhojas inhabited Mṛttikāvatī, situated somewhere on this north-eastern limits of the modern Gujarat.

3. *Ṛkṣavān*—One of the seven principal mountains in India.

4. *Śūktimatī*—Identification not certain. Śūktimatī range might be the southern portion of the Eastern Ghats and the hills of Mysore. General Cunningham's identification of Śūktīmat mountains where the town Śuktimat was laid out, with the high range of mountains to the south of Sehoa and Kanker, which gives rise to Mahānadī, Pairi and Seonath Rivers is challenged by F.E. Pargiter (Mar. Pu. p. 285).

17. He gained victory in another battle and captured a virgin thereat: Slightly afraid the king told his wife—"Here is your daughter-in-law".

18-19. On hearing this she said to him—"O lord, pray tell me whose daughter-in-law she is? On hearing it, the noble king Jyāmagha said:—

The king said:

"I have brought this girl as the wife of the son who will be born to you".

Lomaharṣaṇa said:

20. Due to severe penance of that virgin, that fortunate chaste woman Śaibyā, in her old age, gave birth to the son Vidarbha.

21. Vidarbha begot of this daughter-in-law, a princess, two learned heroic sons Kratha and Kaiśika who became experts in warfare.

22. Bhīma was Vidarbha's son and Kunti was his son. The valorous son Dhṛṣṭa was born to Kunti. He was very bold in battle.

23. Three heroic sons of very great virtue were born to Dhṛṣṭa, Viz., Āvanta, Daśārha and the powerful Viṣahara.

24. Vyoman was the son of Daśārha. It is said that Jīmūta was Vyoman's son. Jīmūta's son was Vikṛti and Bhīmaratha was his son.

25. Navaratha was Bhīmaratha's son and his son was Daśaratha. Śakuni was born to him.

26-27. From him was born Karambha king. Devarāta was the son of Karambha and his son was Devakṣatra. Daivakṣatri, was the son of Devakṣatra. He looked like a divine child. He earned great fame. King Madhu of sweet speech was also born to him. It was he who perpetuated the line of Madhu.

28-29. Purudvān the most excellent man was born of Madhu in his wife Vaidarbhī (daughter of the Vidarbha king). Madhu had another wife Aikṣvāki (born of the family of Ikṣvāku). Satvan endowed with good qualities was born of her. He enhanced the glory of Sātvats: After knowing this creation of Jyāmagha of noble soul one attains pleasure and is always blessed with progeny.

Lomaharṣaṇa said:

30-38. Kauśalyā bore many sons to Sātvata richly endowed with pious qualities viz.—Bhāgin, Bhajamāna, the divine king Devavṛdha, Andhaka of mighty arms, Vṛṣṇi and Yadunandana (?) The detailed narrative of the four has been glorified here.

Bhajamāna had two wives viz Bāhyaka Sṛñjayī and Upabāhyaka Sṛñjayī. Many sons were born to him in these two wives. Krimi, Kramaṇa, Dhṛṣṭa and the heroic Purañjaya, these were born to Bhajamāna in Bāhyaka Sṛñjayī.

Ayutajit, Sahasrajit, Śatajit and Daśaka—these were born to Bhajamāna in Upabāhyaka Sṛñjayī.

King Devavṛdha who had performed sacrifices resolved thus—"A son endowed with good qualities should be born to me." Accordingly he performed an elaborate penance. While performing penance, it was the water of Parṇāsā[1] river that he used always (for drinking and bathing purpose). The river did everything to please him. She was worried with thoughts about him. She could not decide what to do. That excellent river thought thus in view of the auspicious nature of that king—"He has not yet found out a woman in whom he can beget such a son (endowed with all good qualities). Hence, I shall myself go and become his wife."

39. She became a young maiden assuming a fine physical form. She wooed the king and the lord too liked her.

40-41. The liberal king impregnated her with a brilliant foetus. On the tenth month, the most excellent of women gave birth to Babhru Devavṛdha who was endowed with good qualities.

In this context, those who are conversant with the Purāṇic lore are heard singing thus about this race glorifying the good qualities of the noble Devavṛdha.

42-44. Whether we look at him in front or from far or at close quarters, Babhru is the most excellent among men. Devabṛdha was equal to Devas. Seven thousand sixtysix men attained

1. *Parṇāśā,* or (Varṇāśā) is the modern Banas, there are two rivers of this name, (1) a tributary of the Chambal rising near Udayapur and (2) a stream rising near mount Abu and flowing in the Rann of Kacchh.

immortality due to Babhru Devavṛdha. He performed many sacrifices, he was the lord of donors, most intelligent, favourably disposed towards the brahmins; he held weapons with a steady grasp. His family was very big. The Bhojas of Mṛttikāvatī belonged to his family.

45-48. The daughter of Kāśya bore four sons to Andhaka—Viz. Kukura, Bhajamāna, Śaśaka and Balabarhis.

Vṛṣṭi was the son of Kukura. Kapotaroman was the son of Vṛṣṭi. His son was Tittiri. Punarvasu was born to him. Abhijit was born to Punarvasu. It is said that twin sons were born to Abhijit. They were known as Āhuka and Śrāhuka. They were the most excellent of all who earned renown.

49-54. In this context they cite the following verses about Āhuka. "The exalted Āhuka resembles a youth, is endowed with eighty coats of mail, goes ahead with attendants in white livery. The following shall not go in front of him—He who has no son, he who has not given one hundred gifts, who is not destined to live for a thousand years, who is not of pure activities and who does not perform sacrifices. To the East ten thousand elephants marched along with ten thousand chariots rumbling like clouds. Their banners scraped the lap of the moon (i.e. they flowed and fluttered at a great height). They were fitted with protective fenders. Twentyone thousand huge boxes filled with silver and gold accompanied them. To the northern quarter as many thousands of these had parched. The Bhojas were the protectors of entire Earth. Their hands are scared with the tinkling bells and bowstrings."

They say this also—The Andhakas gave their sisters in marriage to Avantis.

55. Two sons were born of Kāśya and Āhuka—Devaka and Ugrasena. Both of them were on a par with divine children.

56. Four sons comparable to Devas were born to Devaka—Devavān, Upadeva, Sudeva and Devarakṣita.

57-61. He had seven daughters who were married to Vasudeva—Devakī, Śāntidevā, Sudevā, Devarakṣitā, Vṛkadevī, Upadevī and Sunāmnī.

Ugrasena had nine sons. Kaṁsa was the eldest. Others were Nyagrodha, Sunāman, Kaṅka, Subhūṣaṇa, Rāṣṭrapāla, Sutanu, Anāvṛṣṭi and Puṣṭimān.

Five excellent ladies were their sisters—Kaṁsa, Kaṁsavatī, Sutanu, Rāṣṭrapālī and Kaṅka.

Ugrasena of the family of Kukura has been described along with children.

A man who retains in memory the race of the Kukuras of unmeasured prowess shall attain an extensive family for himself after being blessed with children.

CHAPTER FOURTEEN

How the Syamantaka Jewel was brought back ?

Lomaharṣaṇa said :

1. Vidūratha, a prominent chariot-warrior was the son of Bhajamāna. The heroic Rājādhideva was the son of Vidūratha.

2-3. The following valiant sons were born to Rājādhideva viz.—Datta, Atidatta, Śoṇāśva, Śvetavāhana, Śami, Daṇḍaśarman, Dantaśatru and Śatrujit. Śravaṇā and Śraviṣṭhā were their sisters.

4. Pratichatra was the son of Śami. Svayambhoja was the son of Pratichatra. Hṛdīka was born to Svayambhoja.

5-6. All his sons possessed great valour. Kṛtavarmā was the eldest among them. Śatadhanvā was the middle one. The other sons were Devānta, Narānta, Vaitaraṇa, who was a physician, Sudānta, Atidānta, Nikāśya and Kāmadambhaka.

7-8. The wise Kambalabarhiṣā was the son of Devānta. He had two sons Asamaujas and Nāsamaujas. No son was born to Asamaujas. His brother gave his sons Sudaṁṣṭra, Sucāru and Kṛṣṇa to Asamaujas.

Thus Andhakas have been described.

9. Gāndhārī and Mādrī were the wives of Kroṣṭṛ. Gāndhārī gave birth to Anamitra of great might.

10. Mādrī gave birth to Yudhājit (known as) Devamīḍhuṣa. She gave birth to Anamitra who conquered the enemies and who was never defeated in battlefield.

11. Nighna was Anamitra's son. Two sons were born to Nighna: Prasena and Satrājit. Both of them conquered the armies of enemies.

12. Prasena was a resident of Dvāravatī. He came to acquire a great Jewel, named Syamantaka[1] from sun.

13-23. The sun was his close friend, a friend no less than his own vital breath. Once, as the night was about to pass off, the king, the most excellent one among the chariot-warriors, went to the banks of the river in his chariot in order to bathe and worship the deity. Even as he was praying to Sun-god the deity appeared in his presence. The lord revealed his physical form with the halo of brilliant refulgence. The king addressed the sun-god standing before him thus—"O lord of Luminaries I see you standing in front of me with your brilliant disc in the same manner as I see you in the firmament. What special significance has been accorded to me as a result of your being my associate ?"

On hearing this, the lord took off the excellent jewel Syamantaka and kept it aside. Then the king saw him in his (bare) physical form. On seeing him he became pleased and chatted with him for a short while. Then Satrājit spoke to him as he rose up to go—"O lord, you illuminate the worlds continuously. Hence, it behoves you to give me this excellent jewel."

Then the Sun gave him the Syamantaka jewel. The king tied it round his neck and entered the city. The people rushed at him shouting "Here goes the sun". The king made his city and the harem wonder-struck. He gave that excellent Jewel to his brother Prasenajit lovingly.

24. The jewel exuded molten gold in the abode of Vṛṣṇis and Andhakas. The clouds showered rains at the proper season. There was no fear from sickness.

25. Lord Kṛṣṇa desired to get the excellent jewel from him.

28. The Vṛṣṇis and Andhakas had come to know that Kṛṣṇa had requested for the jewel. Hence they suspected him to be the cause of Prasena's death.

29. Being suspected thus the righteous Kṛṣṇa who had not

1. *Syamantaka.* The details of this fabulous gem are found in this and the following chapter. It is not possible to identify this gem with the Kohinoor that adorns the British crown.

perpetrated that felony took the vow "I will fetch that jewel" and went to the forest.

30-33. He wandered all over the places where Prasena had been hunting. He got the footsteps of Prasena traced through trust-worthy persons.

Searching through the excellent mountains Ṛkṣavān and Vindhya he became tired. Then the lofty-minded Kṛṣṇa saw Prasena lying slain along with his horse but did not get that jewel. Then, not far off from the dead body of Prasena the lion was seen killed. A bear was indicated (as the culprit) by the footsteps. Following those footsteps lord Kṛṣṇa went to the abode of the bear.

34-35. In the cave he heard the words uttered by a woman. O brahmins, they had been uttered by the nurse who was holding the boy, the son of Jāmbavān and who was playing with the jewel. The words "Do not cry" had been uttered by her.

The Nurse said:

36. "The lion killed Prasena. The lion was killed by Jāmbavān. O gentle boy, do not cry. This Syamantaka is yours".

37-38. Since the words were clear he hastened to the cave. He placed Yadus along with his brother Balarāma at the entrance to the cave. He himself entered the cave quickly. He saw Jāmbavān staying inside the cave.

39. Then he fought a hand-to-hand fight with Jāmbavān within the cave for twentyone days.

40. After Kṛṣṇa had entered the cave (and did not come out for long) Balarāma and others returned to Dvāravatī and announced that Kṛṣṇa was slain.

41. Kṛṣṇa defeated Jāmbavān of great might and obtained Jāmbavatī the daughter of the king of bears, acclaimed (by all).

42. He took the Syamantaka jewel in order to clear himself (of false accusation). After consoling the king of bears he came out of the cave.

43-45. With humble attendants going ahead of him, Kṛṣṇa returned to Dvārakā. Bringing the jewel and clearing himself of the false charge he gave it to Satrājit in the open assembly of Sātvatas. Thus Kṛṣṇa the slayer of foes who had been falsely accused, redeemed the Syamantaka and cleared himself.

Satrājit had ten wives and hundred sons in them.

46. Three of them were well renowned. Bhaṅgakāra was the eldest. Others were the heroic Vātamati and Vasumedha. O excellent brahmins, his three daughters too were famous in the quarters.

47-50. Satyabhāmā was the most excellent among them. Others were Vratinī of steady holy rites and Prasvāpinī. He gave (Satyabhāmā) to Kṛṣṇa. The sons of Bhaṅgakāra were Sabhākṣa and Nāveya, the most excellent men. They were endowed with good qualities, well renowned and richly enduced with handsome features. Yudhājit was born as the son of Mādrī and Vṛṣṇi (?). Śvaphalka and Śīgraka were born as the sons of Vṛṣṇi. Śvaphalka married the daughter of the king of Kāśi.

51. She was Gāndinī by name. Her father gave him many cows. The mighty son well known as Śrutavān was born of her.

52-59. Then the highly blessed Akrūra who distributed wealth in gift was born. (The other sons were)—Upamadgu, Madgu, Mudara, Arimardana, Ārikṣepa, Upekṣa, Arimejaya the slayer of foes, Dharmabhṛt, Dharma, Gṛdhrabhoja, Andhaka, Āvāha and Prativāha. There was a fair-complexioned daughter Sundarī. She was the crowned queen of Viśrutāśva. His daughter was Vasundharā who was endowed with beauty and blooming youth. She was the most charming among all Sātvatas; Akrūra begot of Ugrasenā two sons Vasudeva and Upadeva. They had divine refulgence and delighted the race. Citraka's sons were—Pṛthu, Vipṛthu, Aśvagrīva, Aśvabāhu, Supārśvaka, Gaveṣaṇa, Ariṣṭanemi, Dharma, Dharmabhṛt, Subāhu and Bahubāhu. He had two daughters Śraviṣṭhā and Śravaṇā.

False accusations never befall him, nay they never touch him who understands false accusation of Kṛṣṇa that has been cited here.

CHAPTER FIFTEEN

Akrūra Obtains Syamantaka

Lomaharṣaṇa said:

1. Babhru Akrūra got the excellent jewel Syamantaka which Kṛṣṇa had handed over to Satrājit, stolen through Śatadhanvan of the Bhoja family.

2. Akrūra had sought Satyabhāmā, the uncensured lady. He was waiting for an opportunity to seize Syamantaka jewel.

3. The mighty Śatadhanvā killed Satrājit at night, took away the jewel and handed it over to Akrūra.

4-5. O brahmins, Akrūra took the excellent jewel and contracted alliance with Śatadhanvan—"I should not be exposed by you. If you are attacked by Kṛṣṇa we will come to your support. Undoubtedly the whole of Dvārakā abides by me today."

6-7. When her father was killed, Satyabhāmā became extremely dejected. She rode in her chariot to the city of Vāraṇāvata and informed her husband (Kṛṣṇa) of what had been committed by Śatadhanvan of the Bhoja family. After intimating everything to her husband, the aggrieved lady shed profuse tears.

8. After performing the obsequies and offering libations of water to the Pāṇḍavas who were (supposed to have been) burned, Hari engaged Sātyaki for the condolence rites for the Pāṇḍavas.

9. Śrīkṛṣṇa then, hastened to Dvārakā and spoke to Balarāma, his elder brother.

Śrīkṛṣṇa said:

10-11. Prasena was killed by the lion, Satrājit by Śatadhanvan. Syamantaka must come to me. O lord, I am its owner. Hence, O mighty one, get into the chariot quickly. After killing the mighty Bhoja we shall take possession of Syamantaka.

Lomaharṣaṇa said:

12-19. Then a tremendous battle took place between Bhoja and Kṛṣṇa. Śatadhanvan searched for Akrūra all round.

On seeing Bhoja and Śrīkṛṣṇa engaged in a duel, Akrūra, though capable did not show sympathy on account of a curse (?). The frightened Bhoja resolved to run away on Hṛdayā (his mare) who raced a hundred and odd Yojanas. She was known to be capable of running a hundred Yojanas at a stretch, O brahmins, it was the mare he rode when he fought with Śrī Kṛṣṇa. After he had covered a hundred Yojanas he found Hṛdayā exhausted. She was killed. The vital airs went up due to fatigue and misery. Kṛṣṇa said to Rāma.

Śrīkṛṣṇa said:

"O mighty one, stay here. I have detected some defects in the horse. I shall go on foot and seize the excellent jewel Syamantaka." O Brahmins, Śrīkṛṣṇa who was fully conversant with the excellent missiles went on foot and at the outskirts of Mithilā he killed Śatadhanvan.

20-21. But he did not find the Syamantaka jewel on his person. Rāma said to him when he returned after killing the mighty Bhoja "Give me the jewel." K ṛṣṇa said—"It is not with me." Then Rāma became furious, rebuked him vigorously uttering "Fie on you, fie on you" and spoke thus.

Balarāma said:

22. "I excuse you because you happen to be my brother. Goodbye I am going to leave you for ever. I have nothing to do with you, nor with Dvārakā, nor with the Vṛṣṇis".

23. Then Rāma, the suppressor of foes, entered Mithilā where he was honoured by the king with coveted gifts.

24. In the meantime Babhru Akrūra the most excellent one among the intelligent persons performed many sacrifices unrestrictedly.

25. For obtaining Syamantaka, the excessively famous son of Gāndin donned the coat of mail in the form of initiation as a protective means.

26. For sixty years the virtuous soul displayed jewels and other precious stones in the sacrifice alone.

27. The sacrifices of that noble soul are known as Akrūrayajñas. Dainty food and monetary gifts were distributed in all of them. Whatever was sought by a person was given to him.

28. It was then that lord Duryodhana went to Mithilā and received training from Balarama in the exercise of divine missiles.

29. Later on, Rāma was appeased by Vṛṣṇi leaders and

Andhakas as well as by the noble Kṛṣṇa who brought him back to Dvārakā.

30-34. After getting Satrājit killed while he was asleep along with his kinsmen, Akrūra of great might, the leader of men, had also left Dvārakā. He too was persuaded to return along with the Andhakas. Kṛṣṇa condoned his guilt because he was afraid of creating split amongst his own people.

After the departure of Akrūra there had been no shower in that realm. Due to drought the land had become lean. Then the Kukuras and Andhakas appeased and propitiated Akrūra. When that lord of charitable gifts re-entered Dvāravatī the thousand-eyed lord (Indra) rained profusely over the Kakṣa region.

O excellent sages, as a token of affection the intelligent Akrūra gave to Śrīkṛṣṇa his sister of approved conduct in marriage.

35. Then, by his Yogic power Kṛṣṇa understood that the jewel was with Babhru Akrūra. In the open assembly Śrikṛṣṇa said to Akrūra.

Śrīkṛṣṇa said:

36-37. O lord worthy of honour, hand back that excellent jewel which is in your possession. Do not commit anything ignoble. O sinless one, the fury that has been surging within me for the last sixty years has grown terribly. Much time has elapsed. It brooks no further delay.

38-40. Then, at the instance of Kṛṣṇa, Babhrū handed over the jewel without a strain in the assembly of Sātvatas.

Kṛṣṇa, the suppressor of foes, was delighted in his mind when the jewel was secured by straightforward means from Babhru. But he returned it to Babhru.

Tying the excellent jewel Syamantaka round his neck after it had been handed over to him by Kṛṣṇa the son of Gāndinī shone on earth as the sun shines in the sky.

CHAPTER SIXTEEN

Seven Continents[1]

The sages said:

1-9. A wonderfully great narrative has been related by you. The stories of Bharata kings, of Devas, Dānavas, Gandharvas, Nāgas, Rākṣasas, Daityas, Siddhas, and Guhyakas have been narrated; their wonderful exploits, activities and holy rites have been recounted. Different divine stories and excellent nativities have been mentioned. O highly intelligent one, the creation of Brahmā, Prajāpatis, Guhyakas and celestial nymphs has also been narrated by you. How the mobile and immobile beings were born, how the manifold universe originated has been told by you, O highly blessed one. This beautiful narration has been heard by us. The ancient tradition that yields meritorious benefits has been mentioned in sweet and smooth flowing words. It delights our mind as well as our ear. It is on a par with nectar. Now we wish to hear about the entire zone of the earth. O omniscient one, it behoves you speak it out. We are very eager to hear. How many are the oceans, continents sub-continents, mountains, forests, sacred rivers and holy spots of Devas etc. O highly intelligent one, what is the magnitude of each, what is their support? Of what nature are they? It behoves you to narrate the stance of this universe precisely.

---

1. Seven Continents : (1) Jambū (2) Śāka, (3) Kuśa, (4) Plakṣa, (5) Puṣkara, (6) Śālmali (7) Krauñca. A short description of these continents is as follows: (1) Jambū—It is the central one of the seven continents surrounding the mountain Meru, so called either from the Jambū trees abounding in it or from an enormous Jambū tree on Mount Meru visible like a standard to the whole continent. See S. M. Ali, Op. cit., chapters V-VII *on Jambūdvīpa*.

(2) Śāka can be identified with Malaya, Siam, Indo-China and Southern China or the South-Eastern corner of the land mass of which Jambūdvīpa occupied the centre.

(3) *Kuśa* included Iran, Iraq, the south-western corner of the land mass round Meru.

(4) *Plakṣa* identified with the basin of Mediterranian since Plakṣa or Pākhara tree is the characteristic of warm temperate or Mediterranian lands identifiable with Greece and adjoining lands.

(5) *Puṣkara* covered the whole of Japan, Manchuria and the south-eastern Siberia.

Lomaharṣaṇa said:

10. O sages, please hear as I succinctly relate it to you. A full detailed description of it is impossible even in the course of a hundred years.

11-12. O brahmins, there are seven continents viz—Jambū, Plakṣa, Śālmala, Kuśa, Krauñca, Śāka and Puṣkara. These are encircled by seven oceans, the briny ocean, sea of the sugar-cane juice, wine, ghee, curds, milk and sweet water.

13. The Jambūdvīpa is situated in the middle. In its centre, O leading brahmins, is the Meru the mountain of gold.

14-15. Its over-all height is eightyfour thousand Yojanas. Sixteen thousand Yojanas of it constitute the portion beneath the ground. The peak portion extends to thirtytwo thousand Yojanas. At its root the extent all-round is sixteen thousand Yojanas. This mountain stands as the pericarp of the lotus of the earth.

16. The Himavān, Hemakūṭa and Niṣadha are the Varṣa mountains to its South. The Nīla, Śveta and Sṛṅgin are the Varṣa mountains in the north.

17. The two in the middle extend to a hundred thousand (Yojanas) and others are ten (thousand Yojanas) less. They are two thousand Yojanas in height and girth.

18-24. Bhārata is the first sub continent, then is the Kimpuruṣa Varṣa O brahmins, these and another varṣa viz. Hari-

---

(6) *Śālmala*—the tropical part of Africa bordering the Indian Ocean on the West. It included Madagasgar—the Zenj of the Arab and Persian geographers, the Hariṇa of the Purāṇas and the Śaṁkhadvīpa of some other writers.

(7) *Krauñca* is represented by the basin of the Black Sea.

(8) *Upadvīpas* (sub-continents): (1) Bhārata (2) Kimpuruṣa (3) Hari-varṣa (4) Ramyaka (5) Hiraṇmaya (6) Uttarakuru (7) Ilāvṛta (8) Bhadrāśva and (9) Ketumāla. According to P.E. (p. 342) there are eight long mountain ranges which divide the island Jambu into 9 countries which look like nine petals of the lotus flower.The two countries of the north and south extremities (Bhadra and Ketumāla) are bow-shaped. Four of the remaining seven are longer than the rest. The central country is known as Ilāvṛta.

varṣa are to the South of Meru. Ramyaka is a northern subcontinent. Next to it, is Hiraṇmaya. The northern Kurus are like Bhārata. O excellent brahmins, each of these extends to nine thousand Yojanas. There is the Ilāvṛta Varṣa. In its centre stands the lofty golden Meru. O highly blessed ones, the Ilāvṛta Varṣa extends to nine thousand Yojanas in all directions from Meru. There are four mountains here which stand as the extensive supporting pillars of Meru. They extend to ten thousand Yojanas. The mountain Mandara lies in the east, Gandhamādana is to the south. Vipula is to the west and the Supārśva is to the north. There stand the following trees—Kadamba, Jambū Pippala and Vaṭa as the flag staff of mountains. They extend to eleven hundred Yojanas. O excellent brahmins, the Jambū tree gives the name Jambūdvīpa to this continent.

25. Each of the fruits of this Jambū tree is of the size of a huge elephant. These fruits fall all over the top of the mountain and get shattered and scattered.

26. By the juice of these, the famous Jambū river flows and it is being drunk by the people staying there.

27. The people there are hale and hearty and sound in mind because they drink it. They never even perspire. No bad odour comes out of their bodies. They do not experience old age or debility of sense-organs.

28. The clay on the banks gets soaked in the juice. When it gets dry by the gentle wind that blows there it becomes gold. It is called Jāmbūnada. The ornaments for Siddhas are made thereof.

29. The Bhadrāśva subcontinent is to the east of Meru, Ketumāla is to the west. O excellent sages, between these two Varṣas lies the Ilāvṛta Varṣa.

30. The park of Caitraratha is in the east; the Gandhamādana is in the south; the Vaibhrāja is in the west and the Nandana is in the north.

31. There are four lakes frequented and enjoyed by Devas—the Aruṇoda, Mahābhadra, Asitoda and Mānasa.

32. The Kesara mountains to the east of Meru are—Śāntavān, Cakrakumbha, Kurarī, Mālyavān, Vaikaṅka and others.

33. Trikūṭa, Śiśira, Pataṅga, Rucaka, Niṣadha and others are the Kesara mountains to the south of Meru.

34. Śikhivāsa, Vaidūrya, Kāpila, Gandhamādana, Jānudhi etc. are the Kesara mountains to the west.

35-39. They are very proximate to the Meru and are stationed in its belly. Śaṅkhakūta, Ṛṣabha, Haṁsa, Nāga, Kālañjara etc. are the Kesara mountains to the north.

O leading brahmins, at a height of fourteen thousand Yojanas on the Meru is the great city of Brahmā. All round it in the eight quarters are the excellent and famous cities of Indra and other guardians of the quarters.

Originating from the foot of Viṣṇu and flooding the disc of the moon Gaṅgā falls down from Heaven to the city of Brahmā and flows all round. Having fallen there it flows into four streams in the four directions.

40-46. They are Sītā, Alakanandā, Cakṣu and Bhadrā in order.

The Sītā flows along the firmament to the East from mountain to mountain. Then through Bhadrāśva, the Varṣa in the east, it flows into the ocean.

Similarly, O excellent brahmins the Alakanandā flows to the south, approaches Bhārata and splitting itself into seven streams it flows into the ocean.

The Cakṣu crosses the western mountains and reaches Ketumāla the western Varṣa and then flows into the sea.

O excellent brahmins, the Bhadra crosses the northern mountains and the northern Kurus and then flows into the northern ocean.

The mountains Mālyavān and Gandhamādana extend upto Nīla and Niṣadha mountains. The Meru is in the centre of these two. It is stationed in the form of pericarp.

The Bhāratas, Ketumālas, Bhadrāśvas and Kurus are the petals of Loka mountain outside the mountains of boundary.

The Jaṭhara and Devakūṭa are the two mountains of boundary. They extend from south to north between Nīla and Niṣadha mountains.

47-51. The Gandhamādana and the Kailāsa extend from west to east, to eighty thousand Yojanas. They are stationed in the ocean. Niṣadha and Pāriyātra—the two mountains of boundary—extend from south to north between Nīla and Niṣadha. They are stationed to the east and west of Meru.

The Triśṛṅga and the Jarudhi are the northern Varṣa mountains. They extend from east to west and are stationed within the ocean; they extend from one ocean to another.

Thus, O brahmins, the boundary mountains have been mentioned by me. They are stationed in pairs within the belly of Meru in all the four quarters.

52-53. Around the Meru the Kesara mountains are situated. They have already been mentioned alongwith Śītānta and others. O brahmins, the water troughs amongst those mountains are very charming. They are frequented by Siddhas and Cāraṇas. The forests and the cities in them are very beautiful.

54. There are excellent shrines of Lakṣmī, Viṣṇu, Agni, Sūrya and Indra in them, O excellent sages. They are frequented by men and Kinnaras.

55. Gandharvas, Yakṣas, Rākṣasas, Daityas and Dānavas sport about in those charming water troughs day and night.

56. O brahmins, these places are heavens on earth. They are abodes of the righteous. Those who commit sins never go there even after hundreds of births.

57. O brahmins, in the Bhadrāśva sub-continent lord Viṣṇu stays as Hayaśiras with the head of a horse; in the Ketumāla he stays in the form of a boar and in the Bhārata he assumes the form of a tortoise.

58. Eternal Govinda stays in the Kurus in the form of a fish. Hari, the lord of all, stays everywhere in his Viśvarūpa (Universal form).

59-62. O brahmins, he is the support of all and identical with all.

O excellent brahmins, in the eight Varṣas, Kimpuruṣa etc. there is neither misery, nor fatigue, neither strain nor fear of hunger.

The subjects are healthy and sound, free from agony and devoid of distress. They live upto ten or twelve thousand years. No earthly worries such as hunger or thirst assail them, O brahmins. In these sports there is no such division of time: Kṛta, Tretā, Dvāpara and Kali.

In each of these Varṣas there are seven mountains called Kulācalas.[1] O excellent sages, hundreds of rivers flow there.

CHAPTER SEVENTEEN

Jambūdvīpa

Lomaharṣaṇa said:

1. To the north of ocean and to the South of Himālayas is the sub-continent Bhārata. The subjects are called Bhāratis.

2. O leading sages, its extent is nine thousand Yojanas. This is the land of holy rites to those who opt for heavenly pleasure and absolution.

3. The seven Kulaparvatas are Mahendra, Malaya, Sahya, Śūktimān, Ṛkṣa, Vindhya and Pāriyātra

4. It is from here, O brahmins, that the heaven is attained; one attains absolution too from here, men attain the state of different species of animals or fall in hell from here alone.

5. It is from here alone that men go to heaven or realize absolution at the end of their series of birth. Nowhere else on the earth are holy rites prescribed for men.

6-8. Listen to the nine divisions of this sub-continent.[2] The are Indradvīpa, Kaserumān, Tāmraparṇa, Gabhastimān, Nāgadvīpa, Saumya, Gāndharva and Vāruṇa.

---

1. *Kulaparvatas*—Kulaparvata is a chief mountain range. Kulaparvatas are seven in number. Any one of these is supposed to exist in each Varṣa or division of a continent. The principal seven ranges of Bhārata Varṣa include (1) Mahendra (2) Malaya (3) Sahya (4) Śuktimat (5) Ṛkṣa (6) Vindhya and (7) Pāriyātra. (See 17.3)

2. Bhārata itself is a group of nine islands each separated from the other by oceans and not made easily accessible between each other. They are (1) Indradvīpa (2) Kaśerumān (3) Tāmraparṇa (4) Gabhasti (5) Saumya (6) Gāndharva (7) Vāruṇa (8) Nāga (9) Bhārata. In some of the Purāṇas, *Saumya* is replaced by *Siṁhala*; in others *Siṁhala* is substituted for Gandharva.

S. M. Ali identifies the nine islands as follows:

(1) *Aindra*—the Trans-Brahmaputra region.

(2) *Kaśerumat*—the coastal plain between the deltas of Godāvarī and Mahānadī.

Bhārata, the ninth among them, is an island encircled by the ocean. This island extends from South to North a thousand Yojanas.

Kirātas stay in the East, Yavanas stay in the West.

9. Brahmins, Kṣatriyas and Vaiśyas stay in the centre. Śūdras stay everywhere. These people have their means of subsistence in sacrifice, battle, trade and service.

10. O sage, the Śatadrū, Candrabhāgā and other rivers have their source at the foot of the Himavān. The Vedasmṛti and other rivers originate from the Pāriyātra.

11-14. The Narmadā, Surasā and other rivers flow from the Vindhya. The Tāpī, Payoṣṇī, Nirvindhyā, Kāverī and other rivers flow from the foot of the Ṛkṣa mountain and as it is well known they dispel sin.

The Godāvarī, Bhīmarathī, Kṛṣṇaveṇī and other rivers originate from the foot of Sahya. As it is said they dispel the fear of sins. The Kṛtamālā, Tāmraparṇī and other rivers start from Malaya. The Trisandhyā, Ṛṣikulyā and other rivers have their source in Mahendra. The Ṛṣikulyā, Kumāra and other rivers flow from the foot of Śūktimān.

15-19. There are thousands of tributaries and branches of these rivers. The people of this land bathe in and drink their waters. They are the Kurus, Pañcālas, the people of middle land, eastern lands, residents of Kāmarūpa; people of southern territories such as Pauṇḍras, Kaliṅgas and others. The Parāntyas westerners) Saurāṣṭras, Śūdras, Ābhīras, Arbudas, Murukas, Mālavas, residents of Pāriyātra, Sauvīras, Saindhavāpannas, Śālvas, residents of Śākala territory, Madrārāmas, Ambaṣṭhas, Pārasīkas and others. They drink waters of these rivers and stay on their banks. They are highly blessed, hale and hearty.

---

(3) *Tāmravarṇa* or Tāmraparṇa (associated with the river Tāmraparṇī)—the sector of the Indian peninsula south of Kāverī river.

(4) *Gabhastimān*—the hilly belt between Narmadā and Godāvarī rivers.

(5) *Nāga*—colonies and kingdoms extended all over the mountainous belt between Narmadā ranges upto Chhota Nagpur.

(6) *Kaṭāha*—Kathiawad region.

(7) Siṁhala—Ceylon, not mentioned in this Purāṇa.

(8) Vāruṇa—the western coast of India. The Arabian Sea has long been known as the abode of Varuṇa.

(9) Bhārata is the ninth division.

According to Cunningham Greater India was divided into nine Khaṇḍas.

20. O great sage, the four Yugas, viz. Kṛta, Tretā, Dvāpara and Kali are reckoned only in Bhārata and nowhere else.

21. The ascetics perform penance here; the Yajvins perform sacrifices; people give charitable gifts with devotion to obtain heaven.

22. Here, in the Jambūdvīpa the Supreme Being is worshipped through sacrifices. It is Viṣṇu who is identified with sacrifice that is worshipped. In other Dvīpas he is worshipped otherwise.

23. O great sage, in the Jambūdvīpa, it is the subcontinent Bhārata which is most excellent since it is the land of holy rites and activities. Others are the regions of enjoyment.

24. Here, O excellent one, after thousands and thousands of birth alone does a creature attain human birth sometimes through the accumulation of merits.

25-29. It is said that Devas sing (its praise thus):—"Blessed are they who are born (again and again) as men in Bhārata which is the source of heavenly pleasures as well as liberation.

Holy rites should be performed in utter disregard of their benefits. They must be dedicated to Viṣṇu identical with the Ātman. Those who are pure attain birth in the land of holy rites (i.e. Bhārata) and get merged into that infinite Being (after death)'. We do know that when the merit that had originally yielded heavenly pleasures subsides, those who are blessed will be re-born in the land of Bhārata and not those who are devoid of intelligence.

O brahmins, this Jambūdvīpa, which consists of nine subcontinents and which extends to a hundred thousand Yojanas has been mentioned by me.

O brahmins, the briny sea that extends to a hundred thousand Yojanas and that is like a bangle in shape encircles the Jambūdvīpa externally.

CHAPTER EIGHTEEN

The Magnitude of Oceans and Continents

Lomaharṣaṇa said:

1. Just as the Jambūdvīpa is encircled by the briny sea so also the briny sea is encircled by the Plakṣa dvīpa.

2. The extent of Jambūdvīpa is one hundred thousand Yojanas. O brahmins, twice that is cited as the extent of Plakṣa-dvīpa.

3-4. Medhātithi, the overlord of the Plakṣadvīpa, had seven sons. The eldest was Śāntabhaya by name. Śiśira was the next one. Others were Sukhodaya, Ānanda, Śiva, Kṣemaka and Dhruva. All of them were kings in Plakṣa Dvīpa.

5. The sub-continents are Śāntabhaya, Śiśira, Sukhada, Ānanda, Śiva, Kṣemaka and Dhruva.

6. There are Varṣaparvatas, the mountains demarcating the boundary. They are only seven, O excellent sages. Listen to their names.

7. They are Gomeda, Candra, Nārada, Dundubhi, Somaka, Sumanas and Vaibhrāja.

8. O sinless ones, accompanied by Devas and Gandharvas the subjects live in the charming Varṣa mountains and lands.

9. The countries and territories therein are holy. People are born after long periods (of gestation). Neither mental agony nor ailments afflict them. They feel happy throughout the year.

10. There are seven rivers in these Varṣas which flow into the oceans. I shall name them. Their mention dispels sins altogether.

11. They are Anutaptā, Śikhī, Vipāśā, Tridivā, Kramu, Amṛtā and Sukṛtā. These are seven rivers there.

12. O brahmins, the mountains and rivers mentioned here are the main ones. Small rivers and mountains are in thousands there.

13. The people of the region drink waters thereof and feel delighted. Every river, O brahmins, flows downwards and no river flows up.

14. O excellent brahmins, the different Yugas are not reckoned in these seven climes. The time is perpetually like that of the Tretā-yuga.

15. O Brahmins, in all these continents beginning with Plakṣa and ending with Śaka the people live for five thousand years without any ailment.

16-17. Dharma is of four types among them in accordance with the divisions of Varṇas (castes) and Āśramas (stages of life). The Varṇas are four.

O learned men, I shall mention them to you, O excellent sages, they are Āryakas, Kurus, Vivasvats and Bhāvins. They are brahmins, Kṣatriyas, Vaiśyas and Śūdras.

18. In the centre, there is a big tree of the size of Jambū tree. It is the Plakṣa tree from which O excellent brahmins, the continent derives its name.

19. Hari identical with all, lord of all, creator of the universe is worshipped in the form of Soma (Moon) by those Varṇas, Āryakas and others.

20. The Plakṣa is encircled by the ocean of Sugarcane juice. It is of the same size as the continent Plakṣa and it emulates a halo around it.

21. Thus, O excellent sages, the Plakṣa continent has been recounted to you briefly. Now I shall tell you the history of Śālmaladvīpa.

22-23. O brahmins, the overlord of Śālmaladvīpa is the heroic Vapuṣmān. O excellent brahmins, his sons are Śveta, Harita, Jīmūta, Rohita (Harita?) Vaidyuta, Mānasa and Suprabha. There are seven Varṣas named after them.

24. The ocean of Sugarcane juice is encircled by Śālmaladvīpa twice its size in extent.

25. It should be known that there are seven mountains there, the source of jewels. They signify the different Varṣas. There are seven main rivers too.

26-27. The mountains are: Kumuda, Unnata, Balāhaka, Droṇa that abounds in great medicinal herbs, Kaṅka the fifth mountain, Mahiṣa the sixth and Kakudmān the seventh. Now, O brahmins I shall mention names of the rivers.

28. They are Śroṇī, Toyā, Vitṛṣṇā, Cakrā, Śukrā, Vimocanī and Nivṛtti. Merely on being remembered they quell sins immediately.

29-32. The seven Varṣas are Śveta, Lohita, Jīmūta, Harita,

Vaidyuta, Mānasa and Suprabha. These Varṣas contain the four Varṇas.

O excellent brahmins, in the Varṣas of Sālmala Dvīpa the Varṇas stay. They are Kapilas (tawny), Aruṇas (pink), Pītas (yellow) and Kṛṣṇas (black). They are brahmins, Kṣatriyas, Vaiśyas and Śūdras. They worship lord Viṣṇu, the lord of all, the unchanging Ātman, in the form of wind. They worship by performing sacrifices. They worship the lord stationed in Yojanas.

33. In this charming place there live Devas. Śālmalī is the tree which gives the continent its name.

34. This is encircled by the ocean of wine which in extent is equal to Śālmaladvīpa itself.

35. The ocean of wine is encircled by Kuśadvīpa twice the size of Śālmala in extent.

36-38. Jyotiṣmān is the overlord of Kuśadvīpa and has seven sons. They are Udbhida, Venuman, Svairatha, Randhana, Dhṛti, Prabhākara and Kapila. The Varṣa mountains are named after them. Human beings stay there along with the Daityas and Dānavas. So also stay Devas, Gandharvas, Yakṣas, Kimpuruṣas and others. There also live four Varṇas interested in carrying out their duties.

39. O excellent brahmins, they are Damins, Śuṣmins, Snehas and Mandehas. They are to be cited in order as brahmins, Kṣatriyas, Vaiśyas and Śūdras here.

40-42. Since their authority declines by the performance of holy rites the people in Kuśadvīpa worship Janārdana as Brahman and dispel Ugra, the fierce deity, the bestower of the benefit of Adhikāra.

O excellent brahmins, the following are the seven Varṣa mountains in that Dvīpa:—Vidruma, Hemaśaila, Dyutimān, Puṣṭimān, Kuśeśaya, Hari and Mandāra mountain.

43-44. The rivers are seven. Listen to their names in order. They are Dhūtapāpā, Śivā, Pavitrā, Sammati, Vidyudambhas, Mahī and unnamed river. All these dispel sins of the worshipper. There are thousands of other small rivers and mountains.

45. There is a stump of Kuśa grass in the Kuśa Dvīpa and this gives the continent its name. This Dvīpa is encircled by an ocean of ghee of an equal size.

46. The ocean of ghee is encircled by Krauñca Dvīpa. O excellent sages, Krauñcadvīpa is another great continent. May the account of the same be heard attentively.

47. It extends to twice the size of Kuśadvīpa In Krauñcadvīpa, Dyutimān is the over-lord and the noble Dyutimān had seven sons.

48-54. The king named Varṣas after the names of his sons. They were—Kuśaga, Mandaga, Uṣṇa, Pīvara, Andhakāraka, Muni and Dundubhi. O brahmins, these were his seven sons.

O excellent sages, there are Varṣas, mountains very charming and frequented by Devas and Gandharvas. Now, I shall mention their names. They are Krauñca, Vāmana, Andhakāraka, Devavrata, Dama, Puṇḍarīkavana and the great mountain Dundubhi. The latter ones are twice in size of the previous ones. Just as one Dvīpa is twice another Dvīpa in size, the mountains also are twice in size. In these charming Varṣas and on these excellent Varṣa mountains the subjects live without agony along with the groups of Devas. O excellent brahmins, they are known as Puṣkalas and Puṣkaras. They are brahmins, Kṣatriyas, Vaiśyas and Śūdras cited in due order. O excellent sages, listen to the names of rivers which they drink from.

55-61. There are hundreds of local rivers but the following seven are chief:—Kumudvatī, Sandhyā, Rātri, Manojavā, Khyāti and Puṇḍarīkā. These seven are Varṣa rivers.

The lord Janārdana, in the form of Yogirudra is also worshipped there by the Varṇas, Puṣkara and others at the holding of a sacrifice.

The Krauñca Dvīpa is encircled all round by the ocean of the skin of curds of equal magnitude. O excellent sages, the ocean of the skim of curds is encircled by Śākadvīpa, whose magnitude is twice as that of Krauñca dvīpa.

Bhavya the noble lord of Śākadvīpa had seven sons and he gave them seven Varṣas.

The sons were—Jalada, Kumāra, Sukumāra, Manīraka, Kusumoda, Moaaki and Mahādruma. The seven Varṣas, are named after their names in due order.

62-64. There are seven mountains in that continent which demarcate the boundary of Varṣas. The mountains are Udayagiri, Jaladhāra, Raivataka, Śyāma, Ambhogiri, Āstikeya and Kesarī the most excellent of all mountains.

Śāka is the great tree here. It is frequented by Siddhas and Gandharvas. On coming into contact with the wind blowing from its leaves, great delight is experienced.

65. Many realms are there consisting of four castes. Noble souls devoid of agony and calamity stay there.

66-67. There are highly meritorious rivers here. They dispel sins and fears thereof. They are :—Sukumārī, Kumārī, Nalinī, Reṇukā, Ikṣu, Dhenukā and Gabhasti. O excellent brahmins, there are ten thousands of other small rivers there.

68-70. There are hundreds and thousands of mountains also. Those who are stationed in clouds etc drink joyously the water of those rivers. The realms in the Varṣas are equipped with the fourth aim of life (i.e. liberation). The rivers too are holy and they descend to Earth from heaven. There is no loss of Dharma, no struggle, no sorrow. Nor is there any action repugnant to the limits of decency in those seven regions.

71-74. The four Varṇas are Magas, Māgadhas, Mānasas, and Mandagas. The Magas are brahmias; Magadhas are Kṣatriyas; Mānasas are Vaiśyas and Mandagas are Śūdras.

Viṣṇu, who has assumed the form of the sun is worshipped by the residents of Śākadvīpa by performing appropriate holy rites in the manner they are laid down. The residents have perfect control of their souls and minds.

O brahmins, Śākadvīpa is encircled by the ocean of milk of the size of Śākadvīpa. It is as though encircled by a girdle.

O brahmins, the ocean of milk is encircled by Puṣkaradvīpa.

75-76. Puṣkaradvīpa is twice as much as the Śākadvīpa in size.

In Puṣkaradvīpa the over-lord is Savana and his sons are Mahāvīta and Dhātaki. The two Varṣas are named after them —Mahāvīta and Dhātakikhaṇḍa.

77. O highly blessed ones, there is only one Varṣa mountain named Mānasottara. It is well renowned. It has the shape of a girdle. It is in the centre of Dvīpa.

78. It is fifty thousand Yojanas high and extends to many Yojanas. It is cylindrical in shape.

79. This mountain is so stationed that it appears to divide

the circular Dvīpa in the middle. Hence, the two Varṣas are separated.

80. Each of the two halves is circular in shape and the great mountain is between them. Men there live upto ten thousand years.

81-84. They are devoid of ailments and sorrow. They are free from passion and hatred. O brahmins, there is no distinction of the base and excellent, of the killer and the killed among them. They do not have malice, jealousy, fear, fury, defect or greed and similar base qualities.

The Mahāvīta Varṣa adorned by the Dhātaki-khaṇḍa is frequented by Devas, Daityas and others on the Mānasottara mountain.

In that Dvīpa called Puṣkara there is neither truth nor falsehood. There are neither rivers nor mountains. Men have similar dresses and features. They are similar in form to Devas.

85. The continent is devoid of Varṇas, Āśramas and the conduct of life as such. It is devoid of holy rites. There is neither the Vedic lore, nor the Science of polity, neither business manual nor the code of service.

86. Consisting of two Varṣas, O brahmins, it is called the terrestrial heaven. The time passes happily with everyone devoid of old age and sickness.

87. Such is the situation O brahmins, in the Puṣkara, Dhātakikhaṇḍa and Mahāvīta.

In the Puṣkaradvīpa the holy fig tree is the excellent abode of Brahmā.

88-89. Brahmā stays there, worshipped by Devas and Asuras.

Puṣkara is encircled by the ocean of meat, water equal in size and extent to it.

Thus the seven Dvīpas are surrounded by the seven oceans.

90. The Dvīpa and the ocean that surrounds it are equal. The latter one is twice in size as the earlier one.

The water in each of these oceans remains always the same in volume.

91-94. They do not become less or more in the manner that water in a pot becomes less when heated by fire.

When the moon waxes, the water in the ocean does not

increase. Waters move up or down in the same volume, neither more not less.

O excellent sages, during the moonrise and moonset in the two halves of the lunar month the waters of the ocean are seen moving up or down one thousand five hundred Aṅgulas.

The diet of the people in the Puṣkara Dvīpa comes to them by itself.

95-99. O brahmins, there the subjects enjoy foodstuffs of all the six tastes always.

All round the ocean of sweet water a world is seen stationed. It is twice the size of the ocean. The ground is golden but devoid of all creatures.

Beyond that is the mountain Lokāloka extending to ten thousand Yojanas. That mountain is as many thousand Yojanas in height also.

Beyond that is darkness. It has encircled the mountain all round. That darkness is enveloped by the cauldron of the Egg (Aṇḍakaṭāha).

This universe extends to fifty crores of Yojanas along with the Aṇḍakaṭāha, Dvīpas, oceans and mountains.

O excellent brahmins, this earth is the support of all worlds. It is superior to all other creations, it is noble and excellent.

CHAPTER NINETEEN

The Magnitude of Netherworlds

Lomaharṣaṇa said :

1. O excellent sages, the extent of the Earth has been related. Its height (above the lowermost of the nether worlds) is said to be seventy-thousand Yojanas.

2-8. O excellent sages, each one of the nether worlds is a thousand Yojanas above the lower one. The seven netherworlds are—Atala, Vitala, Nitala, Sutala, Talātala, Rasātala and Pātāla.

The grounds of these nether worlds are black, white, pink, yellow, gravelled, rocky and golden. O leading brahmins, excellent palaces adorn them.

In them the communities of Dānavas, Daityas and kins, men of Nāgas of huge bodies live, O excellent brahmins:

Nārada who entered the heavenly assembly coming straight to heaven from the nether regions said that the nether worlds were more charming than the heavenly world.

There are pure jewels of brilliant lustre which delight the onlookers. The ornaments of the Nāgas, the residents of the nether regions shine splendidly in heaven; there is nothing that is equal to it.

Who is not attracted and delighted by the right of nether regions which are rendered splendid by the lasses of Daityas and Dānavas ? Even a liberated soul is drawn to it. During daytime, rays of the sun spread diffused light but not the glaring sunlight.

9-20. During the night the light of the moon is not utilised for its coolness but only for illumination.

Since that passes away is not taken notice of by the Nāgas who enjoy with gaiety the foodstuffs and the edibles they consume and the great beverages they drink. Nor are Danujas and others aware of it.

O brahmins, the forests, rivers, lakes, and lotus ponds, the cooing of the cuckoo and other sweet birds, the pleasing skies, the unguents and the continuous notes and sounds of musical instruments such as the lute, flute and Mṛdaṅga drums, O brahmins—all these and other beautiful things are enjoyed by virtue of their good luck by Dānavas, Daityas and Nāgas residing in Pātāla. The Tāmasī form of Viṣṇu, named Śeṣa is beneath the lower regions.

Daityas and Dānavas are not capable of recountig his good qualities. He is honoured by Devas and celestial sages. He is spoken of as Ananta. He has a thousand hoods and he is clearly bedecked in Svastika ornaments devoid of impurities. He illuminates all quarters by thousand jewels on his hoods.

For the welfare of the universe he deprives the Asuras of their prowess. His eyes whirl and rove due to intoxication. He has only one earring at all times.

Wearing a crown and garlands he shines like a white mountain aflame with fire.

He is clad in blue garments. He is intoxicated with pride. He is resplendent with white garlands. He is lofty like the mountain of Kailāsa where the celestial Gaṅgā falls. He has placed his hand on the plough-share; he holds an excellent iron club. He is attended upon by the embodied splendour of Varuṇa.

At the end of the Kalpa, Rudra in the form of Saṅkarṣaṇa comes out of his mouth, blazing like the flame of poisonous fire and devours the three worlds.

He holds the entire sphere of the world rising above like a peak.

21-27. Worshipped by the entire hordes of Devas Śeṣa is stationed at the root of Pātāla. His prowess, power, form and features cannot be described or known even by the gods. The whole of the Earth is turned into pink by the flames of jewels on his hoods. It acts as a floral garland for Śeṣa. Who will be able to recount his prowess? When Śeṣa with his eyes rolling and roving due to intoxication, yawns and stretches himself, the whole of the Earth along with its rivers, forests and mountains, quakes and moves.

The Gandharvas, Apsaras, Siddhas, Kinnaras, Nāgas and Rākṣasas never reach the end of his good qualities. Hence, he is Ananta. He is unchanging. The Nāga lasses apply red sandal paste on him as unguent. Wafted by the wind of respiration it acts as the perfumed powder for the quarters. It was by propitiating him that the ancient sage Garga understood the luminaries factually and the predictive astrology based on omens.

The Earth is thus held on his head by the noble Nāga. He holds universe including Devas, Asuras and human beings.

CHAPTER TWENTY

Hells in nether regions

Lomaharṣaṇa said :

1. Thereafter, O brahmins, the hells are situated beneath the waters. The sinners are hurled down into them. Now, hear about them attentively, O excellent brahmins.

2-6. They are Raurava, Śaukara, Rodha, Tāna, Viśasana, Mahājvāla, Taptakumbha, Mahālobha, Vimohana, Rudhirāndha, Vaitaraṇī, Kṛmīśa, Kṛmibhojana, Asipatravana, Kṛṣṇa, Lālabhakṣa, Pūyavaha, Pāpa, Vahnijvāla, Adhaḥśiras, Sadaṁśa, Kṛṣṇasūtra, Tamas, Avīci, Śvabhojana, Apratiṣṭha and a second Avīci. There are other similar hells extremely terrible which fall under the jurisdiction of Yama. They terrify by means of weapons and fires. The persons who are engaged in sinful activities fall into them.

7. He who commits perjury, he who speaks with partiality and he who utters falsehood falls into Raurava hell.

8. O excellent sages, he who destroys a foetus, he who murders his preceptor, he who slays cows and he who suffocates others—all these fall into terrible Raurava hell.

9. He who drinks wine, he who slays a brahmin, he who steals gold and he who comes into contact with these—all these fall into Śūkara hell.

10. He who murders a king, a Vaiśya and a royal soldier, he who defiles the bed of his preceptor and he who indulges in sexual intercourse with his sister—all these fall into Taptakumbha hell.

11. He who sells his chaste wife, he who keeps wine for sale, he who sells saffron and he who discards a devoted friend or servant—all these fall into Taptaloha hell.

12-13. He who indulges in sexual intercourse with his daughter or daughter-in-law is hurled into Mahājvāla hell. He who insults preceptors and elders, he who reviles at them, he who slanders the Vedas, he who sells the Vedas and he who cohabits with the forbidden women falls into Sabala hell, O brahmins.

14-17. A thief falls into Vimoha hell, so also the person who defiles the line of demarcation of boundary.

He who hates Devas, brahmins and Pitṛs, he who spoils jewels—falls into Kṛmibhakṣa hell.

He who performs an ill-conducted sacrifice falls into Kṛmīśa hell.

The base man who takes food prior to Pitṛs, Devas and guests falls into Lālābhakṣa hell. The maker of arrows falls into Vedhaka hell.

Those who make arrows with knots, those who make swords and other destructive weapons fall into the terrible hell Viśasana.

He who receives gifts from indecent men falls into Adhomukha hell.

18. He who performs a sacrifice on behalf of a person not entitled to that privilege, he who foretells by studying stars and he who partakes of sweet cooked food all by himself falls into Kṛmipūya hell.

19. O brahmins, the brahmin who sells lac, gravy, gingelly seeds and salt falls into the same hell.

20. O excellent brahmins he who rears or eats poultry, goats, pigs and birds falls into the same hell.

21-22. He who subsists on the stage or the trade of fish, he who partakes of food from the hand of the bastard, he who administers poison, he who adopts the profession of a spy or a secret informer, he who rears buffaloes, or being a brahmin indulges in sexual intercourse on Parvan days, he who commits arson, he who hates friends, he who behaves as a deceptive and he who performs a sacrifice on behalf of all and sundry in the village and he who sells Soma juice falls into hell Rudhirandha.

23-24. He who destroys honey, he who commits multi-murder of villagers falls into hell Vaitaraṇī.

Those who drink semen, those who break boundary lines or flout limits of decency, those who do not observe pollution (i.e. after birth of an infant or death of kinsman) and those who maintain themselves on deception fall into Kṛcchra hell. He who cuts off a forest in vain falls into hell Asipatravana.

25. Those who hunt wild goats, sheep, or deer fall into hell Vahnijvāla. O brahmins, they too who burn things that should not be burnt, fall into hell.

26. He who commits omissions in the observance of holy

rites and he who errs while performing duties of his stage (āśrama) fall into Sandaṁśa hell and endure its tortures.

27. Those men and religious students who have vowed to celibacy but who discharge semen by day or during dreams, at night and those who are taught by their sons fall into Śvabhojana hell.

28. These are the main hells, there are hundreds, and thousands of similar hells where the perpetrators of heinous crimes are cooked by day and night and tortured.

29. These sins and thousands of similar sins are atoned for by men who are brought to suffering to one or other of these hells.

30. Those who act contrary to the tenets of disciplined life of Varṇas and Āśramas mentally, physically or verbally, fall into these hells.

31. The gods in heaven are seen by the people of hells with their heads directed above. The gods see the residents of hells far below, their heads directed below.

32-33. The following beings attain absolution in that order:—the immobile beings, worms, aquatic animals, birds, animals, men, righteous persons and Devas. The latter ones of these constitute a thousandth part of the former ones among them. All these, O highly blessed ones, progress till they achieve salvation.

34. There are as many dwellers in hell as there are creatures in heaven. He who commits sins but is averse to expiate for them, falls into hell.

35. Holy rites of expiation have been mentioned by great sages in proportion to sins. They have mentioned them being fully aware which particular expiation is capable of quelling the particular sin.

36. O leading brahmins, Manu and other sages have mentioned rites of atonement—elaborate ones if the sin is elaborate and minor ones if the sin is minor.

37. The acts of expiations are in the nature of austerities or holy rites. Of all of them the remembrance of Śrī Kṛṣṇa is the most effective.

38. After committing a sin if a person repents for it, he should remember Viṣṇu—which is the sole rite of expiation for him. This is the greatest of all holy rites.

39. Remembering Viṣṇu at dawn, night, dusk or midday the man attains Viṣṇu because his sins are immediately quelled.

40. By remembering Viṣṇu his pains and strains perish immediately and they attain absolution. Attainment of heaven is an obstacle into him.

41. O leading brahmins, the benefits such as attaining the status of Indra as a result of Japa, Homa, worship etc are obstacles to a man whose mind is set on Vāsudeva.

42. Where is the attainment of heaven characterised by a return once again to the Earth? Where is the Japa of Vāsudeva which is the most excellent cause of absolution (where there is no return to this earth) ?

43. Hence, no brahmin, no man, who remembers Viṣṇu day and night, falls into hell. If he has incurred sins they perish immediately.

44. That which delights the mind is heaven. That which is contrary in effect is hell. O excellent brahmins, good and evil are given the appellations of heaven and hell.

45. The one and the same object is conducive to misery as well as happiness. It produces malice and wrath. Hence there can never be an object solely of the nature of sorrow?

46. The same object generates pleasure at the outset, but later on, it yields misery. The same object causes pain, wrath but later on gives pleasure.

47. Hence, there is nothing which is solely of the nature of sorrow or solely of the nature of pleasure. It is the changed phase of mind that is characterised by happiness or sorrow.

48. Knowledge alone is the greatest Brahman; knowledge alone is effective for removing bondage. The universe is of the nature of knowledge. There is nothing greater than knowledge.

49-50. O brahmins let this be understood that knowledge alone is learning and ignorance.

Thus the sphere of Earth has been recounted to you by me. Similarly, O brahmins, I have recounted the nether regions, hells, oceans, mountains, continents subcontinents and rivers succinctly. Everything has been mentioned to you. What else do you desire to know ?

CHAPTER TWENTYONE

Upper Regions

The sages said :

1-2. Everything has been mentioned to us by you. We wish to know further about the upper worlds Bhūr, Bhuvar, Svar etc. We also wish to know how the planets are stationed and what their magnitude is. O highly blessed Lomaharṣaṇa, mention these precisely.

Lomaharṣaṇa said :

3. That area which is illuminated by the rays of the sun and the moon is known as earth. It consists of oceans, rivers and mountains also.

4. The extent and magnitude of the sky is the same as those of the earth.

5. O brahmins, the disc of the sun is stationed a hundred thousand Yojanas away from the earth. The disc of the moon is stationed a hundred thousand Yojanas away from the sun.

6. Full hundred thousand Yojanas above the moon, the entire sphere of the stars shines.

7. O brahmins, mercury (Budha) is two hundred thousand Yojanas above the sphere of stars. Venus Uśanas is stationed so many Yojanas above Mercury.

8. Mars (Aṅgāraka) is stationed so many Yojanas above Venus. The preceptor of Devas, Jupiter, is stationed two hundred thousand Yojanas above Mars.

9. Saturn (Sauri) is stationed two hundred thousand Yojanas above Jupiter. The sphere of seven sages (the Great Bear), O excellent brahmins, is stationed a hundred thousand Yojanas beyond it.

10. Polestar Dhruva that is the pivot of entire luminaries is stationed a hundred thousand Yojanas above seven sages.

11. O excellent sages, the three worlds have been succinctly mentioned. This is the ground for the benefit of sacrifice. The sacrifice is established here.

12. The Maharloka is a crore of Yojanas above Dhruva. It is here that the Kalpavāsins reside.

13. The Janaloka is two crores of Yojanas above Mahar-

loka. It is here that Sanandana and other sons of Brahmā live. O brahmins, they are pure-minded.

14. Four times that distance above Janaloka (i.e. eight crores of Yojanas) is the Tapas region. It is there that the gods called Vairājas are stationed. They are devoid of physical forms.

15. Six times that distance above the Tapas region (i.e. 48 crores of Yojanas) shines the Satyaloka. This region releases one from the bondage of death (that which does not kill again) and is known as the world of Brahmā.

16. Wherever there is earthly ground or object that can be traversed by foot, it is called Bhurloka. Its extent has been mentioned by me.

17. O excellent sages, the space between the earth and the sun, frequented by the sages, Siddhas and others, is called Bhuvarloka. It is the second of upper worlds.

18. The space between Dhruva and the sun which extends to one million four hundred thousand Yojanas is said to be Svarloka by those who are conversant with the geography of the worlds.

19. This set of three worlds is called Kṛtaka (artificial) by the brahmins. The three worlds Jana, Tapas and Satya are called Akṛtaka (Natural).

20. In between the two, Maharloka is known as Kṛtakā-kṛtaka. At the end of a Kalpa it becomes empty but is not annihilated entirely.

21. O brahmins, these seven upper worlds have been mentioned by me to you as also the seven nether worlds. This is the detailed description of the cosmic Egg.

22. This is enveloped by the cauldron of the Egg (Aṇḍaka-ṭāha) all round, at the sides above and below like the seeds of an apple fruit.

23. The Egg is enveloped by water ten times its size. The encircling volume of water is enveloped by fire.

24. O brahmins, the fire is enveloped by wind; and the wind is enveloped by Ether. O excellent sages, the Ether is enveloped by Mahat.

25. These seven are such that the outer one is ten times the size of the inner one. The Pradhāna stands enveloping the Mahat.

26. It is infinite and endless. It has no reckoning since it cannot be measured by any unit, nor calculated by any figure.

27. O brahmins, it is the cause of entire creation. It is the great Prakṛti. There are thousands and thousands of such cosmic Eggs.

28-30. There are eggs like these, crores and hundred crores in number.

Just as there is fire in the wood, or oil in the gingelly seed so also the Puruṣa is stationed in the Pradhāna which it provides. He is known as the conscious Ātman.

O excellent brahmins, the Pradhāna and the Puruṣa are sustained by the Energy of Viṣṇu that is the soul of all living beings. They mix together in their activity. Thus the energy of Viṣṇu alone is the cause of separation and integration of Puruṣa and Pradhāna.

31-36. O excellent sages, at the creation of the universe it is the cause of agitation.

Just as wind contains chillness of each and every drop of water so also the Energy of Viṣṇu contains both Pradhāna and Puruṣa together.

A tree with its roots, stem and branches grows out of the first seed. Many seeds come out of that thereafter. From those seeds grow other trees. These have the same characteristics, causes and parts.

In the same manner the Mahat etc are evolved, at the outset from the unevolved Pradhāna. From the Mahat to Viśeṣa this is the process of creation. Therefrom the gods and others are born. Their sons are born, their sons and grandsons. It goes on.

Just as there is no deficiency or decline in the tree due to the growth of another tree from its seeds so also the elements do not dwindle by the creation of other elements.

37. Just as the Ether, time, etc. are as the cause of the tree by their mere presence, nearly so also Viṣṇu is the cause of universe without undergoing transformation.

38-40. In the seed of a grain all these are present in latent form—viz—the root, stalk, sprout, leaf, stem, ovary, flower, milk (soup), rice-grain, husks and the bits of grain. O excellent sages, when all the complements of causes for the growth are present, these parts, already present within manifest themselves.

In the same manner, the physical forms of gods and human beings are already present in the diverse activities. They grow up, by coming into contact with the energy of Viṣṇu.

41-44. That Viṣṇu is the great Brahman from whom this universe evolves, in whom it subsists and in whom it is dissolved.

That Brahman is the greatest abode; and the great region beyond Sat and Asat. The universe consisting of mobile and immobile beings is identical with him.

He alone is the Primordial Nature. He alone is the universe when his form becomes manifest. In him alone everything is evolved and dissolved.

He is the agent of rites; he is worshipped; he alone is the sacrifice and the benefit thereof; he alone is the means of sacrifice. There is nothing which is separate and different from him.

CHAPTER TWENTYTWO

Pole Star

Lomaharṣaṇa said :

1. Pole Star is situated at the tail end of the form of lord Viṣṇu in heaven which consists of constellations and which has the shape of Śiśumāra[1] (the Gangetic porpoise).

2. He himself revolves and he makes the moon, sun and other planets too revolve. The constellations follow him in a circular orbit.

3. Along with the planets, the sun, moon, stars and constellations are tied to Dhruva by *gaseous* rows and lines.

4-5. Viṣṇu is the greatest abode. He is the support of that luminous form in heaven with the shape of Gangetic porpoise mentioned above.

1. *Śiśumāra* (the Gangetic porpoise) is a constellation, so called because it is in the shape of a crocodile. It is said to be the starry form of Viṣṇu. At the tail-end of it is Dhruva which automatically rotates and also makes planets like the sun and the moon to rotate. Stars follow the self-rotating Dhruva and rotate like a wheel.

(Meditating on the lord) in his heart, the son of Uttānapāda, Dhruva propitiated the Patriarch Brahmā and stationed himself at the tail end of the stellar Gangetic porpoise.

6. The support of Siśumāra is Viṣṇu the presiding deity of all humanities. The Śiśumāra is the support of Dhruva and the sun is supported by Dhruva.

7. This entire universe including Devas, Asuras and human beings is supported by the sun. O brahmins, now listen, by what method he supports the universe.

8. For eight months the sun absorbs water in the form of juice. Then he showers water in the form of rain. That gives rise to foodgrains. This entire universe rests on food.

9-10. After absorbing water from the universe by his hot rays, the sun nourishes the moon. By the water-essence passing through the gaseous nerves the moon is held aloft over the clouds having their forms evolved out of smoke, fire and wind. The clouds are called Abhras because they hold waters and do not let them fall off.

11. When nudged by the wind the waters in the clouds fall off. O brahmins, they attain the impressions of previous actions activised by the opportune time, and become pure.

12. O brahmins, the sun-god absorbs four types of waters, viz. those of rivers, oceans, earth and those present in the living beings.

13-14. The multi-rayed sun absorbs water from the celestial Gaṅgā and immediately discharges it on to the earth without allowing it to get entangled with the clouds.

O excellent brahmins, the man who has washed the dirt of all sins due to his contact with it never falls into hell. Indeed, it is said to be a divine bath.

15. On seeing the sun, that water falls from heaven without the clouds acting as intermediary. That water from the celestial Gaṅgā is absorbed and cast off by the rays of the sun.

16. The water that falls from heaven on seeing the sun during Kṛttikā and other stars should be known as the water of Gaṅgā poured out by the elephants of quarters.

17. The water that falls down during the even numbered (i.e. Rohiṇī, Ārdrā etc) from heaven after being absorbed by the sun is immediately scattered by the rays of the sun.

18. O brahmins, both of them are extremely meritorious to human beings. They dispel sins. O excellent brahmins, one can have divine absolution with the waters of celestial Gaṅgā.

19. O brahmins, the water that is showered by the clouds nourishes living beings and makes the medicinal herbs grow well. It is the nectar that enlivens all.

20. All kinds of medicinal plants increase thereby. Until they are mature and ripe they continue to be the means to the people.

21. Day by day men with the sacred scriptures as their guides perform sacrifices in the manner they have been laid down and thereby nourish the gods.

22-23. The entire universe consisting of mobile and immobile beings is supported by rain. Thus the sacrifices, Vedas, castes beginning with the brahmins, Devas, animals and the rest of living beings—everyone is supported by rain. O excellent sages that rain is generated by the sun.

24. O excellent sages the support of the sun is the Polar Star and that of the Polar Star is Śiśumāra and that support of Śiśumāra is Viṣṇu.

25-26. Viṣṇu is stationed in the heart of Śiśumāra. He maintains all living beings. He is the primordial cause and eternal.

Thus, O excellent sages, the cosmic egg has been cited by me along with the divisions of the earth, oceans etc. What else do you desire to know ?

CHAPTER TWENTYTHREE

Holy Centres : Their Greatness

The sages said :

1. O Sūta conversent with piety, it behoves you to narrate the tale of holy shrines and centres over the earth. We are inclined to hear the same.

Lomaharṣaṇa said:

2. He whose hands and feet are clean, whose mind is fully restrained and who has learning, penance and fame, enjoys the benefit of visiting holy shrines.

3. The pure mind is the holy centre unto men. So also the control over speech and the restraint on the sense-organs. There are holy centres present in the physical body itself. They make the man understand the path of heaven.

4. The wicked mind situated within does not become purified by ablutions in the sacred water in the holy centres, like the unclean mudpot of stale liquor which cannot become pure even when washed with water a hundred times.

5. Neither holy centres, not charitable gifts nor holy rites, nor penance groves can purify the man whose mind is wicked, who takes delight in arrogance or who has not conquered his sense-organs.

6. Wherever a man stays after keeping his sense-organs fully under his control—the holy centres of Kurukṣetra, Prayāga and Puṣkara are present there.

7. Hence listen. I shall mention holy centres and sacred shrines—whatever there are on the earth, O excellent sages.

8-9 They cannot be explained in detail even in the course of hundreds of years.

O excellent brahmins I shall mention holy centres of Puṣkara, Naimiśa forest, Prayāga and Dharmāraṇya as the foremost among holy spots.

There are Dhenuka, Campaka and Saindhava forests.

10. The meritorious Sagarāraṇya forest, Daṇḍaka forest, Gaya, Prabhāsa, Śrītīrtha, and the divine Kanakhala.[1]

11. Bhṛgutuṅga, Hiraṇyākṣa, Bhīmakanyā, Kuśasthalī Lokārgala, Kedāra and Mandāra forest.

12. Mahālaya, Koṭitīrtha, that dispels sins, Rūpatīrtha, Śūkara and Cakratīrtha of great benefit.

13. Vyāsatīrtha, Somatīrtha, Śākhoṭakatīrtha, Kokāmukha tīrtha and the holy Badarī mountain.

---

1. *Kanakhala*—A holy place of pilgrimage on the bank of Gaṅgā. Kālidāsa refers to this place in his Meghadūta. This is the place where Dakṣa Prājāpati performed the sacrifice.

14. Somatīrtha, Tuṅgakūṭa, Skandāśramatīrtha, Sūryaprabha, Dhenusaras and the seventh āyuṣmika.?

15. Koṭitīrtha at Dharmodbhava, the Sārva-kāmika-tīrtha, Sūryaprabha, Mahākuṇḍa and Somābhiṣecanatīrtha.

16. Mahāśtotra, Koraka, Pañcadhāras Tridhāra, Saptadhāra, Ekadhāra and Amarakaṇṭakatīrtha.

17. Śālagrāma, Cakratīrtha, the excellent Kadalīhrada, Vidyutprabha, Devahradatīrtha, and Viṣṇuprabha.

18. Śaṅkhaprabha, Devakuṇḍa, Vajrāyudhatīrtha, Vastrāpada, Barhapada and Lokārohaṇa.

19. Svayaṁvaṭa, Bhadrabala, Kauśāmba, Divākara, Sārasvata Dvīpa, Vijayadvīpa, and Kāmaja Dvīpa.

20. (?) Sollayāṅgopacāra, Cavarambana, Pūrṇavat (?) Snānakuṇḍa, Prayāga and Guhā Viṣṇupada.

21. Kanyākuṇḍa, Vāyukuṇḍa, Jambūmārga the excellent holy centre, Gabhastitīrtha and the clean Yayāti Pattana.

22. Bhadravaṭa Koṭitīrtha, Mahākālavana, the great Narmadātīrtha, Tīrthabīja and Arbuda.

23. The Pañcatīrtha including Vasiṣṭhatīrtha, Priyasaṁjñaka, Vārṣika and the splendid Pañjiraka.

24. Sutīrtha, Brahmarudra, Kanyākumārika, Śakratīrtha, Pañcanada and Reṇukātīrtha.

25. The pure Paitāmahatīrtha, the excellent Raudrapāda, Maṇimanta, Kāmākhya, Kṛṣṇatīrtha and Kuliṅgaka.

26. Śrīśakrayajana, Brahmavālukā, the holy Vyāsatīrtha, Puṇḍarīka and the excellent Maṇimantha.

27. Dīrghamantha, Haṁsapādatīrtha, Sayana, Daśāśvamedha, Kedāra and Tamasodbheda.

28. Rudrakūpa, Saṁyamanītīrtha. Saṁtrāvanāsika, Syamantapañcaka, and Brahmatīrtha very pleasing to look.

29. Pṛthivītīrtha, Pāriplava, Pṛthūdaka, Daśāśvamedhika, Sākṣida and Vijaya.

30. The Koṭitīrtha at Pañcanada, Varāha, Yakṣiṇīhrada, Puṇḍarīka, Somatīrtha, and the excellent Muñjāvaṭaratha.

31. The Babūravanatirtha situated in the forest Badarīvana, Svarlokadvāraka and Kapilātīrtha.

32. Sūryatīrtha, Varusthāna, Bhavābhavana, Yakṣarākṣasatīrtha, and Brahmatīrtha the excellent holy centre.

33. Kāmeśvara, Mātṛtīrtha, Śātavana, the abode of the earthly Haṁsa (swan) and the Sārasatīrtha.

34. Daśāśvamedha, Kedāra, excellent Brahmajña Saptarṣikuṇḍa and the well-delimited tīrtha of the goddess.

35. Ihāspada (the support here, on earth) Koṭikṛta, Kiṁvāna, Kiṁjaya, Kāraṇḍava, Viśvatīrtha and another Triviṣṭapatīrtha.

36. Pāṇikhātatīrtha, Miśrakatīrtha, Madhukaṇṭatīrtha, Manomayatīrtha, the divine Kauśikītīrtha and the excellent Kanyātīrtha.

37. The Brahmatīrtha, Manastīrtha, the sacred holy centre, Saugandhika the holy forest, Maṇitīrtha and Sarasvatītīrtha.

38. The most excellent holy centre Īśānatīrtha, the holy Pañcayajñaka, Triśūladhara, Mahendra, and the divine abode Mahālaya,

39. The divine holy centre Śākambharītīrtha, Suvarṇākhya, Kapīmada, Kṣīreśvara, Virūpākṣa, Bhṛgutīrtha and Kuśodbhava.

40. Brahmāvarta, Brahmayoni, the mountain Nīlaparvata, the eddy Bhadrakarṇa and the eddy Śakrakarṇa.

41. Saptasārasvata, the holy centre of Auśanasatīrtha, Kapālamocana, Avakīrṇa and Pañcakatīrtha.

42. Catussāmudrika, Satkāñcanasahasrika, Reṇuka, Pañcakaṭaka and Ainasa-Vimocanatīrtha.

43. Sthāṇuthīrtha, Tīrtha of Kuru, Svargadvāra, Kuśadhvaja, Viśveśvara, Vāmakara and the hermitage of Nārāyaṇa.

44. Gaṅgāhrada, the holy Vaṭa and Badarī, Indramārgaṇakṣetra and Jirikāvāsa.

45. O brahmins, Somatīrtha, the meritorious Koṭitīrtha, the holy spot of Koṭitīrthasthalī, an eddy by Bhadrakālī.

46. The holy forest of Arundhatīvana, the excellent Brahmāvarta, Aśvadevī, Kubjavana and Yamunāprabhava.

47. Vīra-Pramokṣa, Siddhārtha, Māyāvidyodbhava, Mahāhrada, Vetasikārūpa and Sundarikāśrama.

48. Brahmāṇītīrtha, which is very great, Gaṅgodbhavasarasvatī, Bāhukātīrtha and Vimalāśokatīrtha.

49. Gautamītīrtha, Airāvatītīrtha, Śatasahasrikātīrtha, Koṭitīrtha in the abode Bhartṛsthāna and the excellent Kāpilītīrtha.

50. The Pañcanadatīrtha of the intelligent Mārkaṇḍeya, Somatīrtha, Śivoda and Matsyodarītīrtha.

51. Sūryatīrtha having the lustre of the sun, the holy forest Somakavana, Aruṇāspada, Vāmanaka and the Sūryatīrtha abounding in sands.

52. The Tīrtha called Avimukta, the Nīlakaṇṭhahrada, Piśācamocana, and Subhadrāhrada.

53. Vimalakuṇḍa, Tīrtha of Caṇḍīśvara, Śreṣṭhasthāna-hrada and Samudrakūpa.

54. The forest of Jaigīṣavya, the forest of Hṛṣīkeśa, Ajāmu-kharasa, and the whirlpool of Ghaṇṭākarṇa.

55. Puṇḍarīkahrada, the tank of Kāṣṭhaka, Śmaśāna-stambha, Kumbhatīrtha and the Vināyakahrada.

56. The well born of the Siddhas, the holy lake Brahma-saras Bhadrāvāsa, Nāgatīrtha and Somatīrtha.

57. Bhaktahrada, the lake of milk, Pretādhāra, Kumāra-katīrtha, Brahmāvarta Kuśāvarta and the holy centre Dadhi-karṇodaya.

58. The great holy centre of Śṛṇgatīrtha, the excellent holy centre of Mahānadī, the divine lake Brahmasaras, and the holy Akṣayavaṭa at Gayāśīrṣa.

59. Gomayatīrtha in the South, Hayaśāntika in the north, Kapilāhrada, Gṛdhrakūṭa and Sāvitrīhrada.

60. The forest Gītavana that destroys sins, Yonidvāra, Dhainuka, Dhanvaka, Lohika and Mataṅgahrada.

61. Pitṛkūpa, Rudrakūpa, Matitīrtha, Sumālin, Brahma-sthāna, Saptakuṇḍa, and Maṇiratnahrada.

62. The hermitage of Mudgala, the whirlpool of Mudgala, the holy centre Janakakūpa, and the holy Tīrtha Vinaśana.

63. The holy centre Śoka, Bhāratatīrtha, Jyeṣṭhālika, Viśveśvara of hundredfold merits, and Kanyāsaṁvedha.

64. Nidhitīrtha, Rāmabhavatīrtha, the hermitage of Vasiṣṭha, Devakūṭa, Devakūpa and the hermitage of Kauśika.

65. Kulakarṇahrada, Kauśikīdruma, Dharmatīrtha, Kāñ-canatīrtha and the holy centre Uddālaka.

66. Daṇḍātmā, Mālinītīrtha, Vanacaṇḍikātīrtha, San-dhyātīrtha, Kālatīrtha, Kapilātīrtha and Lohitārṇava.

67. Śoṇodbhava, Vaṁśagulma, the centre of Rāma Bhaṅ-

gīka, Puṇyāvartahrada, Śrīmattīrtha and the hermitage Badarikāśrama.

68. Rāmatīrtha, Vitastā, Merujātīya, the Rohiṇī and the lake of Indradyumna.

69. Avasarga, Mahendra, Śrītīrtha and the holy centre Iṣutīrtha, Vārṣika, and the abode of Kubera.

70. Kanyātīrtha, Gokarṇa, the abode, of Gopati Saṁvarta, Viśvāsa and the group of seven deep pools named Saptagodāvarīhrada.

71. Another Badarīhrada, Brahmasthānavivardhana, Jātihrada, Devahrada, and Kuśaprathana.

72. Sarvadevavrata, Kanyāśramahrada, Mahārājahrada, the holy Śakratīrtha and Kundaka.

73. Āṅgāratīrtha, the forest Rudrāraṇyaka, Medhāvin, Devahrada and the holy centre Amaravartana.

74. The holy Mandākinīhrada, Kṣama, Māheśvara, Gaṅgātīrtha, Tripuruṣa, and Bhīmatāṇḍavamukha.

75. Pṛthukūṭa, Śālvakūṭa, Śoṇa, Rohitaka, Kapilahrada, Mālya and Kapilāhrada belonging to Vasiṣṭha.

76-79. The eddies, the holy waterspots of Vālakhilyas, the seven sages, other great sages and the Akhaṇḍita-hrada.

The man who is endowed with faith who takes his bath duly in these sacred water spots and holy centres should observe fast and control his sense-organs. He should perform Tarpaṇa rites for Devas, sages and Pitṛs. After worshipping the deities he should stay there for three nights.

O brahmins, benefits are derived severally from each of these holy centres. Undoubtedly, the man obtains the benefit of a horse-sacrifice by making journeys to these places.

He who listens to this narrative daily, or who narrates this greatness of holy centres is liberated from sins.

CHAPTER TWENTYFOUR

A Dialogue between Brahmā and Sages

The sages said :

1. O Sūta the most excellent among the eloquent ones, tell us about the most excellent place on earth, that bestows virtue, love, wealth and salvation and that is the most excellent of all holy centres.

Lomaharṣaṇa said :

2. O excellent brahmins formerly, the great sages asked my preceptor this very question that you ask me just now. I shall mention it.

3-8. My preceptor Vyāsa, the holy sage was seated in his hermitage in Kurukṣetra. The hermitage was rendered splendid by different varieties of flowers. It abounded in different kinds of trees, creepers and herds of different animals. There were the following trees—Punnāga, Karṇikāra, Sarala, Devadāru, Śāla, Tāla, Tamāla Panasa, Khadira, Pāṭala, Aśoka, Bakula, Karavīra, Campaka and other trees, all in full bloom. My preceptor was an expert in sacred scriptures. He had composed the great Mahābhārata. He was the foremost among intellectuals. He was omniscient and engaged in activities conducive to the welfare of all living beings. He was engrossed in spiritual quests. He had mastered the Vedas and Vedāṅgas. He had expounded the Purāṇas and Āgamas. He was the son of Parāśara. He was handsome with eyes as wide as the petals of the lotus.

The sages of holy rites came there to see the calm sage.

9-14. The following were the sages who came viz.—Kaśyapa, Jamadagni, Bharadvāja, Gautama, Vasiṣṭha, Jaimini, Dhaumya, Mārkaṇḍeya, Vālmīki, Viśvāmitra, Śatānanda, Vātsya, Garga, Āsuri, Sumantu, Bhārgava, Kaṇva, Medhātithi, Guru Māṇḍavya, Cyavana, Dhūmra, Asita, Devala, Maudgalya, Tṛṇabāhu, Pippalāda, Akṛtavraṇa, Saṁvarta, Kauśika, Raibhya, Maitreya, Hārīta, Śāṇḍilya, Agastya, Durvāsas, Lomaśa, Nārada, Parvata, Vaiśampāyana, Gālava, Bhāskari, Pūraṇi, Sūta, Pulastya, Ulūka, Pulaha, Vāyu, Devasthāna, Tumburu, Sanatkumāra, Paila, Kṛṣṇa and Kṛṣṇānubhautika.

15. The intelligent sage, son of Satyavatī surrounded by these and other excellent sages shone like the moon surrounded by the stars.

16. The sage, the knower of the Vedas honoured those sages who came there. They too honoured him in return. Thereafter, they engaged themselves in conversation.

17. At the end of their preliminary talk the excellent sages, the residents of the penance-groves asked Kṛṣṇa (Dvaipāyana), the son of Satyavatī to clarify their doubts.

The sages said :

18. O sage, you know the entire range of sacred lore, viz. the Vedas, Purāṇas, Āgamas and Bhārata. You know the past, present and future.

19-21. O excellent sage, tell us. We ask you the highly pleased soul, the following things on seeing the universe submerging in the ocean of worldly existence without any support and (miserably) unconscious (of the same). This ocean of worldly existence is painful and utterly full of misery. It has no real substance. It is terrible with passions acting like crocodiles, the objects of sense-organs acting like flood waters, the sense-organs like a blended mass of whirlpool, the visible objects like hundreds of confused masses of waves, delusion making it turbid like mud. It is impassable, grave and difficult to be crossed due to covetousness.

22. What is it that is conducive to welfare in this terrible world that causes hairs to stand on end. It behoves you to uplift the worlds by offering advice.

23. It behoves you to recount that rare and extremely great holy centre which bestows liberation, We wish to hear about the land of holy rites on this earth.

24-25. It is only by perfectly performing the holy rites on this earth in the manner they have been laid down that a man attains the greatest perfection. By repugnant activities he falls into hell. The intelligent man attains absolution in the holy centre of salvation. Hence, O highly intelligent one, recount what you have been asked by the excellent brahmins.

26. On hearing the words of those sages of purified souls the intelligent Vyāsa, conversant with the past and future said:

Vyāsa said :

27-30. Listen O sages. I shall mention as you ask, the conversation that formerly took place between the sages and Brahmā on the summit of Meru that is spacious and bedecked with variety of jewels. It abounds in many trees and creepers rendered splendid by diverse kinds of flowers. There the atmosphere is full of chirping sounds of various birds. It is literally scattered with animals with a confusing mass of their offsprings. Many wonderful and mysterious things are present there. Rocks and pebbles of different colour lie scattered embellished with minerals and metals of all kinds. It contains several hermitages thronged with sages.

31-33. The four-faced lord of the universe was seated there. He is the source of origin of the universe. Being the lord and support of worlds, he is worthy of being saluted by all. He was then surrounded by Devas, Dānavas, Gandharvas, Yakṣas, Vidyādharas, serpents, sages, Siddhas, Apsarās and other heaven-dwellers. Some of them were eulogising him. Some were playing on musical instruments and singing songs in his praise. Others were dancing.

34-35. Thus, when the time was joyous and the living beings had gathered together, when the gentle southern breeze served them wafting the sweet odour from different kinds of flowers, Bhṛgu and other sages bowed to lord Brahmā. O brahmins, those excellent sages asked the father this very same topic.

The sages said :

36-37. "O lord, we wish to hear about the land of holy rites on the surface of the earth. O lord of Devas, it behoves you to recount the most inaccessible centre of absolution"

Vyāsa said :

On hearing their words, Brahmā, the lord of Devas, said to them in reply to the questions they asked, O excellent sages.

CHAPTER TWENTYFIVE

Bhārata Subcontinent

Brahmā said :

1. O sages, you listen to what I am going to say now. It is a splendid ancient traditional account connected with the Vedas. It grants worldly pleasures and salvation.

2. The Bhārata sub-continent is the land of holy rites in the whole of the earth. Heaven and hell are the lands for reaping the fruit of those holy rites.

3. O brahmins, by committing sins or performing holy rites in that subcontinent a man necessarily attains the fruit thereof whether auspicious or inauspicious.

4. There is no doubt that by performing their ordained duties in that sub-continent, the brahmins and others of perfect self-control attain the highest success.

5. O excellent brahmins, in that Varṣa, a person of self-control attains everything viz. virtue, wealth, love and liberation.

6. O excellent brahmins, Indra and other Devas have attained the status of a deity after performing splendid holy rites in that sub-continent.

7. Other men too had attained salvation in that Varṣa. They had control over their organs. They were devoid of passion and indecent rivalry.

8. Those persons who are devoid of ailments and who stay in heaven with aerial chariots had previously performed splendid holy rites in that land of Bharata and had attained heaven thereby.

9. Devas do always wish for a residence in Bhārata that yields the benefit of heavenly pleasures and liberation. They often spoke "O when shall we visit Bhārata".

10-13. O most excellent one among Devas, it has just been stated by you that except in Bhārata, rites holy or unholy are not conducive to meritorious or sinful results. But it seems likely that holy rites are not enjoined on men elsewhere. Hence, O Brahmā, recount Bhārata to us in detail, if you are kind to us. O lord, mention everything, how this sub-continent is situated. What are the continent mountains here ? What are its divisions.

Brahmā said :

14. Listen, O brahmins, the Bhārata sub-continent has nine sub-divisions which are separated by oceans. They are equal to one another.

15-16. They are Indradvīpa, Kaseru, Tāmravarṇa (? Tāmraparṇa), Gabhastimān, Nāgadvīpa, Saumya, Gandharva and Varuṇa. Bhārata surrounded by the ocean is the ninth among them. The island extends from south to north and is one thousand Yojanas long.

17. In the east of it, the Kirātas stay. The Yavanas stay in the west. O brahmins, the Brahmins, Kṣatriyas, Vaiśyas and Śūdras stay in the middle.

18-20. They are sanctified by holy rites and worldly pursuits as sacrifice, warfare, trading. Their general behaviour is intelligible through their activities, which cause heavenly pleasures and liberation. They incur merit and sin thereby.

There are seven Kula mountains viz., Mahendra, Malaya, Sahya, Śūktimān, Ṛkṣa, Vindhya and Pāriyātra. There are thousauds of other mountains nearby.

21-24. They are vast, lofty and beautiful. They are immense. Their ridges are of wonderful and variegated nature. They are Kolāhala, Vaibhrāja, Mandara, Dardala, Vātādhvaga, Daivata, Maināka, Surasa, Tuṅgaprastha, Nāga, Godhana, Pāṇḍura, Puṣpa, Vaijayanta, Raivata, Arbuda, Ṛṣyamūka, Gomantha, Kṛtaśaila, Śrī Cakora and hundreds of other mountains. The populated realms are interspersed with these mountains. The Mlecchas live in parts of this territory.

25-27. Excellent waters of these rivers are drunk by those people. O excellent brahmins, know these rivers.

The following rivers rise from the foot of the Himavān :— Gaṅgā, Sarasvatī, Sindhu, Candrabhāgā, Yamunā, Śatadrū, Vipāśā, Vitastā, Airāvatī, Kuhū, Gomatī, Dhūtapāpā, Bāhudā, Dṛṣadvatī, Devikā, Cakṣu, Niṣṭhīvā, Gaṇḍakī and Kauśikī.

28-29. The following rivers originate from the Pāriyātra mountain :—Devasmṛti, Devavatī, Vātaghni, (Kālī) Sindhu, Venya, Candana, Sadānīrā, Mahī, Carmaṇvatī, Vṛṣī, Vidiśā, Vetravatī, Śiprā and Dravantī.

30-32. The following rivers originate from the foot of Ṛkṣa mountain :—

Śoṇā, Mahānadī, Narmadā, Surathā, Kriyā, Mandākinī, Daśārṇā, Citrakūṭā, Citrotpalā, Vetravatī, Karamodā, Piśācikā, Atilaghuśroṇī, Vipāśā, Śaivalā, Samerujā, Śuktimatī, Śakunī, Tridivā and Kramu.

33-34. The following rivers have their source in the foothills of the Vindhya mountain :—Śiprā, Payoṣṇī, Nirvindhyā, Tāpī, Veṇā, Vaitaraṇī, Sinīvālī, Kumudvatī, Toyā, Mahāgaurī, Durgā and Antaḥśilā. These rivers are splendid and their waters are holy.

35-40. The following excellent rivers originate from the foot of Sahya mountain :—Godāvarī, Bhīmarathī, Kṛṣṇavāṇi, Tuṅgabhadrā, Suprayogā, and Pāpanāśinī.

The holy rivers of cool waters rising from the Malaya mountain are Kṛtamālā, Tāmraparṇī, Puṣpavatī and Utpalavatī.

The following rivers originate from the Mahendra mountain: Pitṛsomā, Ṛṣikulyā, Vañjulā, Tridivā, Lāṅgalinī and Vaṁśakarā.

The following rivers take their source from the mountain Śuktimān :—The Suvikālā, Kumārī, Mandagā, Mandagāminī, Kṣayā and Payoṣṇī.

These rivers are holy. They are on a par with Sarasvatī and Gaṅgā. They fall into the sea. They are the mothers of the universe. They may dispel sins. O excellent brahmins, there are thousands of other small rivers too.

41-42. Some of them flow during the rainy season (with plenty of water). Some of them are perennial rivers.

The Middle lands consist of the following climes :—Matsyas, Kumudamālyas, Kratulas, Kāśi, Kośalas, Āndhras, Kaliṅgas, Maśakas and Vṛkas. These are the main realms.

43. That spot of land to the north of Sahya where the river Godāvarī flows is the most charming in the entire earth.

44-50. The city of Govardhana, the residence of the noble Bhārgava is, indeed, very beautiful.

The following lands contain Kṣatriyas, Vaiśyas and Śūdras:—Vāhīkas,[1] Rāṭadhānas, Sutīras, Kālatoyadas, Aparāntas, Śūdras,

1. *Vāhīka-Bāhīka.* The term refers to the people of Punjab who were shut out by the Sarasvatī, Kurukṣetra and other natural features from the central country which remained true to Brahmanism. The term is also applicable to

Bāhlikas[1], Keralas, Gandhāras, Yavanas, Sindhus, Sauvīras, Madrakas, Śatadruhas, Kaliṅgas, Pāradas, Haribhūṣikas, Maṭharas, Kanakas, Kaikeyas, Dambhamālikas.

The following realms comprise the northern lands :—

O brahmins, they are Kāmbojas, Barbaras, Laukikas, Vīras, Tuṣāras, Pahlavas, Dhāyatas (?) Ātreyas, Bharadvājas, Puṣkalas, Daśerakas, Lampakas, Śunaśokas, Kulikas, Jāṅgalas, Oṣadhis, Calacandras, Kirātas, Tomaras, Haṁsamārgas, Kāśmiras, Karuṇas, Śūlikas, Kuhakas, and Māgadhas—These are the northern climes. Now understand the eastern climes.

51-53. Andhas, Vāmāṅkurakas, Vallakas, Makhāntakas, Aṅgas, Vaṅgas, Maladas, Mālavartikas, Bhadratuṅgas, Pratijayas, Bhāryāṅgas, Apamardakas, Prāgjyotiṣas, Madras, Videhas Tāmraliptakas, Mallas, Magadhakas, and Nandas—these are the eastern realms.

54-57. There are other climes, those of the Southern region : The Pūrṇas, Kevalas, Golāṅgulas, Ṛṣīkas, Mūṣikas, Kumāras, Rāmaṭhas, Śakas, Mahārāṣṭras, Māhiṣakas, Kaliṅgas, Ābhīras, Vaiśikyas, Aṭavyas, Sarvas, Pulindas, Mauleyas, Vaidarbhas, Daṇḍakas, Paulikas, Maulikas, Aśmakas, Bhojavardhanas, Kaulikas, Kuntalas, Dambhakas and Nīlakālakas.

These are the Southern realms. Now understand the Western climes :—

58-62. The Śūrpārakas, Kālidhanas, Lolas, Tālakaṭas etc are the residents of Western climes.

Listen to the residents of Vindhya mountains :—The Malajas, Karkaśas, Melakas, Colakas, Uttamarṇas, Daśārṇas, Bhojas, Kiṣkindhakas, Toṣalas, Kośalas, Traipuras, Vaidiśas, Tumburas, Caras, Yavanas, Pavanas, Abhayas, Ruṇḍikeras, Carcaras, Hotravartis.—these are the realms and peoples residing on Vindhya mountains.

Henceforth, I shall mention the climes founded on mountains.

---

the people who were thought to be impure and contemptible for not observing the rules prescribed for the fourfold society of Aryan people.

1. *Vāhlika*—Bāhlīka—Bālhīka. Balkh or ancient Bactrians. But there were two tribes of Vāhlikas—one settled in the plains of Punjab between Chenab and Sutlej rivers and the other among the lower slopes of the Himālayas between Chenab and Bias.

63-66. They are the Nīhāras, Tuṣamārgas, Kurus, Tuṅgaṇas, Khasas, Karṇaprāvaraṇas, Ūrṇas, Darghas, Kuñcakas, Citramārgas, Mālavas, Kirātas and Tomaras.

The Yugas, Kṛta, Tretā, Dvāpara and Kali are followed here. The injunctions befitting the four Yugas are strictly adhered to :

Such is the Bhārata subcontinent situated with its subdivisions. There is a great ocean to its South West and East. The Himālaya mountain stands to its north like the string of a great bow.

O excellent brahmins this Bhārata is the seed of everything.

67-68. It is the cause of different states such as the state of Brahmā, the state of Amareśa (Indra), the state of Devas, Maruts, animals, Yakṣas, Apsaras serpents, reptiles, and immobile beings. O brahmins, people attain these states as a result of their merits or demerits. O brahmins, there is no other holy place of rites in all these worlds.

69. O brahmins, this is the perpetual desire of all Devas—"If we are to fall off from the status of Devas onto the Earth may we attain Bhārata as the place of our birth".

70. What men do cannot be done by Devas and Asuras. Men are engaged in holy rites while Devas and Asuras are eager to obviate their Karman.

71. O brahmins, in the whole of the Earth there is no other sub-continent equal to Bhārata where different Varṇas—Brahmins, Kṣatriyas and others attain their cherished goal.

72. Excellent men who are highly blessed are born in Bhārata. They derive the benefits of virtue, love, wealth and liberation.

73-78. O brahmins, who is competent to narrate the excellent qualities of Bhārata? It is there that the rare benefit of austerities is attained. The fruit of all charitable gifts, all sacrifices, pilgrimage to holy centres, service to the elders and preceptors, rites of propitiation of Deities, the benefit of life of a householder, different holy rites, different sacred scriptures, practice of the virtue of non violence, the benefit of all cherished desires, the fruit of a celibate life, the benefit of self-study of the Vedas, the fruits of residence in the forest, that of the life of a recluse, the benefit of digging wells, etc. and performing sacrifices and the benefit of other holy rites—these are attained only in Bhārata, nowhere else. O excellent brahmins, Devas are always delighted in wishing for a splendid life there.

79-80. Thus the excellent Bhārata sub-continent has been adequately recounted by me. It dispels all sins; it is holy and is conducive to the attainment of wealth. It enhances intellect and wisdom.

He who controls his sense-organs and listens to this account or repeats the same shall be liberated from sins and shall attain the world of Viṣṇu.

CHAPTER TWENTYSIX

The Glory of Koṇāditya

Brahmā said :

1-9. There in the Bhārata subcontinent is a land that bestows heavenly pleasures and liberation. It is situated on the southern ocean and it is well known as Oṇḍadeśa. The region to the north of the ocean is the beautiful Vīraja Maṇḍala. This is the land of those who are habituated to the attainment of good qualities. It is embellished with good attributes. The brahmins born in that land have perfect control over their sense-organs. They are always engaged in penance and study of the Vedas. They are worthy of being honoured and saluted. They are famous for their ability to officiate in the rites of Śrāddha, charitable gift, marriage rites and sacrifices. They are experts in sacred rites. They are of divine origin. The brahmins therein are regularly engaged in performing the six types of holy rites. They are masters of Vedic lore. They are conversant with mythology and Ancient Historical tradition. They are experts in all scriptures. They perform sacrifices regularly. They are devoid of indecent rivalry. Some are engaged in sacrificial rites and some are interested in maintaining holy fires ordained in the Smṛtis. The residents of that land are endowed with sons, wives and riches. They are truthful in speech.

They perform homas. They live in the holy land of Utkala rendered beautiful by sacrifices and festivals. The people belonging to the other three castes, Kṣatriyas and others are righteous. They control their sense-organs. They are calm. They are engaged in their respective duties. Sun-god known as 'Koṇāditya' is the lord in that land. Those who visit lord Bhāskara there are liberated from sins.

The sages said :

10. O excellent one among Devas, we wish to hear further. Tell us now about the holy shrine of the sun in that land where lord sun is stationed.

Brahmā said :

11-17. The holy shrine of the sun is situated on the holy and beautiful shore of the briny sea. The land is endowed with all good qualities. It is full of sands. It abounds in varieties of trees such as Campaka, Aśoka, Bakula, Karavīra, Pāṭala, Punnāga, Karṇikāra, Nāgakesara, Tagara, Dhava, Bāṇa, Atimukta, Kubjaka, Kadamba, Lakuca, Śāla, Panasa, Devadāru, Sarala, Mucukunda, white and red sandal trees, Aśvattha, Saptaparṇa, Āmra, Āmrātaka, Tāla, Arka, coconut, wood apple and many other trees all round. There are flowering plants such as Mālatī, Kunda, Mallikā, Ketakī, etc. which shine with blossoms in all seasons. The shrine of lord sun is famous in the whole world. The region all round to the extent of a Yojana yields worldly pleasures and salvation.

18. The thousand-rayed lord sun is directly present there. He is well known, as Koṇāditya. He is the bestower of worldly pleasures and liberation.

19-27. On the seventh day in the bright half of the Māgha month the devotee should observe fast. After performing purificatory rites he shall take bath in the ocean in the presence of lord Sun. With a pure mind he shall remember him with concentration. After performing Tarpaṇa rites for Devas, sages, mortals and Pitṛs, he shall come out of the sea and wear a pair of cloths free from dirt. They should have been washed and kept dry the previous day itself. With complete purity he shall perform Ācamana after sitting on the seashore. As the

Sun rises up in the morning he shall sit facing him. He shall draw the mystic diagram of a lotus with the red sandal paste. It should have eight petals, filaments and be circular with the pericarp moving upwards. The intelligent devotee shall put gingelly seeds, rice, grains, red flowers, Darbha grass, and red sandal into a copper vessel and pour water therein. If a copper vessel is not available he shall put gingelly seeds in a cup made of the leaf of Arka plant. O excellent sages, he should cover this vessel with another vessel and keep it down. He should then perform Nyāsa rites of hands and limbs. With the heart and other organs he should meditate on the sun as his own self with sincere faith. The intelligent devotee should worship the deity in the petals in the middle as well as in south-east, south-west, north-east and north-west. He shall then worship (once again) in the middle.

28-33. After propitiating the lord for attaining supreme happiness he should worship the mystic lotus. From the sky he should invoke lord Sun and establish him on the pericarp. He should show mystic gestures. After performing the rite of ablution he should meditate on Sun with concentration thus :—He is stationed in the refulgent disc, his eyes are tawny; he is red with two arms, wearing garments pink like the lotus; he is endowed with all characteristics and he is decked in all ornaments. He is calm bestowing boons, bedecked in a halo of great brilliance. After seeing the rising Sun resembling thick paste of saffron he should take that vessel and keep it on the head. Kneeling on the ground he should silently affer Arghya into the Sun. He should concentrate his mind on the lord and repeat the three-syllabled Mantra.

34. He who has not received proper initiation should merely repeat the name of the Sun god and make water offerings with faith and fervour since lord sun can be made favourable through devotion.

35. He should make water offering, in the south-east, south-west, north-east, middle and in the four directions beginning with the east. He shall repeat the following Mantras and make water offerings in the direction indicated :—Hrām, obeisance to the heart (south-east); Hrīm, obeisance to the head (south-west); Hrīm, obeisance to the tuft of hair

(north-west); Hraim, obeisance to the coat of mail (north-east), Hraum, obeisance to the three eyes (in the middle); Hraḥ, obeisance to the missile. (in the four quarters).

36. After the water offering he should offer sweet scents, incense, light and food. After repeating prayers and holy names he should bow to the deity, show mystic gestures and discharge the deity ritualistically.

37-38. Whether Brahmins, Kṣatriyas, Vaiśyas, or Śūdras men or women whoever make water offerings to Sun with perfect control over their sense-organs and mind, with great devotional favour and pure conscience, enjoy the desired pleasures and attain the greatest goal.

39. Those who remember him as the illuminator of three worlds traversing firmament will obtain happiness.

40. The devotee should not worship Viṣṇu, Śiva or the lord of Devas (Indra) unless the water-offering has been made to the Sun-god in the manner prescribed in the Śāstras.

41-42. He who makes water offerings with great concentration to Sun-god on the seventh day after taking bath and remaining pure will obtain the desired benefit. Hence, one should strenuously endeavour to make water offering every day to Sun-god along with sweet scents and beautiful flowers. He shall remain pure too.

43. The ailing man is liberated from sickness, he who seeks wealth will attain wealth; he who seeks learning will obtain learning and he who seeks sons shall be blessed with sons.

44. Whatever desire he may cherish in his mind, the intelligent man shall fully obtain that desire and benefit by offering libation of water.

45. The devotee, whether a man or a woman shall take bath in the ocean, offer libation of water to Sun-god and bow down to the deity. He or she will obtain the desired benefit thereby.

45-A. The man who has taken bath in the waters of Gaṅgā, shall sprinkle water on the head of Sun-god by means of Kuśa grass. Thereby liberated from all sins he passes on to heaven.

46. Thereafter, the devotee shall proceed to the temple of Sun-god taking flowers with him. After entering the shrine he shall circumambulate thrice and worship Sun-god.

47. O excellent sages, on the day of Sun-god the devotee shall worship Koṇārka reciting Vedic Mantras and Tāntrika texts, with great devotion. He shall offer scents, sweet and fragrant flowers, lights, incense and food-offerings.

48-52. He shall prostrate before the deity lying flat on the ground like a long pole. He shall eulogise the lord and shout cries of victory unto him. By worshipping thus the thousandrayed lord of the universe, a man obtains the benefit of ten horse-sacrificcs. He will be liberated from all sins and assume a youthful divine form. O brahmins, he will redeem seven ancestors and successors in his family. He will go to the world of Sun-god on an aeriel chariot that has solar lustre and colour that is excessively refulgent and that can go wherever one likes it to go. He will be sung about by Gandharvas. After enjoying excellent pleasures there till the final dissolution of all living beings, when his merits have been exhausted, he will return to the Earth and be born in the excellent family of Yogins. He will become a pure brahmin learning all the four vedas and engaged in holy rites. After becoming united with the sun he will attain liberation.

53-55. In the bright half of the month of Caitra the devotee should make the holy pilgrimage to *Damana-bhañjakā*. He who makes pilgrimage to that place will obtain the benefit as mentioned before.

During the period of going to bed and rising up of the Sun i.e. during the tropical and equinoctical transits, O brahmins, persons of perfect control over their sense-organs shall perform holy pilgrimage on Sundays, the seventh day of the month or on Parvan days. They go to the world of Sun-god on the aerial chariot having solar lustre and colour.

56-59. Lord Mahādeva is also present on the shore of the ocean. He is known as *Rāmeśvara*. He is the bestower of desired benefits. The devotees should have a dip in the vast ocean and visit the lord, the enemy of lust (Kāma). They should propitiate the lord with sweet scents, fragrant flowers, incense, lights, excellent food-offerings, prostrations, eulogies, songs of prayer and sweet musical instruments. They will become noble souls and attain the benefit of Rājasūya and horse sacrifices. They will attain great success.

60. They will go to the world of Śiva on an aerial chariot that can travel as it pleases and that has clusters of tinkling bells suspended from it. Gandharvas will sing songs in their praise.

61. They will enjoy charming pleasures until the dissolution of all living beings and when their merits have been exhausted they will return to the Earth and be born as brahmins learning the four Vedas.

62-63. Being united with Brahman they will attain liberation.

He who passes away in the holy centre of the Sun will reach the world of Sun-god and rejoice in heaven together with Devas. Reborn as a man he will become a virtuous king.

64-65. Becoming united with the Sun-god he will attain salvation.

Thus, O excellent sages, the rare holy centre of Koṇārka on the shores of the ocean has been recounted by me. It yields worldly pleasures and salvation.

CHAPTER TWENTYSEVEN

Efficacy of Devotion to Sun-god

The sages said :

1-6. O most excellent one among Devas, what has been cited by you about the holy centre of the Sungod that yields worldly pleasures and salvation, has been heard by us. Listening to the pleasing stories coming through your mouth—the holy stories of the sungod that dispel sins—we have not reached the point of contentedness. O most excellent one among Devas, the foremost among the eloquent ones do enlighten us on the following points :— the benefit from the worship of the lord, the benefit of charitable gifts, the benefits of prostration, kneeling down, circumambulation, and the offerings of lights and incense, the rite of scrubbing and cleaning, the benefits of observance of fasts and the merits of taking food only at night. Of what form is water libation and where is it to be offered? How is devotion to be pursued ? How is the lord pleased ? O excellent one among Devas, we wish to hear.

Brahmā said :

7. O excellent brahmins, understand even as they are being recounted, the procedure of water libation of worship, devotion to the Sun-god, and the faith as well as concentration of mind.

8. Devotion is a pure mental feeling; faith is a favourite feeling. Meditation is a perfect concentration. Now listen to what I am going to say.

9. He who narrates the story of the lord with devotion, he who worships him, he who maintains the holy fires, is called the eternal devotee.

10. He is an eternal devotee whose mind dwells on the lord, who thinks about him, who is engaged in the worship of the lord and who renders service unto him.

11. He who praises or permits the holy rites that are performed for the furtherance of the Vedas, O brahmins, is the real devotee. He is really a great man.

12. The man who performs the holy rites of the Sun is a devotee of the higher type. But he should not censure other deities nor be jealous of the devotees of those deities.

13. The man who constantly remembers the Sun-god whether staying or moving about, whether sleeping or waking, while smelling or keeping the eyes closed or open is indeed the greatest devotee.

14-15. The devotion of this nature should be practised by one who knows. All holy observances are performed with devotion and concentration with the mind dwelling on reality. A charitable gift should be given to a brahmin (with devotion) and actually Devas or the Pitṛs accept it.

16. Devas accept whatever is offered with devotion whether it be a leaf or a flower, a fruit, or water. They avoid atheists.

17. Purity of mind, good conduct and due observances should be applied to everyone. Whatever is performed with purity of mind becomes fruitful.

18. One is liberated from sins by the prayer, repetition of

holy names, offerings of presents and the worship of Sun-god together with observance of fast with devotion.

19. There is no doubt about this that he who keeps his head on the ground and performs obeisance is liberated from all sins instantaneously.

20. The devout man who circumambulates the Sungod circumambulates in effect the whole of the earth consisting of seven continents.

21. If a man keeps Sungod in his mind and circumambulates ether, know that Devas have been circumambulated by him.

22-25. O highly blessed ones, the devotee shall take food only for once on the sixth day of the lunar fortnight. Maintaining the holy regulations and restrictions and endowed with devotion, the man shall worship sun-god on the seventh day. He shall attain the benefit of performing horse-sacrifice.

He who worships sun-god after observing fast for day and a night goes to the world of sun-god by means of a vehicle of fiery lustre. One who performs this holy rite on the sixth or seventh day of the lunar fortnight attains the supreme goal.

The devotee who observes fast on the seventh day of the black fortnight and conquers his sense-organs and who worships the sun-god offering all precious stones, goes to the world of the sun-god on a vehicle that has the lustre of a lotus.

26-32. The devout man shall observe fast on the seventh day of the bright fortnight. He shall worship the sungod with the offerings of all white substances. Freed from all sins he goes to the world of sun-god.

On the first day of the following holy rite the devotee shall drink a palmful of water held in a leaf cup of the Arka plant. He shall increase it by one every day for twentyfour days. Then he shall decrease the number by one every day. This process continues for two years and the holy rite is concluded then. This holy rite Arkasaptamī bestows all cherished desires. It is a praiseworthy holy rite.

If a Sunday coincides with the seventh day of the bright lunar fortnight it is called Vijaya Saptamī. Whatever is offered as a charitable gift on that day yields a great benefit. Ablution, charitable gift, penance, sacrifice or fast—everything observed on Vijayasaptamī is destruc tive of all great sins.

Those men who perform Śrāddha on Sundays and worship the deity Mahāśveta derive great benefits. Their holy rites directed to the Sungod are fruitful. No impoverished or sick member is born in their families.

33-37. He who plasters the walls of the temple with white, yellow or red clay,

He who observes fast and worships the Sungod with different fragrant flowers will obtain all cherished desires.

By lighting lamps for the Sun-god with ghee or gingelly oil the devotee will attain longevity and beautiful form. He will never have the deficiency of vision.

A person who is engaged in making charitable gifts of lamps continuously, shall make the lamp of perfect knowledge blaze. With the intellect and the sense-organs clear, the man will be liberated sometimes. The gingelly seeds are extremely sacred. Charitable gift of gingelly seeds is very excellent. Gingelly seed used in holy rites in fire or in lamps is destructive of great sins.

38. He who makes perpetual offerings of lamps to temples, quadrangles and highways shall become blessed and handsome.

39. The first preference should be given to lamps with ghee. The second preference should be given to the juices of medicinal herbs. It should never be offered with the extracts from fat suet or bones.

40. The lamp shall always burn with the flame leaping upwards. It shall never be directed downwards. Thus the person who offers lamps becomes refulgent. He shall never attain the state of an animal.

41. The burning lamp should never be taken away nor should it be destroyed. The remover of a burning lamp may attain imprisonment, destruction, wrath or darkness.

42-45. The donor of lamps shines in the heavenly world like an array of lamps.

He who adorns lamps with saffron, agallochum and sandal paste shall become an excellent man with riches, fame and glorious splendour.

By offering perpetual libations of water at sunrise accompanied by red flowers mixed with red sandal paste, the clean man shall attain success in the course of a year.

The holy rite of the Sun-god should be observed as follows:—

The devotee shall stand facing the sun from sunrise to sunset turning when the sun changes direction. He shall continuously repeat some Mantra or hymn of prayers. This Ādityavrata is destructive of all sins.

46. He who offers everything along with its ancillaries together with the libation of water at the time of sunrise, endowed with faith, is liberated from all sins.

47. He who offers water-libation accompanied by gold, cow, bull, plot of land or cloths will derive benefits lasting for seven births.

48. The libation of water shall be assiduously offered into the fire, water, atmosphere, clean ground, idol or ball of rice.

49. The libation of water shall not be offered to the left or right. It shall be offered straight in front along with ghee and Guggula (Aromatic resin) by one who is endowed with devotion to Sun-god.

50-55. The devotee shall offer all worship in front of the Sun-god. He is instantaneously liberated from all sins undoubtedly.

By offering Śrīvāsa (turpentue) Devadāru (cidar oil), Sarjaka (exudation of the Śāla tree), camphor, agallochum and incense, devotees will go to heaven.

By worshipping Sun-god during his transit to the tropics of Capricorn and Cancer in particular, the devotee is liberated from all sins.

By worshipping Sun-god particularly during the Equinoctical Visuva transits, Saḍaśīti (i.e. transit to Virgo, Sagittarius, Pisces or Gemini) transits and eclipses, one is liberated from sins.

By worshipping Sun-god with devotion whether it is the proper time or otherwise on the seashore or elsewhere, a man is honoured in the world of Sun-god.

By offering oblations to Sun-god with Kṛsaras (cooked gingelly seeds), milk puddings, sweet pies, fruits, roots or rice cooked in ghee he will obtain his cherished desires.

By performing libation of ghee, a man will become excellent of men.

56. By performing libation with milk the devotee is never afflicted by mental distress.

By performing libation with curds, the man attains fruition in his affairs.

57. He who is mentally and physically pure and fetches water for the ablution of sungod from a sacred river or a holy pool attains the supreme goal.

58. By offering an umbrella, banner canopy, flagstaff and chowries to Sun-god with faith, one will attain his desired goal.

59. Whatever article a man dedicates to Sun-god with devotion will be returned to him by Sungod a hundred thousand times more.

60. The devotee wipes off his sin, be it the physical, verbal or mental by offering obeisance to Sun-god.

61. Even by hundreds of sacrifices with adequate monetary gifts as laid down in scriptures one does not attain benefit which is obtained in a single day by the worship of Sungod.

CHAPTER TWENTYEIGHT

Glory of Sun-God

The Sages said:

1-6. The wonderful glory of Sun-god, lord of the universe, has been heard, O most excellent one among gods, even as you are recounting the most rare and inacessible tales among them. O lord of Devas, O lord of universe, tell us again what we are anxious to know. O brahmā, we wish to hear the same. We are extremely eager. Which deity shall a devotee desiring liberation worship, no matter whether he be a householder or a religious student or a forester or a recluse ? Whence can his celestial attainment be assured? Wherefrom is the supreme welfare gained ? What shall he do, while in the heaven, to prevent his falling off therefrom? Who is the god of gods? Who is the father of manes? O lord of Devas, tell us that than which there is no greater Being. O Brahmā, whence is this universe of mobile and immobile beings originated ? Whom does it resort to at the time of dissolution? It behoves you to mention that.

Brahmā said:

7. O excellent brahmins, rising up, Sun-god makes the universe by his rays free from darkness. There is no other lord greater than him.

8. He has neither beginning nor death. He is eternal, unchanging and force. With his rays he scorches the three worlds revolving round.

9. He is identical with Devas. He is the most excellent among the scorchers. He is the lord of entire universe. He is the witness unto every activity, auspicious or inauspicious.

10. He makes the living beings shrink. He creates them once again. With his rays he illuminates and scorches the earth. He causes rain too.

11. He is the creator and dispenser of destiny. He is the first cause of living beings. He purifies all living beings. He never faces decline nor does his disc ever dwindle.

12. He is the father of Manes and the deity of gods. He is known as the steady and steadfast abode from which one never falls off.

13. They say that, at the time of creation, the entire universe is evolved from Sun-god and at the time of dissolution reverts to him.

14. Abandoning their abode—the physical body—innumerable Yogins turn into gaseous state and retire to Sungod who is a mass of refulgence.

15. Just as the birds of sky resort to the branches of trees, the sages and the liberated souls along with the gods resort to his thousands of rays and stay there.

16-17. Householders, Janaka and other kings possessing Yogic virtue, Vālakhilyas and other sages who expound Brahman, others who are forest-dwellers and Vyāsa and other mendicants or recluses—all these acquire Yogic power and enter the disc of the Sun.

18. Śuka, the glorious son of Vyāsa attained Yogic virtue, entered the rays of the Sun-god and got union with him never to be separated again.

19. Brahmā, Viṣṇu, Śiva and others are mentioned in the Vedas as the bestowers of happiness and the Vedas are only words. But lord Sun who destroys darkness is the visible god.

20. Hence devotional pursuits should not be directed elsewhere by him who longs for auspicious benefits, since what is not seen never nullifies what is seen.

21. Hence, Sun-god should always be worshipped by you. Indeed, he is the mother, father and preceptor of the universe.

22-27. The lord without beginning, lord of worlds, lord of universe possessing garlands of rays, stationed in the form of Sun, blazes, O excellent brahmins. Brahmā, devoid of beginning and end, permanent lord devoid of decline, created oceans, continents and the fourteen worlds. For the welfare of the world he stayed on the banks of the river Candrasarit after creating lords of subjects, Prajāpatis and other subjects. Therefore, the unmanifest hundred thousand rayed Sungod divided himself into twelve Ādityas. They are :—Indra, Dhātṛ, Parjanya, Tvaṣṭṛ, Pūṣan, Aryaman, Bhaga, Vivasvat, Viṣṇu Aṁśa (?) (Aṁśumān Varuṇa and Mitra.

O excellent brahmins, this entire universe has been pervaded by the Sungod the supreme soul by these twelve-physical forms.

28. The first form of Āditya named Indra is the king of Devas. It destroys the enemies of Devas.

29. His second form glorified by the dame Dhātṛ is Prajāpati who creates different kinds of subjects.

30. His third form well known as Parjanya is stationed amongst the clouds. It causes rain through the rays.

31. His fourth form well known by the name Tvaṣṭṛ is stationed amidst trees, plants and medicinal herbs all around.

32. His fifth form well known by the name Pūṣan is stationed in grains and edible foodstuff. It accords perpetual nourishment unto the subjects.

33. His sixth form well known as Aryamā is the outer covering of the Wind. It is stationed among Devas.

34. His seventh form well known as Bhaga is stationed

among the elements, living beings and the physical bodies of the embodied souls.

35. His eighth form well known as Vivasvān is established fire; it digests the food-in-take of the embodied souls.

36. His ninth form well known as Viṣṇu incarnates and destroys the enemies of Devas.

37. His tenth form well known as Aṁśumān is established in the Wind; it delights the subjects.

38. His eleventh form called Varuṇa is stationed in the waters; it protects subjects continuously.

39. His twelfth form known as Mitra is stationed on the Candrasarit river for the welfare of the world.

40. Stationed there he performed a penance having air alone as his food.

By the benign glance of his eyes he blessed his devotees bestowing several boons.

41. This first abode was well established later on by the lord. Since Mitra (the Sun-god) stayed there it is known as Mitravana (forest of Mitra).

42. O excellent brahmins, this universe is pervaded by the supreme being Sungod through these twelve forms.

43. Hence, the Sungod should be meditated upon and worshipped by men with devotion as stationed in the twelve forms and their mind shall dwell upon him.

44. Thus, by bowing to the twelve forms of Sun-god, by listening to their accounts and by reading (this account), a man is honoured in the world of Sungod.

The Sages said :

45. If this sun is the primordial eternal lord wherefore did he perform penance desirous of boons like a common person ?

Brahmā said :

46. I shall mention the secret of (Sun-god). This was asked by Nārada the noble-souled sage and explained to him formerly by Mitra.

47. The twelve forms of Sungod have been mentioned to you before. Two of them viz Mitra and Varuṇa performed penances.

48. Among them, Varuṇa performed penance in the Western ocean with water alone as his food-in-take. Mitra performed penance in Mitravana with air alone as his food-in-take.

49-50. Descending from the peak of *Meru* during his sojourn through the worlds, Nārada the Yogin of self-control reached *Gandhamādana*. He came to the place where Mitra was performing penance. Seeing him engaged in penance Nārada's curiosity was aroused.

51-52. He thought thus—"This Mitra is devoid of decline and is unchanging. He is manifest and unmanifest. He is eternal. The whole of the three worlds has been held as one unit by this noble-souled Being. He is the father of all Devas. He is greater than the greatest Being. Which deity did he worship then ? Which ancestors did he propitiate ?" After reflecting thus Nārada spoke to the lord.

Nārada said :

53. "In Vedas and their ancillary (subsidiary) sections and in the Purāṇas you are glorified as the unborn, perpetual creator of great and excellent form.

54-56. Everything whether past, present or future is founded in you, O lord, the four stages of life worship you every day. You have assumed different forms. You are the father and mother of everyone. You are the ever-present deity. We do not know which forefather or lord you worship."

Mitra said :

57. This eternal great secret cannot be adequately expressed, even if it should be explained. O brahmin, I shall mention it precisely to you since you are endowed with devotion and piety.

58-61. That which is subtle, incomprehensible, unmanifest, steady and devoid of sense-organs, sensual objects and elements is the immanent soul of all living beings. He is called the knower of shrine, the immortal soul. He is the being that lies latent in the mind conceived of as separate from three attributes. He is known as lord Hiraṇyagarbha. In the Yoga treatises he is known as the cosmic intellect, great principle and the chief Being. In the systems of Sāṁkhya and Yoga he is said to be of various natures and names. He has three features; he is the soul of the universe; he is known as One and Imperishable.

62. As a matter of fact the whole of the three worlds is one unit. Himself unembodied, he is present in all the bodies.

63. Though he stays in different bodies he is not tarnished by physical activities. He is your immanent soul, mine too, as well as of all those others stationed in bodies.

64. He is the witness unto all living beings. He cannot be comprehended by anyone at any place. He is identical with the universe, with attributes and without attributes. He is known as comprehensible through perfect wisdom.

65. He has the extremities of feet, hands, eyes, heads and mouths all round; he has ears all round; he stands enveloping everything.

66. The universe is his head; the universe constitutes his arms, feet, eyes and nose. He moves about in the body happily and comfortably as he wills.

67. The body is meant by the word Kṣetra. The Supreme being, the Yogic Ātman, comfortably knows everything concerning the body. Hence, he is called the knower of the body.

68. He is called Puruṣa because he lies latent in the unmanifest city—the cosmic mind. The word Viśva connotes the knowables of diverse kinds. It is called sarva (the composite whole), pervading the universe.

69. Since he has many forms he is known as Viśvarūpa. The ultimate greatness belongs solely to him. He is called Puruṣa.

70. The sole, eternal Being, holds the title Mahāpuruṣa. Endowed with Sattva quality, intelligence and efficiency he creates his own soul by his own self.

71. By his own soul he creates many souls hundredfold, a thousandfold, in hundred thousands, in crores.

72. Just as the water that falls from firmament undergoes a change in taste by virtue of diverse tastes present in the Earth so also the soul undergoes change in attributes due to its various contacts.

73. Just as the singular air within the body functions as five organic airs, so also the supreme Being has unity and diversity undoubedly.

74. Just as fire undergoes changes in name by virtue of particularity of different sects so also the individual souls undergo different titles such as Dhruva, Brahmā etc.

75. Just as a single lamp lights up thousands of lamps, so also he, though single, gives birth to thousands of forms.

76. When he realizes his self he becomes alone and single. When singleness dissolves, diversity and multiplicity begin to function.

77. There is no living, mobile or immobile, who is permanent in this universe. The supreme self alone is called indeclinable (immeasurable, incomprehensible) and omnipresent.

78. O excellent sages, the unmanifest consisting of three attributes originated from him. That which is unmanifest, that the form of which is not clear, is called primordial nature.

79. Understand that primordial nature is the womb of Brahman; he who is of the nature of existent and non-existent is worshipped in the world, in the holy rites pertaining to Devas and manes.

80. O brahmins, there is none greater than he; therefore he the father or lord is greater than every being. Hc is comprehensible through the soul. Hence I worship him.

81. The embodied beings who are present in heaven make obeisance to him. Thereby, O celestial sage, they attain the benefit and goal as directed.

82. Devas who have assumed different forms, who are stationed in their respective stages of life, devoutly worship that primordial Being. He bestows salvation on them.

83. He is called omnipresent and devoid of attributes. Having heard thus and having understood it, I worship the lord.

84. Those who are sanctified by him resort to the sole and single entity. This is a further achievement unto them that they enter the sole and single entity.

85. Thus, O Nārada, the secret doctrine has been narrated to you. O celestial sage, by virtue of your devotion to us, the greatest fact has been revealed to you.

86. All those sages who imbibed this ancient knowledge devote themselves to the worship of Sungod.

Brahmā said :

87. Thus, this had been formerly recounted to Nārada by Sun-god—through his form—Mitra. O excellent brahmins, thus, the story of sun-god has been mentioned to you.

88. O excellent brahmin this narrative recounted by me should be mentioned only to the good. This should never be imparted to one who is not a devotee of the solar deity.

89. There is no doubt that the man who listens to this account and narrates the same to another, will enter the lord of thousand brilliant rays.

90. The agonized will be liberated from ailment by listening to this story from the beginning. Those who are desirous of knowing shall derive perfect knowledge and the desired goal.

91. O sage, he who reads this account obtains the path of salvation instantaneously. Whatever one wishes for, one undoubtedly attains it.

92. Hence, lord Sun should be worshipped by you all. He is the creator, dispenser of destiny and the preceptor of all.

CHAPTER TWENTYNINE

Name of Sun-god

Brahmā said :

1. O excellent sages, the three worlds have the sun as their source of origin. The entire universe including Devas, Asuras and human beings originates from him.

2-3. The brilliance of the deities viz—Rudra, Upendra and Mahendra, the splendour of the leading brahmins and heaven-dwellers of great refulgence, nay the refulgence of all the worlds is lord Sun—the soul of all, the lord of all—Devas as well as human beings. The sun alone is the root cause of three worlds. He alone is the greatest deity.

4. The ghee offerings duly consigned to the fire produce clouds which in turn generate rain. Rain originates food-grain whereby the subjects are nourished.

5. Everything is born of him; everything is dissolved in him. He is the cause of origin and destruction of the universe.

6. The meditation of those who meditate, the liberation of those who are liberated centre round Sungod. They are absorbed in him but are reborn of him. This happens frequently.

7-8. The following units of time have their origin in the Sun-god—moments, Muhūrta (units of 48 nets), days, nights, fortnights, months, years, seasons and Yugas. These cannot be reckoned without him; without calculation of time there is no holy observance, there is no holy rite in the sacrificial fire.

9-10. Without sun-god who steals water and then showers it, how can the seasons be classified ? How can fruits and flowers occur ? How can vegetation be produced ? How can grasses and medicinal herbs grow ? It is due to his power that these occur in the universe. Otherwise, there will be an absence of all dealings among the creatures here and hereafter.

11. The sun does not blaze if there be no rain; the sun is not happy if there be no rain; the sun has no halo if there is no rain; the sun blazes due to water.

12-13. The sun is tawny in spring; during summer he resembles gold, he is white during rainy season; he is pale, grey during autumn; he is copper-coloured in early winter; he is red during late winter. Thus the colours of sun-god caused by the seasons have been recounted.

14-18. With colour naturally belonging to the season, the sun causes welfare and prosperity. There are twelve general names of Sun-god and there are twelve other names severally. I shall mention all of them.

The following are the twelve general names :—Āditya, Savitā, Sūrya, Mihira, Arka, Prabhākara, Mārtaṇḍa, Bhāskara, Bhānu, Citrabhānu, Divākara and Ravi. The Sungod is known by these twelve general names.

The following are the twelve Ādityas reckoned separately :—

Viṣṇu, Dhātṛ Bhaga, Pūṣan, Mitra, Indra, Varuṇa, Aryamā, Vivasvān, Aṁśumān, Tvaṣṭṛ and Parjanya. They are separate forms rising in twelve months respectively :—

19. Viṣṇu blazes in the month of Caitra. Aryamā in Vaiśākha; Vivasvān in Jyeṣṭha and Aṁśumān in Āṣāḍha.

20. Parjanya blazes in the month of Śrāvaṇa, Varuṇa in Prauṣṭhapada, Indra in Āśvayuja and Dhātṛ in Kārttika.

21. Mitra blazes in the month of Mārgaśīrṣa; Puṣā, Bhaga in Māgha and Tvaṣṭṛ in Phālguna.

22. Viṣṇu blazes with one thousand two hundred rays. Aryamā with one thousand three hundred rays.

23-26. Vivasvān with one thousand four hundred rays; Aṁśumān with one thousand five hundred rays; Parjanya and Varuṇa like Vivasvān; Bhaga is like Mitra one thousand and four hundred rays; lord Tvaṣṭṛ with one thousand and one hundred rays; Indra with one thousand and two hundred rays; Dhātṛ with one thousand and one hundred rays; Mitra with a thousand rays and Pūṣan with nine hundred rays.

During the northern transit of the sun, the rays increase; during the southern transit the rays decrease. Thus, sun-god sustains worlds by thousands of rays.

27. The means of protection in different seasons is manifold. The sun has a set of twentyfour names. They have been mentioned already. The sun has another set of one thousand names. They have been glorified in detail.

The sages said :

28. O Prajāpati, O great lord, what is the merit and the goal of those who eulogise the sun-god with those thousand names ?

Brahmā said :

29-30. O leading sages, listen to the eternal truth. Enough of those thousand names, should one recite the following auspicious prayer. Listen, I shall relate to you those secret, sacred and splendid names of the Sun-god.

31-33. *The Prayer of Twentyone names.*

The twentyone names of Lord sun are Vikartana, Vivasvan, Mārtaṇḍa, Bhāskara, Ravi, Lokaprakāśaka, Śrīman, Lokacakṣuṣ, Maheśvara, Lokasākṣi, Trilokeśa Kartā, Hartā, Tamisrahā, Tapana, Tāpana, Śuci, Saptāśvavāhana, Gabhastihasta, Brahmaṇya and Sarvadevanamaskṛta. These are twentyone names of the Sun-god. This prayer is always liked by Sun-god.

34. This prayer is called 'Royal'. It is well known in the three worlds. It is conducive to the health of body. It causes increase in riches and enhances glory.

35. O excellent brahmins, he who remains pure and eulogises the Sun-god with this hymn at the two junctions viz sunrise and sunset, is liberated from all sins.

36. By repeating this hymn but once in the presence of the sun all sins perish whether they are mental, physical or verbal or caused by other activities.

37. Repetition of this hymn for once is the Mantra for Homa, and worship during the twilight, it is the mantra for incense, for Arghya and for oblations too.

38. If this great Mantra is accompanied by the gift of cooked rice, or obeisance or circumambulation it dispels all sins. It is splendid.

39. Hence, you all should eulogise the lord, the bestower of boons, one who grants all cherished desires, assiduously, by reciting this hymn, O brahmins.

CHAPTER THIRTY

Nativity of Sun-god

The sages said :—

1-2. The sun-god has been mentioned by you as the eternal lord who is devoid of attributes. What is heard by us as mentioned by you now is that he was born in twelve forms. How was that lord of great lustre, the mass of refulgence born of womb of a woman ? Our doubt in respect to this is very great.

Brahmā said :—

3. Dakṣa had sixty excellent splendid daughters viz:—Aditi Diti, Danu, Vinatā and others.

4. Dakṣa gave thirteen of his daughters to Kaśyapa. Aditi gave birth to Devas the lords of three worlds.

5. Diti gave birth to Daityas; Danu to Dānavas who were

haughty on account of their strength. Vinatā and others gave birth to mobile and immobile beings.

6. O sage, with the sons and daughters and their sons and grandsons, the entire universe is pervaded.

7. Devas were important among the sons of Kaśyapa. They are purely of Sattva quality. The other sons were of Rajas and Tamas qualities.

8. The creator Parameṣṭhin, the most excellent one among those conversant with the Brahman, Prajāpati made Devas the partakers of shares in sacrifices and the lords of the three worlds.

9-10. Due to enmity, Daityas and Dānavas harassed them collectively.

The Rākṣasas too joined them. The combat raged furiously, continued for a thousand years according to divine calculation. Devas were tortured. Daityas and Dānavas were victorious, in the battle.

On seeing the sons routed by Daityas and Dānavas and the three worlds destroyed, O excellent sages, Aditi was afflicted. On seeing her sons deprived of shares in sacrifices and afflicted by hunger she became distressed.

11. She endeavoured much for propitiating the sun. Restraining her diet and concentrating her mind she resorted to the holy observances of regulations. She eulogised Sun-god stationed in the firmament as a mass of refulgence.

Aditi said :

12-15. Obeisance to you who bear inimitable lustre, that is very subtle and worthy of homage. O lord of rays, I bow to you, the eternal support of refulgence, lord of refulgent ones. I bow to that fierce form which you have, while taking up the juice at the proper time for rendering service to the worlds. I bow to that fierce form you have when you hold the watery juice taken during eight months. I bow to that form of yours that is combined with Rajas during the two junctions (i.e. at dawn and at dusk). Obeisance to you, that soul with attributes that will bestow on me what I desire in my mind. I bow to that blazing form you have by virtue of unification of Ṛk, Yajus and Sāman (the three Vedas).

16. Obeisance to you, the lustrous one that scorchest the three worlds. The form that is beyond it is meditated upon by utterring Om. It is gross and non-gross. It is free from impurities, O eternal lord, obeisance to that form.

Brahmā said :

17. O brahmins, desirous of propitiating Sun-god, that gentle lady eulogised thus day and night. She maintained the observance of all holy rites. She abstained from taking food.

18. O excellent brahmins, after a long time, the sun-god became visible to that daughter of Dakṣa.

19. She saw a massive peak of refulgence enveloping the sky and standing on the ground. She saw the sun-god extremely unbearable by virtue of dense mass of flames.

20. On seeing him, the gentle lady became excessively awe-struck.

Aditi said :

21-23. O lord of rays, the original cause of the universe, I am unable to look at you. O sun-god, be pleased with me; let me see the form you possess. O lord, sympathetic with devotees, protect my sons, your devotees.

Thereupon, the sun-god came out of that mass of refulgence. The lord sungod was then seen resembling copper.

The sun-god said to that gentle lady who bowed to him reverentially.

"Choose any boon from me; whatever you wish"

24. Touching the ground with her knees she bent her head and replied to Sungod the bestower of boons who stood near her.

Aditi said :

25. O lord, be pleased. The three worlds that belonged to my sons and their shares in sacrifices, have been taken away by Daityas and Dānavas of superior valour and might.

26. On that account, O lord of rays, grant me a favour. With a part of yours adopt their brotherhood, my son, and destroy their enemies.

27-28. O sun, be pleased and favour them with sympathy,

O lord, so that they may once again be the partakers of their shares in sacrifice and be overlords of the three worlds. O unsevering lord, the remover of distress of those who resort to you, you are one who can do this work.

29. Thereafter, O brahmins, lord Sun the thief of waters, the lord who had a pleasant gentle face, spoke to Aditi who bowed to him.

30. "With the thousandth part of mine I shall be born in your womb. Efficient that I am, I shall, ere long, kill the enemies of your sons and become delighted".

31. Having spoken thus, lord Sun vanished thereafter. Having secured everything she had desired she ceased from her activities in pursuit of penance.

32-34. In order to fulfil her desire, at the end of a year thereafter, the Sungod took up his residence in the womb of Aditi by means of one of his rays Suṣumnā amongst a thousand. With great concentration and mental purity she performed several holy rites: Kṛcchra, Cāndrāyaṇa, etc. O brahmins, it was with this viz. "I shall conceive this divine foetus with great purity" that she performed those holy rites. Thereupon Kaśyapa spoke to her, with words full of wrath.

35-37. "Why do you destroy the Egg of the foetus by observing a perpetual fast ?" Provoked by his query she spoke furiously to him—"See the foetus for yourself. It is not killed. He will certainly cause a death-blow to the enemies". Infuriated by the utterance of her husband she uttered these words and discharged the terrible foetus that was dazzling with splendour. On seeing that the foetus had the refulgence of the rising sun, Kaśyapa bowed and eulogised respectfully in words of high order.

38. Even as he was eulogised the lord revealed himself out of the Egg of the foetus. He had the lustre and colour similar to those of the petals of a lotus. He pervaded the quarters by means of his splendour.

39. Addressing Kaśyapa the excellent sage and his wife from the firmament an unembodied voice as grave and majestic as the rumbling sound of the cloud uttered thus :—

The Voice said :

40. O sage, since this foetus of Aditi was pronounced slain by you, this son of yours will come to be called Mārtaṇḍa.

41-42. He will slay Asuras, the enemies who took away shares from sacrifices.

On hearing the voice from the firmament, Aditi felt excessively delightful since without a war Dānavas had their prowess crippled, Indra challenged Daityas for a fight.

43. In the company of Devas he felt very joyous: Dānavas rushed against him. The battle of Devas with the Asuras was terrible.

44-46. With the intervening spaces between the worlds brightened up by the continuous shower of weapons and missiles the combat raged furiously. On being stared at by sungod, Asuras were burnt by his refulgence and were reduced to ashes in the course of that battle making the heaven-dwellers attain unparalleled delight. They eulogised Aditi and the sun-god, the source of the mass of refulgence. They regained the lost rights and their due shares in the sacrifice.

47. Lord Sun too exercised his rights. Enveloped by his rays beneath and above like the blossoms of Kadamba he resembled a ball of fire. His physical form appeared clearly.

The sages said:

48. How did the sun-god, later on, attain the shining form like the globular blossoms of the Kadamba? O lord of the universe, recount it to us.

Brahmā said:

49. After bowing to him and propitiating him, the Prajāpati Tvaṣṭṛ Viśvakarmā, gave his daughter Saṁjñā to the Sun-god.

50. The lord of the rays begot three children of her, two highly blessed sons and a daughter, Yamunā.

51. The sun-god scorched the three worlds consisting of the mobile and immobile beings with his abundant refulgence.

52. Seeing the form of the sun-god like a ball of fire and

unable to bear the excessive splendour, Saṁjñā spoke to her shadow—Chāyā.

Saṁjñā said:

53. O splendid lady, welfare unto you. I shall go to my father's house. At my bidding you stay there itself without being affected in the least.

54. These two boys of mine and this faircomplexioned daughter should be brought up by you. This secret should not be divulged to the lord at any rate.

Chāyā said:

55. Unless I am seized by tresses, until I am cursed I shall never reveal your secret. You may go wherever you have desire to go.

56-57. Assured thus Saṁjñā went to the abode of her father. She continued to stay in her father's house for a thousand years. Frequently pressed by her father to return to her husband she assumed the form of a mare and went to the northern Kurus.

58-61. O excellent brahmins, desisting from food the chaste lady performed a penance there.

When Saṁjñā had gone off to her father's place, Chāyā who had assumed her form abided by her instructions and approached the sun-god. Taking her to be Saṁjñā, the sun-god begot of her two sons and a daughter. The Earthly Saṁjñā (i.e. Chāyā) did not show as much affection to the children born before as she showed to her own children. Manu (the elder son) did not mind it but Yama (the younger son did not brook it.

62. Afflicted in many ways by his step-mother he became extremely sad. Whether it was due to anger or to childishness or to the force of his inevitable future he threatened her with his lifted foot but he did not let it fall on her form.

Chāyā said:

63. Since you have threatened your father's wife senior to you (in age), this foot of yours will undoubtedly fall off.

Brahmā said:

64. Yama became extremely afflicted in mind due to that curse. Accompanied by Manu, that righteous soul intimated everything to his father.

Yama said:

65-66. O lord, our mother does not treat us with equal affection. Leaving off the elder ones she desires to nourish the younger ones with devoted love. Of course the foot was lifted up but it did not touch her body; whether this was due to my childishness or delusion it behoves you to forgive the same.

67. O father, I, the son, have been cursed by this mother in great anger. Hence, O foremost one among those who blaze, I do not consider her as my true mother.

68. O lord of rays, think of the ways and means whereby, your grace, my foot may not fall off as a result of my mother's curse.

The Sun-god said:

69. O son, certainly a great reason must lie behind this affair since you, conversant with virtue and holy rites, have been swayed by wrath.

70. There are remedies for all curses but there is none to ward off the curse of one's mother.

71. It is not possible to negative the curse of your mother. But I shall do something to attenuate the effects of the curse.

72. Worms will take off flesh from your foot and go down to the earth. Thereby your mother's curse will be carried out and you will also be saved.

Brahmā said:

73-74. Āditya said to Chāyā:—"When the sons are equal why did you treat one with more affection? Certainly, you are not the real mother: Saṁjñā has gone away somewhere. A real mother will not curse her children even if they are worthless fools.

75. Afraid of being cursed by Sungod she who had been avoiding it so far, revealed herself to him.

76. On hearing that, the sun-god went to his father-in-law. (Tvaṣṭṛ) of holy rites, honoured the sun-god of great splendour. As the god appeared at the point of burning him up in his wrath, he pacified him.

Viśvakarmā said:

77. This form of yours, permeated by excessive refulgence is unbearable. Unable to bear it, Saṁjñā is performing a penance now in the forest.

78. Today you will see her. Of auspicious conduct she is performing a penance for your gentler forms and features, in the forest.

79. Brahmā's statement has been heard by me. O lord, if it pleases you, I shall make your form more lovely and glossy, O lord of heaven.

Brahmā said :

80-81. Thereupon the sun-god said to Tvaṣṭṛ 'So be it'. Permitted by the sun-god Viśvakarmā mounted him on his lathe in the Śākadvīpa and began to whet the disc that had been originally circular and rough.

82. When the sun, the central pivot of the worlds, began to rotate, the Earth along with the oceans, mountains and forests rose up into the sky.

83. O brahmins, O highly blessed ones, the entire firmament including the moon, planets and stars came tumbling as if pulled down and agitated.

84. Waters of oceans splashed up. The great mountains crumbled down with their rows of ridges broken up and scattered.

85. The abodes having Dhruva the Pole Star for their support came down, O excellent sages, as the cords of rays that held them together, snapped.

86. Thousands of huge clouds were tossed up by gusts of wind as they fell and whirled about with great velocity. They rumbled terribly as they were shattered to pieces.

87. O excellent sages, with the Earth, sky and nether regions whirling about along with the rotating Sungod the entire cosmos became excessively agitated at that time.

88. On seeing the three worlds thus whirled about, the celestial sages and Devas eulogised the sun-god alongwith Brahmā.

89-92. "You are the primordial lord of Devas. You are born for the prosperity of Earth. You stand by in three forms at the time of creation, sustenance and dissolution. Hail to you, O lord of Universe, O Sun-god, O bestower of virtue."

As the lord was being whetted and scraped Indra and other Devas eulogised thus :—

"O lord, O lord of the universe, be victorious. O lord of cosmos, be victorious".

The seven sages, Vasiṣṭha, Atri and others eulogised him by various hymns. They said: "Hail, Hail".

The Vālakhilyas[1] too eulogised sun-god by their excellent worlds and passages of the Vedas.

93-96. Aṅgiras and others were extremely joyous and they eulogised Sungod who was being whetted.

"O lord, you bring salvation to those who are desirous of liberation. You are the object of meditation for those who meditate. You are the goal of all living beings following the section of the Vedas on Rituals. O lord of Devas, you are worthy of being worshipped. O lord of worlds, may we achieve welfare. May we the bipeds have welfare. Let welfare befall the quadrupeds."

The Vidyādharas, Yakṣas, Rākṣasas and Nāgas joined their palms in reverence. With heads bent they made obeisance to Sun-god. They uttered different words pleasing to ears and minds.

97-100. "May your splendour be bearable to the living beings. O sanctifier of living beings."

Then Hāhā, Hūhū, Nārada and Tumburu[2] all experts in the art of music—began to sing in praise of Sun-god. They were experts in Ṣaḍja, Madhyama and Gandhāra notes. Their

---

1. *Vālakhilyas*—sixty thousand hermits of the size of half a thumb live in the solar region. Wearing hides of animals they travel in front of the sun in the shape of birds.

2. Hāhā Hūhū, Nārada and Tumburu were distinguished musicians in Ancient World. Puranic literature is full of their anecdotes. Similarly, Viśvācī, Ghṛtācī, Urvaśī, Tilottamā, Menakā, Sahajanyā and Rambhā were celestial courtezans highly skilled in the art of instrumental music.

songs were pleasing by virtue of their soft Modulation, intonation (beating of time and mode of performance).

While Sungod, lord of the worlds, was being whetted, the celestial damsels danced. They were Viśvācī, Ghṛtācī, Urvaśī, Tilottamā, Menakā, Sahajanyā and Rambhā, the most excellent one among the celestial nymphs.

101-102. They showed various gestures and dancing tricks. Emotions were tickled by their poise, elegant movements and seductive twists.

Various musical instruments such as lutes, flutes, gongs, drums of diverse kinds such as Paṇavas, Puṣkaras, Mṛdaṅgas, Paṭahas, Ānakas and Dundubhis, and hundreds and thousands of conches were played.

103. A great tumult arose as they were singing, dancing and playing on instruments such as Turyas and Vāditras. Gandharvas and Apsaras raised their pleasing sounds everywhere.

104. Then, with their palms joined in reverence, with their bodies bending low with devotion, the deities made obeisance, even as the thousand-rayed Sun-god was being whetted.

105. Amidst that sonorous din, in the assembly of living beings, Viśvakarmā went on whetting slowly and steadily.

106. The Sun-god was whetted carefully and skilfully up to the knees by Viśvakarmā. He did not approve of further whetting. Hence, he was brought down from the lathe.

107. As the surplus refulgence was shed off, the unbearable form vanished. It increased in pleasing lustre and attractive shape.

108-109. By listening to this story of whetting of Sungod who is the cause of seasons when snow falls, clouds shower water and heat increases and who is praised by Śiva, the lotus-seated Brahmā and Viṣṇu, one goes to the world of Sungod at the final departure from this world.

Thus it was, O excellent sages, that Sun-god took birth formerly. His excessively beautiful form has already been recounted by me.

CHAPTER THIRTYONE

One Hundred and Eight Names of Sun-God

The sages said :

1-2. Please tell us more stories about Sun-god. Listening to the pleasing stories we never reach the point of satiety. The Sungod iș brilliant. He has great refulgence like that of mass of fire. O lord, we wish to know this—whence is the greatness and power of that god ?

Brahmā said :

3-4. When the worlds were enveloped in darkness, when mobile and immobile beings perished at the outset, the cosmic intellect was born of Primordial Nature. It was the cause of the attributes. Ego, the activiser of great elements, was born thereof. Then wind, fire, waters, Ether and Earth originated. Thereafter, the (Cosmic) Egg was born.

5. It is in this Egg that these seven worlds are founded. The Earth is inclusive of seven continents and seven oceans.

6. Lord Viṣṇu, lord Śiva and I (Brahmā) were stationed there alone. All of us were deluded by all-enveloping darkness. We were meditating on the supreme god.

7. Thereafter, Sun-god the dispeller of darkness, the deity of great brilliance, appeared. Then he was recognized as Savitṛ (Sun-god) by us by our Yogic power of meditation.

8. After realising him as the Supreme Soul we eulogised him by means of divine hymns.

9. Prayer: You are the primordial lord of Devas. By your power of lordship you are called Īśvara. You are the first maker of all living beings. You are the cause of daylight and the lord of Devas.

10. You are the enlivener of all living beings. Devas, Gandharvas, Rākṣasas, sages, Kinnaras, Siddhas, Nāgas and birds.

11. You are Brahmā, Śiva, Viṣṇu. You are Prajāpati. You are the wind god, Indra, Moon, Sun-god and Varuṇa.

12. You are time, the creator, annihilator and sustainer.

You are the lord. You are the rivers, oceans, mountains, lightning and Rainbow.

13-14. You are (the cause of) dissolution and origin. You are Eternal, manifest and unmanifest. Beyond Īśvara is Knowledge. Beyond Knowledge is Śiva. You alone are the lord greater than Śiva. You are Parameśvara. You have the extremities of feet and hands all round. You have eyes, hands and mouths all round.

15. You have thousand rays, thousand faces, thousand feet and thousand eyes. You are the cause of Elements. You are the worlds Bhū, Bhuvaḥ, Svaḥ, Mahar, Satya, Tapas and Jana.

16. The form that the leading Devas praise is divine, brilliant, and difficult to comprehend. It dazzles, it illuminates the world. Obeisance to you.

17. The form that you possess is resorted to by Devas and Siddhas. You are eulogised by Bhṛgu, Atri, Pulaha and others. Your form is extremely unmanifest. Obeisance to you.

18. The form that you possess is comprehensible to those who know the Vedas. It is accompanied by omniscience. You are the overlord of all Devas. Obeisance to you.

19. The form that you possess is identical with the world. It is the creator of Universe. It is worshipped by Fire-god and Devas. It is stationed everywhere, yet incomprehensible. Obeisance to you.

20. The form that you possess is greater than sacrifice, greater than the Veda, greater than the world, greater than heaven. It is famous as the supreme soul. Obeisance to you.

21. The form that you possess is unrealisable, unobservable and unchanging. It is not realized in meditation. It has neither a beginning nor an end. Obeisance to you.

22. Obeisance to the causes. Obeisance to you who liberate from sins. Obeisance to you honoured by Aditi. Obeisance to you who dispel ailments.

23. Obeisance, obeisance to you who bestow boons. Obeisance to you who bestow happiness. Obeisance, obeisance to you who bestow riches. Obeisance, obeisance to you who bestow intellect.

24. When eulogised thus, the lord assuming the brilliant

form expressed inauspicious worlds—"what boon shall be given to you ?".

Devas said :

25. "O lord, none will be tempted to bear this excessively brilliant form of yours. For the welfare of the world, may that form become bearable."

26. Saying "Let it be so," the Sungod the cause of all creation began to bestow heat, rain and snow for the fulfilment of all worldly affairs.

27. Ever since, the adherents of Sāṅkhya, Yoga and other systems of thought who seek salvation meditate on you who are seated in heart.

28. Even if a man is devoid of good traits, even if he is imbued with heinous sins, he surmounts all by resorting to your feet.

29. The holy rite of Agnihotra, Vedas and sacrifices wherein much wealth is distributed as gifts do not deserve even a sixteenth part of devout obeisance of the devotee being offered to you.

30. Devotees resort to you who are on a par with the greatest of all holy centres, the most auspicious of all auspicious things and the holiest of all holy objects.

31. Those who bow down to you, who are eulogised by Indra and others are liberated from sins and go to your world.

The sages said:

32. O Brahmā, for a very long time we had been cherishing this desire to hear. Tell us the hundred and eight names of Sun-god which had previously been mentioned by you.

Brahmā said:

33. O brahmins, even as I recount to you the hundred and eight names of the Sungod, they constitute a great secret which yields celestial pleasures and salvation.

One Hundred and Eight Names of Sun-God

34-45. (1) Sūrya (2) Aryaman (noble-splendoured) (3) Bhaga (fortune) (4) Tvaṣṭṛ (5) Pūṣan (nourisher) (6) Arka (7)

Savitṛ (one who begets subjects) (8) Ravi (9) Gabhastimān (possessed of rays) (10) Aja (unborn) (11) Kāla (Time) (12) Mṛtyu (Death) (13) Dhātṛ (creator) (14) Prabhākara (cause of lustre) (15) Identical with Earth (16) Water (17) Fire (18) Ether (19) Wind (20) Parāyaṇa (the greatest resort) (21) Soma (Moon) (22) Bṛhaspati (Jupiter) (23) Śukra (Venus) (24) Budha (Mercury) (25) Aṅgāraka (Mars) (26) Indra (27) Vivasvān (possessing riches) (28) Dīptāṁśu (having bright rays) (29) Śuci (pure) (30) Śauri (31) Śanaiścara (Saturn) (32) Brahmā (33) Viṣṇu (34) Rudra (35) Skanda (36) Vaiśravaṇa (Kubera) (37) Yama (38) Vaidyuta (lightning) (39) Jaṭhara Agni (gastric fire) (40) Aindhana (fuel fire) (41) Tejasāṁ Pati (Lord of brilliance) (42) Dharmadhvaja (banner of Virtue) (43) Vedakartā (creator of the Vedas) (44) Vedāṅga (ancillary of the Vedas) (45) Vedavāhana (having Vedas for Vehicle) (46) Kṛta (47) Tretā (48) Dvāpara (49) Kali (50) Sarvāmarāśraya (support of all immortal beings) (51) Identical with time units such as Kalā, Kāṣṭhā, Muhūrta, Kṣapā (night) Yāmas, and Kṣaṇas (52) Saṁvatsarakāra (cause of the year) (53) Aśvattha (holy fig tree) (54) Kālacakra (Wheel of Time) (55) Vibhāvasu (having lustre as riches) (56) Śāśvatapuruṣa (permanent Being) (57) Yogin (58) Vyaktāvyakta (Manifest and Unmanifest) (59) Sanātana (Eternal) (60) Kālādhyakṣa (Presiding deity of Time) (61) Prajādhyakṣa (lord of subjects) (62) Viśvakarmā (of universal activities) (63) Tamonuda (dispeller of darkness) (64) Varuṇa (65) Sāgarāṁśa (part of the Sea) (66) Jīmūta (cloud) (67) Jīvana (enlivener) (68) Arihā (destroyer of enemies) (69) Bhūtāśraya (support of Elements) (70) Bhūtapati (Lord of living beings) (71) Sarvalokanamaskṛta (bowed by all the worlds) (72) Sraṣṭṛ (creator) (73) Vivartaka (transformer) (74) Yajñī (Possessor of sacrifices) (75) Sarvasya Ādi (cause of all) (76) Alolupa (non-greedy (77) Ananta (without an end) (78) Kapila (79) Bhānu (80) Kāmada (bestower of desires) (81) Sarvatomukha (having faces all round) (82) Jaya (Victorious) (83) Viśāla (extensive) (84) Varada (bestower of boons) (85) Sarvabhūtahitarata (engaged in the welfare of all living beings) (86) Manaḥ (mind) (87) Suparṇa (88) Bhūtādi (cause of elements) (89) Śīghraga (moving fast) (90) Prāṇadhāraṇa (sustainer of life) (91) Dhanvantari (92) Dhūmaketu (comet) (93) Ādideva (first lord) (94) Aditeḥ Sutaḥ (Son of Aditi) (95) Dvādaśātmā (having twelve forms) (96) Ravi (97) Dakṣa (Efficient) (98) Pitā, Mātā, Pitāmaha (father, mother, grandfather) (99) Svargadvāra (gateway to heaven) (100) Prajādvāra (entrance to the Subjects) (101) Mokṣa-dvāra (entrance to Salvation) (102) Triviṣṭapa (heaven) (103) Dehakartā (creator of the body) (104) Praśāntātmā (of calm soul) (105) Viśvātmā (soul of the universe) (106) Viśvatomukha (having faces all round) (107) Carācarātmā Sūkṣmātmā (the subtle soul of the mobile and immobile beings (108) Maitreya Karuṇānvita (son of Mitra endowed with mercy).

46. O excellent sages, this is the beautiful hymn of one hundred and eight names of the Sungod of unmeasured splendour. He is worthy of being glorified. It has thus been recounted by me.

47-49. For the welfare of all I make my obeisance to the sun-god who is served by Devas, manes and Yakṣas, who is saluted by Asuras, moon and Siddhas, and who has the lustre of gold and fire.

The man who reads this hymn with great concentration at sunrise shall obtain sons, wives, riches, heaps of precious gems, faculty of remembering previous birth, perpetual memory and the finest of intellects.

The man who repeats this prayer of the most excellent of Devas, with pure mind and concentration, is liberated from conflagration of miseries and ocean of sorrows. He obtains all objects of his desire.

CHAPTER THIRTYTWO

Penance of Umā

Brahmā said:

1-3. The omnipresent lord Rudra who was famous as the enemy of the three cities[1] the three-eyed, beloved of Umā, and

1. *Tripurāri*—Śiva who destroyed three cities of gold, silver and iron in the sky, air and earth built for Asuras by Maya.

moon-crested drove out all Devas, Siddhas, Vidyādharas Gandharvas, Yakṣas, Nāgas and sages who had assembled at Dakṣa's sacrifice. The lord destroyed sacrifice which was in progress, which had all the requisite materials fully stocked, including precious gems (as gifts to the priests).

4. O brahmins, Indra, and other gods were frightened by his valorous exploits. They could not desire peace and tranquility. They sought refuge in heart.

5-6. O excellent sages, it is this lord who is present in the holy centre, Ekāmraka in the land of Utkala. He is the trident-bearing full-bannered lord who bestows boons. He is the Pināka-armed lord who destroyed the sacrifice of Dakṣa. He is clad in the hide of Elephant and bestows all desires.

The sages said:

7. Why did lord Śiva who is interested in the welfare of all living beings, destroy Dakṣa's sacrifice adorned by Devas, Yakṣas, Gandharvas and others?

8. O lord, we think that the reason thereof cannot be insignificant. We wish to hear this account. Our eagerness is inordinate.

Brahmā said:

9. Dakṣa had eight daughters who were living with their husbands. The father once invited them at house and honoured them.

10-13. O brahmins, honoured well by him, they stayed on in the house of their father. The eldest of them was Satī, the wife of lord Śiva. Dakṣa had not invited her because lord Śiva never bowed to Dakṣa. As he stood in natural brilliance he never offered obeisance to his father-in-law. Satī came to know that her sisters had arrived at their father's house. Although she was not invited she too went to her father's abode. The father accorded her a welcome less ardent than that extended to others because she was not liked by him. The gentle lady who was infuriated on this count said to her father in anger.

Satī said:

14. O Lord, indeed, I am more excellent than my younger sisters. Why don't you honour me? Considering my position, you have totally neglected me and I stand despised. Being the eldest and the most excellent I deserve welcome from you.

Brahmā said:

15-19. Addressed thus, Dakṣa spoke to her with his eyes turned red.

Dakṣa said:

My younger daughters are more excellent, greater and more worthy of welcome than you. O Satī, their husbands are honoured and respected by me. They are far greater than the three-eyed lord. They have realized Brahman. They perform holy rites. They are great Yogins and righteous. They are superior to Śiva and more worthy of praise. My excellent sons-in-law are—Vasiṣṭha, Atri, Pulastya, Aṅgiras, Pulaha, Kratu, Bhṛgu and Marīci. Śiva contends with them always and they too vie with him. Śiva indeed is antagonistic to me. Hence, I do not encourage you."

20. So said Dakṣa with a deluded mind which provoked her curse on him and the sages. Thus addressed, the infuriated Satī spoke to her father:

Satī said:

21. Since you rebuke and disrespect him who is undefiled verbally, mentally and physically I eschew this body, O father, that has originated from you.

Brahmā said:

22. Due to that insult Satī was infuriated. She felt miserable. After bowing to the self-born lord Sati uttered these words:

Satī said:

23. Where I am going to be reborn, may I be born righteous and undeluded with a refulgent physical body. I should

attain the status of the virtuous wife of the intelligent three-eyed lord.

Brahmā said:

24-25. The infuriated gentle lady seated herself there alone and entered into self-meditation. She performed the rite of Āgneyī Dhāraṇā[1] within her soul. The soul being raised from all limbs, went out of the body. Urged by the wind, fire emerged from all limbs and reduced her body to ashes.

26. On hearing about the death of Satī and the factual cause thereof, the trident-bearing lord Śiva was very angry and prompted to destroy Dakṣa.

Śiva said:

27-28. Since Satī who had come suddenly was insulted and since the other daughters were praised along with their husbands, these great sages, O Dakṣa, will be born in the Vaivasvata Manvantara in your second sacrifice as persons not born of a womb.

29-32. After pronouncing the curse on the seven sages he cursed Dakṣa:

You will become a human king in the Cākṣuṣa Manvantara as the grandson of Prācīnabarhis and the son of pracetas.

You will be born of Māriṣā the daughter of the trees when Cākṣuṣa Manvantara arrives. You will be known as Dakṣa. O Suvrata, I shall frequently put obstacles in your way at that time also

33-35. Dakṣa who was thus cursed, cursed Rudra in return.

Dakṣa said:

O ruthless one, since you have cursed even the sages on account of my activities, the brahmins will not worship you in

1. *Āgneyī Dhāraṇā*. A yogī could reduce his body to ashes by the process of Yoga. Compare Kālidāsa. "Yogenānte tanūtyajām". The kings of Raghu dynasty used to burn up their bodies by taking recourse to Yoga. In this process, the yogī feels no pain while his body is aflame with fire. It is said that the fire becomes as cool as the moon till his whole body is reduced to ashes.

any sacrifice along with Devas. After pouring ghee for you in the holy rites, O cruel deity, they shall touch water. Abandoning heaven, you will stay here alone in the world till that age comes to a close. Thereafter, you will never be worshipped on the Earth together with Devas.

Rudra said:

36-38. Devas and others who partake of shares in sacrifice will be bound by the discipline of four castes. Hence, I shall not take food with them. I shall take food separately. The world of the Earth is the first among the worlds. Alone and single-handed I sustain it at my will and not at your behest. When it is supported the other worlds abide perpetually. Hence I stay here always out of my own accord and not at your bidding.

Brahmā said:

39. Thereafter, Dakṣa who was cursed by Rudra of unmeasured splendour left off his body as the son of the selfborn lord and was reborn among human beings.

40. At that time, lord Dakṣa, the lord of sacrifices performed all sacrifices along with the gods. He worshipped them by means of sacrifices as a householder.

41. The king of mountains begot of Menā, a daughter called Umā, in the Vaivasvata Manvantara. She had previously been Satī.

42. That girl had been Satī formerly. Later on, she was born as Umā. She became the wife of Rudra.

43-49. Rudra is never left off by her as long as he wishes for an abode in the course of Manvantaras.

The following gentle ladies never forsake their husbands:—Goddess Aditi always follows Kaśyapa, son of Marīci. Śrī is always with Nārāyaṇa. Śacī follows Indra, Kīrti follows Viṣṇu, Uṣā follows Sun. Arundhatī follows Vasiṣṭha.

Similarly, in the Cākṣuṣa Manvantara Dakṣa was born as the son of Pracetas and grandson of Prācīnabarhiṣ. He was born as a king. He was born of Māriṣā and Pracetas. It is heard by us that he took his second birth due to the curse of Rudra. The great sages, Bhṛgu and others were born at first in the

Tretā Yuga in the Vaivasvata Manvantara in the course of sacrifice of the great lord who had assumed the body of Varuṇa. They repented remorsefully in the course of their subsequent birth as a result of the mutual curse of Dakṣa and lord Śiva.

50. Never can a creature gain glory by enmity. It is never conducive to prosperity even if he takes another birth because he is always affected by both auspicious and inauspicious things. No enmity should be pursued by one who knows this.

The sages said:

51-54. How did Satī the daughter of Dakṣa come to be born in the abode of the lord of the mountains after casting off her body in anger? How did she have a body in the later life? How was she united with Rudra? How did they converse together? How did the Syayaṁvara marriage happen in that hoary past? O lord of the universe, how was that marriage full of wonderful incidents, celebrated? O Brahmā, it behoves you to narrate all this in detail. We wish to hear that meritorious story which is extremely delightful to the mind.

55. O leading sages, listen to the story that is destructive of sins. Listen to the story of Umā and Śiva. It is a story that bestows desirable benefits.

56. Once Himavān asked Kaśyapa the most excellent of human beings who had arrived at his abode, about the various happenings in the world, conducive to welfare and glory.

57. "By what means are the ever-lasting worlds and great glory obtained? How is the state of being worthy of worship by good men attained? Mention it to me, O sage."

Kaśyapa said:

58. O mighty one, all this is obtained through a child. My all-round glory is due to my children. So also in regard to Brahmā and the sages.

59. Don't you see this yourself, O lord of mountains, wherefore do you ask me? O lord of mountains I shall recount what happened previously in the manner it was seen by me.

60. While I was once going to Vārāṇasī I saw a brand new and divine aerial chariot stationed in the sky. It was unparalleled and magnificent.

61. Beneath it in a hollow spot I heard the shout of agony. I knew it by my power of penance. I stood there hiding myself.

62. Then, O leading lord of mountains, a brahmin who was pure and who observed virtuous rites came there. He was purified by ablution in the holy waters. He was in the midst of a great penance.

63. As he was going along, the brahmin was extremely frightened by a tiger. O lord of mountains, he entered the spot where there was a hollow pit.

64. That distressed brahmin then saw his departed ancestors hanging by a Vīraṇa reed beneath the pit. He asked them who seemed to be highly dispirited.

The Brahmin said :

65. O sinless ones, pray, who are you ? You are hanging down suspended upside down in the Vīraṇa reed. You are dispirited. By what means, is your liberation possible ?

The Pitṛs said :

66. We are your forefathers, grandfathers and great-grandfathers. You had performed meritorious deeds. But we are afflicted by your wicked action.

67. O highly blessed one, this is a hell stationed here in the form of this hollow pit. You are the Vīraṇa reed, we hang on to you.

68. O brahmin, we can stay, only as long as you live. When you are dead we will be falling into the hell; we are sinful.

69. If you marry and beget a virtuous son, we will be liberated from this sin thereby.

70. O son, it cannot be by any other means whether penance or the fruit of pilgrimage to holy centres. O highly intelligent one, do this and redeem us, your forefathers, from our fear.

Kaśyapa said :

71-73. He promised, saying—"So be it." He propitiated the bull-bannered lord, redeemed his forefathers from their fear and became the lord's attendant. By the name of Suveśa he became a favourite of Rudra. He became the chief of Gaṇas of Rudra, approved of by all and devoid of dirt.

Hence, O lord of mountains, perform a severe penance and beget a virtuous child, a fair-complexioned daughter.

Brahmā said :

74. Thus advised by the sage, the lord of mountains took up holy observances and performed an unparalleled penance. I was pleased thereby.

75. I rushed to him and said :—"I am the bestower of boons. O lord of mountains, of good holy rites, I am delighted at this penance. Tell me what you want.

The Himavān said :

76. O lord, if you are pleased with me grant me this boon. I wish for a son adorned by all good qualities.

Brahmā said :

77. O brahmins, on hearing those words of the king of mountains, I granted him the boon the object of his wish.

Brahmā said :

78-81. O lord of mountains of good holy rites, a daughter will be born to you as a result of this penance. By virtue of your favour you will obtain splendid fame. You will be worshipped by all Devas. You will be surrounded by crores of holy centres and sacred rivers. She will be your eldest daughter. Two other splendid daughters shall follow her.

Brahmā said :

After saying this I vanished there itself. In due course of time the lord of the mountains begot of Mena three daughters Aparṇā, Ekaparṇā and Ekapāṭalā.

82-86. These daughters performed great penance. Ekaparṇā ate a leaf of the holy fig tree in the course of a thousand years. Ekapāṭalā ate one leaf of the Pāṭala tree in the course of a thousand years. Their penance continued for a hundred thousand years. It was such a penance as could not be performed by either Devas or Dānavas.

Aparṇā completely abstained from food. Her mother said to her forbidding such a course. She was distressed due to her motherly affection. She said "U mā" (O, not). The gentle lady who performed such a difficult penance was thus addressed by her mother. Hence, she became known by that name. She was honoured by Devas.

87. Thus the universe of mobile and immobile beings had this noble set of the three virgins. The story of the austerities of these virgins will be told as long as the Earth lasts.

88. All those three maidens adopted Yogic means. Penance itself sustained their bodies. All of them were highly blessed. All of them had perpetual youth.

89. They are the mothers of worlds and celibate ladies. By means of penance they bless the worlds.

90. The fair-complexioned Umā was the eldest and the most excellent among them. She was endowed with great Yogic power. She went over to Great Lord as his spouse.

91. (?) Dattaka was the son of Uśanas. His son was a scion of family of Bhṛgu. Ekaparṇā bore a son Devala to him.

92. The third of those girls Ekapāṭalā approached Jaigīṣavya, son of Alarka as his spouse.

93-94. Śaṅkha and Likhita are known as her two sons not born of the womb.

Umā the fair-complexioned lady performed penance. Observing that all the three worlds were fumigated by her penance and Yogic practice I spoke to her :

95. "O goddess, O splendid lady, why do you scorch all worlds by austerities ? This entire visible world has been created by you. Once you have made it do not destroy it.

96. Indeed, you sustain these worlds by your own splendour. O mother of the universe, be pleased with us. Tell me what is it that is sought by you ?

The goddess said :

97. O Sire, you know whatfor I am engaged in the performance of this penance. Then why do you ask ?

Brahmā said :

98. Then I spoke to her—O splendid lady, he for whom you perform this penance, will approach you here itself and will woo you.

99. O splendid lady, Śiva the most excellent of the lords of all worlds is your husband. All of us are his servants the most submissive ones.

100-101. O goddess, that lord of Devas himself will approach you. He is the self-born lord of elegant form. His external features may seem deformed but there is no one equal in handsome features to him. My lord is a resident of the world of mountains. He is the primordial lord of mobile and immobile beings. He is incomprehensible and immeasurable. Without the crescent moon whose lustre is like that of Indra he appears to have assumed a terrifying form.

CHAPTER THIRTYTHREE

Testing of Pārvatī

Brahmā said :

1-8. Devas rushed to Pārvatī and said : "O goddess, Śiva, that lord of Devas, by whom you have been created and who cannot remain without you, shall be your husband. Do not perform penance." Thereafter, O brahmins, Devas circumambulated her and vanished. She stopped her activities of penance and resorted to the Aśoka tree that grew at the entrance of her hermitage.

At that time, lord Śiva who dispels the agony of Devas came there. The moon constituted the ornamental mark on his forehead. He had assumed a deformed body short in stature and simian in features. His nose was split and the hair was tawny. He was hump-backed too. With twisted contracted face he said— 'O gentle lady, I woo you'.

Umā who had achieved Yogic power knew that it was Śiva who had come. She honoured and worshipped him with Arghya, Pādya and Madhuparka[1] (water for washing the feet

1. *Madhuparka.* A mixture of honey, milk, curd and butter as an offering to a guest specially to a bridegroom when he first arrives at the bride's house.

and materials of greeting). Respectful to brahmins she offered flowers to that brahmin. With her mind purified by inner emotional fervour and desirous of obtaining his mercy through her activities she spoke :

The goddess said :

9-10. "O lord, I am not free. I have my father and mother. O leading brahmin, I am only a simple girl. My father alone is competent to give me away. Go to my father, the prosperous lord of the mountains and request him. O brahmin, if he gives me to you that is acceptable to me also".

Brahmā said :

11. Then the lord approached the king of mountains with the same deformed body and said, "O lord of mountains, give me your daughter."

12. At the sight of his deformed body he understood that he was the eternal Rudra. Dispirited because he was afraid of his curse he spoke :—

The lord of mountains said :

13-14 O lord, I do not insult or disrespect the brahmins. They are gods on the Earth[2]. O highly intelligent one, hear what had already been thought of and desired by us. I am arranging *Svayaṁvara*[3] of my daughter. My plan has been approved by the brahmins.[4] Whomsoever she may choose he will become her husband.

---

2. The lines indicate the position which the Brāhmaṇas had attained during the age of Purāṇas. The term Bhūdeva as the synonym of a Brāhmaṇa supports the view that like the consecrated monarch the Brāhmaṇa was considered to be a deity. Compare verse 48 of this chapter where Pārvatī tells the crocodile to spare the Brāhmaṇa boy because Brāhmaṇas were favourite to her, and again in verse 55 where she says, "I consider Brāhmaṇas to be most excellent among castes."

3. *Svayaṁvara*—Self-choice, the election of a husband by a princess or daughter of a Kṣatriya at a public assembly of suitors.

4. This shows that the consent of Brāhmaṇas (clergymen) was necessary for holding Svayaṁvara where a princess could select a husband of her own choice.

15. On hearing the words of the mountain lord, the lofty-minded, full-bannered lord came near the goddess and said :—

Śiva said :

16. O gentle lady, I hear that your Svayaṁvara has been approved by your father. O sinless lady, it is said that he whom you choose therein will be your husband.

17. Hence, O good-faced lady, I shall take leave of you and go. You are inaccessible to me. Leaving off a handsome person how can you woo one like me ?

Brahmā said :

18-20. Thus addressed by him she pondered over what he had said. Realising her mental emotion directed towards Rudra, as well as the clarity of her mind, she said to the lord of Devas—"Do not misunderstand me. I shall woo you. It is by no means surprising. O lord, if at all you have feelings of suspicion about me, I shall woo you here itself, O highly blessed one. You are already present in my mind."

Brahmā said :

21-22. Pārvatī stood there with a bunch of flowers in her hands, placed it on Śiva's shoulders and said "You have been chosen."

Thereupon, the lord, who was chosen by Pārvatī spoke as if resuscitating the Aśoka.

Śiva said :

23-28. Since I have been wooed with holy bunch of flowers you will have no old age. You will become immortal. Your form is loveable. Your flowers are lovely. You bestow love. You are my favourite. You will be a steadfast beloved of Devas. You will always possess flowers that will serve as your ornaments. You will be having flowers that will yield fruits which you will eat as food. You will smell as nectar. You will have sweet scents. You will be devoid of fear. Extremely happy you will traverse worlds. Henceforth, the hermitage will be known as Citrakūṭa. The seeker of merit who comes to this hermitage will attain the benefit of a horse-sacrifice. He who dies here will go to the world of Brahmā. He who performing holy rites casts off his life here shall reap the benefit of your performing penance. He shall be the lord of Gaṇas.

Brahmā said :

29. After saying this, the lord, the creator of the universe, the lord of all living beings took leave of the daughter of Himavān and vanished.

30. When the lord of unmeasured soul had gone, Pārvatī sat on a rock with her face turned to the direction where he had gone.

31. With her face turned to Śiva the great lord, the lord of worlds, she became dispirited like the night devoid of the moon.

32. Then the daughter of the mountain-lord heard the cry of an unhappy boy in a lake near the hermitage.

33. Śiva the lord of Devas had assumed the form of a boy who had gone to the centre of the lake for playing. He was then caught by a crocodile.

34. Adopting the Yogic Māyā the cause of origin of the universe, he assumed that form in the middle of the lake and spoke thus :

The boy said :

35-38. Let some one protect me. I have been seized by a crocodile. Fie on this misery, even as a boy who has not yet realized his cherished desire and purpose. I am courting death in the jaws of this wicked crocodile. Although I am very sad on being seized by the crocodile I am not bewailing for myself, I am bewailing for my parents. On knowing that I am dead after being devoured by the crocodile, they who are fond of me, their only son, will surely cast off their lives. Alas, it is tragic that I, a mere boy who have not yet entered the main stage of life will die after being seized by a crocodile.

Brahmā said :

39. On hearing that cry of the distressed brahmin the splendid lady stood up and proceeded to that place where that brahmin boy happened to be.

40. That moon-faced lady saw the boy of handsome features caught in the jaws of a crocodile and trembling with fear.

41. On seeing Pārvatī approaching, that massive, splendid and glorious crocodile hastened to the middle of the lake taking the boy along with him.

42. On being dragged thus, the lustrous boy cried aloud in distress. On seeing the boy in this miserable state that lady of great holy rites was distressed and spoke thus :

Pārvatī said :

43. O king of crocodiles of great power, huge fangs and terrible exploit, leave of this boy who is the only son of his parents. Leave him off immediately.

The crocodile said :

44-45. O madam, he who comes within my grasp at the outset on the sixth day is ordained as my prey by the creator. O highly blessed daughter of the king of mountains, this boy has come to me on the sixth day. Certainly, he has been urged by Brahmā. By no means will I release him.

Pārvatī said :

46. In exchange of the penance that has been performed by me on the peak of the Himavān, release this boy, O king of crocodiles, obeisance be to you.

The crocodile said :

47. O splendid-faced gentle lady, let there not be any wastage of your penance over a small boy. O excellent one, do what I say. I shall release him then.

48. O lord of crocodiles, speak out quickly. What is not repugnant to good men shall be done. Entertain no doubt about this, since brahmins are very favourites to me.

The crocodile said :

49. Offer me quickly whetever penance has been performed by you whether it be very little or much more. Offer the same to me in entirety. He shall be released then.

The lady said :

50. O great crocodile of powerful grasp, everything has been granted to you, every thing of the merit that has been acquired by me ever since my birth, leave off the boy.

Brahmā said :

51. Then the crocodile blazed on being enveloped by that penance. Like the sun at midday he became too dazzling to be seen. Delighted in mind he spoke to her.

The crocodile said :

52-53. O gentle lady of great holy rites, should this much have been done without thinking deeply ? Gathering the power of penance together is a sad affair. Its eschewal is not commendable. O lady of slender waist, take back your penance as well as this boy. I am pleased with your devotion to brahmins. Hence, I grant this boon unto you. Thus urged by the crocodile, the lady of great holy rites said :—

Pārvatī said:

54. O crocodile, even with my body, the brahmin should be assiduously protected by me. Penance can be acquired by me once again. But the brahmin cannot be secured once again.

55. O great crocodile, it is after pondering over it deeply that the liberation of the boy has been effected by me. Penance is not more valuable than brahmins. I consider brahmins to be most excellent among castes.

56. O leader of crocodiles, after giving away I shall never retake it. It has already been bequeathed to you. No man shall take back what has already been given away, crocodile.

57. This has already been given to you by me. I am not going to take it back, let it rejoice within you. But, let this boy be released.

Brahmā said:

58. (Decisively) told thus, that crocodile praised her, released the boy and bowed down to her. After taking leave of her he vanished there itself.

59. Released near the bank of the lake by the crocodile, the boy too vanished there itself like an object acquired in dream.

60. Considering that her penance had dwindled down, the gentle lady the daughter of the great mountain Himavān began to perform the same once again with strict observance of regulations.

61. Knowing that she was desirous of performing penance once again, O brahmins, Śiva appeared before her and asked her not to perform penance.

62. O gentle lady of great holy rites, as your penance has been granted to me alone, you will get it back a thousand times more and it shall never dwindle down.

63. Thus acquiring the everlasting excellent penance Pārvatī was pleased and delighted. She stayed there eagerly awaiting the Svayaṁvara celebration.

64. The man who always reads this episode of the daughter of the king of mountains will acquire a change of form. He will become the chief of Gaṇas and be equal to Kumāra.

CHAPTER THIRTYFOUR

Pārvatī weds Śiva

Brahmā said:

1-6 In due course, the Svayaṁvara of the daughter of the mountain was celebrated on the lofty peak of the Himavān filled with hundreds of lofty chambers. The Himavān, the king of the mountains, an expert in meditation came to know of the secret talk of his daughter with the lord of Devas. Even after knowing it, with a desire to conform to the traditional procedure he proclaimed the Svayaṁvara celebration of his daughter all over the world. He thought thus—"If my daughter woos Śiva in the presence of Devas, Dānavas and Siddhas, residing in all parts of the world, that alone will be proper, praiseworthy and suitable to my dignity". After thinking thus and keeping lord Śiva in heart, the king of mountains announced Svayaṁvara amongst Devas ending with Brahmā. The most excellent king of the mountains littered his land with precious gems and organized the Svayaṁvara ceremony very carefully.

7. Immediately after the Svayaṁvara of his daughter had been announced, Devas and others, the residents of all the worlds came there assuming divine forms and dresses.

8. Informed by the king of mountains I went there accompanied by Devas. I was seated on my full blown lotus seat and surrounded by Siddhas and Yogins of immeasurable spiritual power.

9-12. Riding on his Airāvata, the chief of the leading elephants, which exuded profuse currents of ichor, the lord of immortal beings (Indra) came there at the head of Devas holding his thunderbolt. The lord of Devas had a thousand eyes and his features were elegant by viture of his divine unguents and garlands.

Seated on his golden chariot with waving flags the son-god came there hurriedly. He brightened the quarters so that he appeared to be equal in lustre to them though he was superior to them in refulgence and power.

One of the sons of Kaśyapa viz. Āditya came there in his chariot equal in lustre to fire and solar splendour. His rays were those of the midday. His ear-rings brightened up by jewels, dazzled all.

Riding on his terrible buffalo, the god of Death Yama hastened to that place. He was holding his sceptre (rod of chastisement). His physical body was yellow in colour. In prowess he was comparable to none. He was unparalleled in brilliance, strength and power of demanding obedience. His limbs were well developed and he wore garlands.

13-16. Riding in his chariot, wind god who sustains the world, came there, beautiful in dress and demeanour. Gold and jewels enhanced his elegance. In height and stoutness his body vied with great mountains.

Coming in the centre of the leading Devas, the fire-god wearing grand apparel, stood there, blazing. Superior to all in splendour, and steeped in excessive brilliance he warmed the leaders of Devas and Asuras.

Riding in an excellent divine aerial chariot, the most excellent in the universe, Kubera the lord of all chiefs of wealth came there in a hurry with his slender staff-like body brightened by different sorts of jewels.

Riding in an aerial chariot of wonderful form studded with great shining precious gems the Moon god arrived there instilling enthusiasm in the leaders of Devas and Asuras by means of his splendour and grand apparel. He was elegant in form and dress.

17-21. Riding on Garuḍa who resembled a mountain, the macebearing lord Viṣṇu hurried to that place. Garlands of sweet scent were tied round his limbs; his dress was wonderful and his slender body was dark-complexioned.

Aśvins, the excellent physicians were seated in the same aerial chariot. Charming in their brilliant and elegant apparel, the two bold and excellent Devas hastened to the venue of the marriage rites.

The noble-souled Nāga king of fiery solar splendour rode in an aerial chariot along with the other Nāgas and arrived there. He had the colour of fire-emitting sparks.

The sons of Diti the great Asuras, refulgent like fire, sun, Indra and the wind-god came there even before Devas clad in nice apparel befitting their excellent features.

At the bidding of Indra the king of Gandharvas arrived there along with Gandharvas and Apsaras. Bedecked in shoulderlets and riding in a divine chariot he had a handsome form wonderful to behold.

22-26. Several other Devas, Gandharvas, Yakṣas, Serpents and Kinnaras too came there, riding in aerial chariots. They were clad in different sorts of beautiful apparel.

The overlord of mountain kings, Himālaya shone amidst the leading Devas, superior to some, equal to others in beauty of form. Delighted himself and delighting others by his power of command and prosperity he beautified the spot of Svayaṁvara ceremony.

It was for accomplishing the task of heaven-dwellers that Satī protested against Dakṣa, died of herself and was reborn in the abode of Himavān. Being the cause of worlds, she gave birth to the universe. She was the mother of Devas and Asuras. She had formerly been the wife of Śiva, the intelligent Puruṣa and she had been praised as the great Prakṛti in the Purāṇas.

Now as Umā she was seated in an aerial chariot covered with gold and studded with jewels. She was fanned (on either side) by the waving chowries. She held a garland of sweet-scented flowers of all seasons. She stood ready to proceed ahead quickly.

Brahmā said:

27-28. As the Umā stood there in the assembly of Devas, holding the divine garland, as Indra and other Devas had come there ready for Svayaṁvara, Śiva assumed the form of an infant (with five tufts of hair) with a desire to test her again. The lord of great lustre lay asleep in the lap of Umā.

29. All of a sudden, Umā saw the infant lying (asleep in her lap). By means of meditation she understood who it was and took him up with great delight.

30. She of pure thoughts attained a husband of her choice. Holding him to his bosom she turned round and sat down.

31. On seeing the infant lying in the lap of Umā Devas were completely deluded. "Who is this infant ?" They muttered to one another and then shouted loudly.

32-33. This slayer of Vṛtra (Indra) seized his thunderbolt and lifted up his hand against the infant. The raised hand of Indra remained in that position stunned by Śiva the lord of Devas in the form of the infant. The slayer of Vṛtra could not hurl his thunderbolt. He could not even move.

34. Then the powerful son of Aditi and Kaśyapa named Bhaga, who too was deluded, lifted up his bright weapon, desirous of cutting up the infant.

35. His hand too was stunned; his strength, splendour and yogic power became ineffective.

36-37. Viṣṇu looked at Śiva shaking his head. When those angry Devas stood thus, I was extremely agitated. By means of meditation I understood that it was Śiva, the lord of the chiefs of Devas who was lying on the lap of Umā.

38-44. On realising that it was lord Śiva, I stood up immediately with reverence. I saluted the feet of Śiva. O brahmins, then I eulogised him with ancient songs and secret names conducive to merit. "You are the unborn lord. You are never old. You are the lord who created the greater and smaller beings. You are the primordial Nature (Prakṛti) as well as Puruṣa. You are the Brahman worthy of meditation. You are the imperishable and undying Being. You are the supreme soul. You are the lord and great cause. You are the creator of Brahmā. You are the maker of Prakṛti. You are beyond Prakṛti. This gentle lady is Prakṛti the permanent instrument unto you in the process of creation. She has assumed the form of your wife and has come to you as the cause of the universe.

O lord, obeisance to you as well as to your glorious consort. O lord of Devas, it was at your bidding and by your favour that these Devas and subjects had been created by me. They are now deluded by your Yogic Māyā. Be pleased with them. May they be as they were before.

O brahmins, after submitting this to the lord I spoke at this occurrence to all those Devas who were stunned.

45-49. "O ye deities, you are confounded. You don't understand lord Śiva. You immediately seek refuge in lord and his divine consort. He is the unchanging great Soul."

Then all those heaven-dwellers who were stunned, bowed to lord Śiva with their minds purified by emotional fervour.

Śiva, the lord of Devas was pleased with them. He immediately restored Devas to their former self. When this process of reviving Devas was going on, the lord of Devas assumed a wonderful body possessed of three eyes.

50-56. Devas, eclipsed and dazzled by the brilliance of Śiva closed their eyes. The lord granted them powerful eyes competent to behold him. Then they looked at the lord of Devas. On seeing the third eye Indra and other Devas recognized him as Śiva.

In the presence of heaven-dwellers the delighted goddess placed garland at the feet of the lord of unmeasured lustre. Saying "Well done, Well done." Devas, once again, bowed to the lord along with the goddess, with their heads resting on the ground.

In the meantime O brahmins, I spoke to Himavān the great mountain of massive splendour. I was accompanied by Devas.

You are worthy of being praised and honoured by all. You are really great. Since you have the alliance with Śiva your prosperity will be great. Let the auspicious marriage rite be performed. There shall be no delay in this matter?

Then after bowing to me Himavān replied:

Himavān said:

57. O lord, you alone are the cause of my all-round rise and prosperity. The favour has come about suddenly and the reason thereof can be you alone. O sire, conduct celebration of marriage after fixing up the programme.

Brahmā said:

58. On hearing the words of the king of mountains, O brahmins, I said thus to the lord—"O lord, let the marriage rite be celebrated".

59-63. Śiva, the lord of the worlds said to me—"As you like". O brahmins, instantaneously I created a city for the marriage. It was made splendid by different sorts of jewels, precious stones and gems of various colours; gold and pearls came in their embodied form and decorated that excellent city. The ground was wonderfully paved with Emerald. It was adorned with columns of gold. Shining crystals constituted the walls. Pearl necklaces were suspended from them. At the entrance to that beautiful city, raised platform was constructed for the marital rites. That place of noble Śiva, lord of Devas, shone well. The moon and the sun (assumed the form of) two brilliant gems and rendered the place warm and cool.

64. Wafting sweet fragrant smell, very pleasing to the mind, the wind-god came there, evincing his devotion to lord Śiva. He was gentle to the touch.

65-68. The four oceans, Indra and other Devas, the celestial rivers, the great terrestrial rivers, Siddhas, sages, Gandharvas, Apsaras, Nāgas, Yakṣas, Rākṣasas, aquatic and Sky-bound birds and animals, Kinnaras, Cāraṇas, Tumbaru, Nārada Hāhā, Hūhū and the singers of Sāman hymns brought with them other sorts of gems and came to the city. Ascetics and sages, experts in singing vedic Mantras chanted holy Mantras of marriage rites with delighted minds.

69. Mothers of the universe and the celestial virgins began to sing joyously in the course of that wedding ceremony of the lord.

70. The six seasons were simultaneously present in their

embodied forms at the marriage function. They spread pleasing scents everywhere.

71-79. In the course of marriage celebration of the daughter of the mountain, the rainy season was present with the following characteristics:—

Resembling the blue clouds, delighted at the chanting sound of the Mantras, the peacocks danced about everywhere producing their crowing notes called 'Kekā'.

It was highly elegant with dangling, rolling tawny, clear like lightning streaks. It was made splendid by the white cranes with lilies for their crest-jewel.

It became refulgent as the freshly grown mushrooms, plantain trees and trees and creepers of other sorts had sprouts coming out. It was rendered noisy by countless frogs that woke up longing for flourishing currents of clear water and that were rendered lethargic by intoxication.

It was accompanied by the delightful crowing Kekā sounds of the peacocks that brought about a break in the haughty anger excited by jealousy in lovely maidens, though lofty-minded. These maidens bore a grudge against their lovers and their anger made them haughty in their minds.

The rainy season shone with the rainbow that was present very near the rainy clouds. The beautiful form of the crooked rainbow shone with various colours. It spread golden splendour everywhere.

In the rainy season the pleasing winds shook the splendid forelocks of celestial damsels. The winds were fragrant because they were blowing against flowers of diverse colours. They were cool by their contact with the waters of fresh and dense clouds.

The disc of the moon was concealed by the rumbling cloud. The beautiful Durvā grass near water-logged spots was sprinkled with fresh water. The rainy season that arrived with such traits was respectfully looked at by the yearning and pining harlot maidens who had been heaving deep sighs rendering the atmosphere as it were filled with smoke.

The rainy season was like a maiden. The cackling sound of the swans was like that of the anklets. The clouds were lifted up and raised. The rolling lightning streaks were the necklaces. The clear lotuses were the eyes.

The black layers of clouds supported the swans in the waters of different colours. The downpour of water made the lilies bend down, the lilies that served the purpose of eyes. Their beauty was enhanced by the fragrant pollen dust.

The Autumn

80-88. The season of autumn was present at the marriage function of Pārvatī, the daughter of lord Himavān.

The quarters looked very beautiful. The autumn was like a lady who had taken out her bodice in the form of a cloud. Buds of lotuses that resemble the breasts made their appearance. The cackling sound of swans was like the tinkling of anklets.

The banks of rivers were like buttocks ample and extensive. The chirping Sārasas served as the girdle. The blue lotuses in full bloom were charming like the dark-coloured eyes.

The ripe red Bimba fruits were like the lower lips. She smiled with Kunda flowers appearing like teeth. The lady of autumn had dark-coloured curly umbilical hairs with the spreading fresh green creepers.

The lady of autumn was sweet-voiced with the humming sound of intoxicated swarms of bees. The rolling clusters of lilies were the charming earrings that heightened her beauty. The lady of autumn had the sprouts growing from the branches of red Aśoka tree for her fingers. She was embellished in garments constituted by its bunches of flowers.

The red lotuses were the tips of her feet. The Jasmine Jāti flowers were her nails. The stems of the plantain trees were her thighs. The moon was her face.

The lady of autumn appeared like a charming beloved full of love. She was richly endowed with all characteristics. She was bedecked in all ornaments.

Divested of her bodice covering, in the form of black cloud, the full moon represented her lovely face; the blue lotuses were her eyes; the lotuses, which blossomed by the rays of the sun, acted as her breasts delighting the mind through the soft winds, rendered fragrant by the pollen dust of different flowers. With the sweet cackling sounds for her tinkling anklets the lady of Autumn was present at the wedding function of Umā.

Hemanta and Śiśira

89. The two seasons Hemanta and Śiśira (the early winter

and the later winter) of great lustre came there flooding the quarters with excessively chill waters.

90. The Himavān the most excellent of mountains was approached by the two seasons. They are showering flakes of snow in quick succession. Enveloped by a shower of flakes Himavān appeared to be as it were an attendant.

91. With the dense shower of snow flakes that fell deep below, the Himālaya shone like the ocean of milk.

92. That great mountain was approached by successive seasons, like a prejudiced person who is gratified by the service of the great.

93. With his peaks covered with layers of snow the mountain shone like a ruler of the Earth with large and white umbrellas.

94. The winds frequently enhanced the passionate love of Devas and their maidens. The lotus ponds were filled with clear water. The lotuses and lilies grew in abundance. With these they appeared to be charming like women who reveal the tips of their breasts slightly.

The Spring season:

95-117. At the marriage of the daughter of the mountain lord Spring was also present.

The celestial elephants full of delight entered the lake filled with waters which were neither too hot nor too cold. They were rendered tawny by the particles of pollen. With the cackling of ruddy geese the atmosphere became resonant. The mango and the Priyaṅgu trees were in full bloom vying with each other. With their bunches of flowers one appeared to threaten the other. Both of them looked admirably splendid.

On the white snow-clad peaks, the Tilaka trees with their blossoms appeared like elderly guests accompanied by infants. They appeared as though they had come for some specific purpose.

The Aśoka creepers in full bloom supported by the big Śāla trees shone like loving maidens with their arms twined round the necks of their lovers.

The following trees were laden with fruits and flowers : They were the mango, Kadamba, Nīpa, Tāla, Tamāla, Sarala,

Kapittha (Wood apple), Aśoka, Sarja, Arjuna, Kovidāra, Punnāga, Nāgeśvara, Karṇikāra, Lavaṅga, Kālāguru (Agalschum), Saptaparṇa, Nyagrodha, Śobhāñjana and Cocoanut. There were other trees also. They were seen everywhere. There were beautiful water reservoirs with waters sparkling like gold. They were filled with blue lilies and fishes. Aquatic birds and animals like ruddy geese, Kāraṇḍavas, swans, Koyaṣṭis, Dātyūhas (water crows) and cranes abounded in them. Birds were seen on the tops of trees with wings of diverse colours and the limbs of various forms. They appeared to be embellished as it were.

Birds and animals with their passion roused and their bodies excited produced cries and sounds as if they were threatening those engaged in amorous sports.

On that mountain, in the course of marriage celebration of the daughter of the mountain-lord winds blew making the limbs delighted and cool. The winds originating from the Malaya mountain slowly blew down the white flowers from the trees.

All reasons of meritorious nature shone with their respective traits intermingled. Those seasons whose special traits have been recounted looked very charming at that place.

The Mālatī creepers shone with their bunches of flowers. Intoxicated swarms of bees were humming amongst them. These creepers appeared as if they were terrifying one another.

The petals of flowers were resorted to by the intoxicated swarms of bees. The waters were rendered blue by the blue lotuses, white by the white lotuses and red by the red lotus stalks.

There were clusters of golden lotuses in lakes of extensive water surface, in some, beautiful flowers grew continuously; in some there were lotuses with stalks like lapis lazuli.

The ponds were very beautiful with lotuses, lilies and other flowers. The rows of golden steps were rendered resonant by various birds O brahmins, the lofty peaks of that mountain, thickly overgrown with Karṇīkāra trees in full blooms shone like golden peaks.

The quarters shone pink in colour on account of the Pāṭala trees with their flowers slightly opened. They were gently shaken by the wind.

There were Kṛṣṇārjuna trees and the blue Aśoka trees on that mountain, ten times their number. They were in full bloom. They appeared to compete with one another in their growth.

Forests of Kiṁśuka trees resonant with sweet sounds shone on all ridges of that mountain.

With groves of Tamāla trees, the Himavān had a special beauty as though groups of clouds were lying hidden in its joints.

With tall sandal and Campaka trees with their branches spreading extensively, and profusely laden with flowers, and with the cooing sounds of intoxicated cuckoos the Himālaya shone very well.

On hearing the low sweet intoxicating cooing sound of the cuckoos the peacocks fluttered their wings and grew sweetly. Lord Kāma found his strength enhanced by their sounds. He stood ready to pierce the celestial maidens in their limbs, keeping his hands fixed to the bow and arrow.

The summer :

118-124. At the time of marriage the summer season came to the Himālaya with the power of sunshine melting water. There remained very little water in the reservoirs.

The summer season too brightened the peaks of the snow-clad mountain all round by means of many trees profusely in bloom.

During that season the winds were very pleasant. They blew and wafted the fragrance of (the flowers of) Pāṭala, Kadamba and Arjuna that grew extensively.

The tanks were made pink in colour due to the pollen dust full blown lotuses. The banks were resonant due to the cackling of swans.

The Kurabaka trees were covered with flowers on the peaks. They were resorted to by swarms of bees.

On the wide side-valleys and ridges of the mountain the Bakula trees put forth lovely flowers all round.

Excellent sages accompanied by various seasons came there to increase the prosperity of the marital rites of Umā and Śiva. The trees abounded in flowers of various sorts. The lands were beautiful by virtue of sweet sounds of different sorts of birds.

125-126. When the living beings had begun to assemble thus, when hundreds of musical instruments were played, I got the daughter of the mountain embellished with befitting ornaments and led her myself into the city, O brahmins.

127-128. Thereafter, I spoke thus to the lord Īśa. "I am present in the capacity of the preceptor. I shall pour the holy ghee into the fire. If you grant permission, holy rites can be carried out immediately."

Śaṅkara, the lord of Devas, the lord of the universe said to me.

Śiva said :

129. "O lord of Devas, O Brahmā, whatever has been thought of, whatever is desired, do it. I shall carry out your directions, O lord of the universe."

130-135. Thereafter, delighted in my mind I took up Kuśas immediately and bound the hands of Śiva and Pārvatī together in the Yogic knot. The fire-god stood there with palms joined in reverence. The auspicious Mantras of Vedas assumed physical forms and were present at the marriage. I performed sacrifice in the manner laid down. The ghee-like necter was poured as offering. I made the lord (and the goddess) circumambulate the fire. The binding knot was untied. Along with Devas, my mental sons and Siddhas, I was delighted within myself. As the marriage rites were over I bowed to the bull-bannered lord. O brahmins it was due to their Yogic power that the marriage of Umā and Śiva was effected.

That great marriage was concluded in this way. Devas did not know how it happened at all.

Thus the details of marriage have been recounted to you. Listen further about the marriage of the lord. It is very wonderful.

CHAPTER THIRTYFIVE

Hymn in Praise of Śiva

Brahmā said :

1. When the marital ceremony of lord Śiva of unmeasured splendour was performed, Indra and other Devas were highly pleased. They eulogised the lord in glorious words and paid obeisance in reverence, in the following way.

Devas said :

2. Obeisance to the lord whose symbol is the mountain. Obeisance to the lord who is the wind in velocity. Obeisance to the lord, the destroyer of pain and the bestower of splendid riches.

3. Obeisance to the lord who has the blue tuft. Obeisance to the lord, husband of Umā. Obeisance to the lord in the form of the wind. Obeisance to the lord of one hundred forms.[1]

4. Obeisance to the deity of terrible form, of deformed eyes, one thousand eyes and one thousand feet.[2]

5. Obeisance to the deity in the form of Devas; obeisance, obeisance to the lord, the ancillary of the Vedas. Obeisance to the deity who stunned the arms of Indra,[3] obeisance to the germinating sprout of the Vedas.

6. Obeisance to the overlord of mobile and immobile beings; obeisance, obeisance to one who suppresses sinners. Obeisance to the deity whose symbol is a water reservoir; obeisance, obeisance to one who annihilates the Yugas.

7. Obeisance to the deity with skulls for garlands; obeisance to the deity who wears skulls for the sacred thread; obeisance to the deity with a skull in his hand; obeisance to the deity holding a staff; obeisance to the deity holding the iron-club.

---

1. *Rudra of one hundred forms*. P. E. has a long anecdote on Śatarudra. The Veda declares emphatically that there is a single Rudra: *Eka eva Rudro vatasthe na dvitīyaḥ* but at the same time it speaks of numerous Rudras that exist on earth: *asaṁkhyātā sahasrāṇi ye rudrā adhibhūmyām.*

2. *Sahasrākṣaḥ Sahasrapāt*—Thousand-eyed, thousand-footed. These epithets are applied to primeval being (*Puruṣa*) in ṚV X.90.

3. Cf. Ch. 34, VV 33-34. The slayer of Vṛtra (Indra) lifted up his arm to strike Śiva in the form of an infant lying in the lap of Pārvatī but his right hand remained stunned and he could not hurl his thunderbolt.

8. Obeisance to the lord, the master of three worlds; obeisance to the deity, interested in the world of mortals. Obeisance to the deity with the iron club in hand; obeisance to the lord who dispels the agony of those who bow down to him.

9. Obeisance to the destroyer of the head of sacrifice; obeisance to him who removed Kṛṣṇa's tresses; obeisance to him who plucked the eyes of Bhaga;[1] obeisance to the deity who removed the teeth of Pūṣan.[2]

10. Obeisance to the wielder of Pināka,[3] trident, sword, dagger and iron-club. Obeisance to the destroyer of the god of Death, obeisance to the deity with the third eye.

11. Obeisance to one who annihilated the god of Death,[4] obeisance to the deity who resides on the mountain; obeisance to the deity with the necklace of gold; obeisance to one wearing ear-rings.

12. Obeisance to the destroyer of Yogic power of Daityas; obeisance to the Yogin; obeisance to the preceptor; obeisance to the deity with the moon and the sun for eyes; obeisance to the deity with an eye in the forehead.[5]

---

1. *Who plucked the eyes of Bhaga*—Bhaga is one of the twelve Ādityas. Devas assembled together and decided upon the share of Yajñas due to each of them and in thus fixing up shares they left out Rudra. Enraged at this neglect Rudra made a bow and fought against Devas. During the fight he extracted the eyes of Bhaga and the teeth of Pūṣan. Ultimately Devas satisfied and pleased Rudra who returned to Bhaga and Pūṣan the eyes and teeth which had been extracted.

2. *Who removed the teeth of Pūṣan.* Pūṣan—one of the twelve ādityas born as sons of Kaśyapa Prajāpati, by his wife Aditi.

In a sacrifice which Śiva attended uninvited there was a fight between Devas and Śiva. In this fight against Śiva Pūṣan lost his teeth (Mbh. Sauptika Parva Ch. 18).

3. *Pināka*—name of Śiva's bow.

4. *Annihilated the god of death.* Śiva gave Mṛkaṇḍu a boon that a pious son would be born to him but he would live only for sixteen years. The child was born and named Mārkaṇḍeya. He was educated in Vedas and Śāstras. When the hour of his death arrived, the boy embraced the liṅga idol of Śiva. When Yama, the god of death came to fetch him, the angry Śiva arose out of the idol and killed Yama. At the request of gods Yama was revived to life but Mārkaṇḍeya was granted youth for ever.

5. *An eye in the Forehead*... The two eyes of Śiva represent the Sun and the Moon; the third eye in the forehead is the eye of wisdom. But it emits fire when it opens at the time of Dissolution or even earlier when Śiva is angry.

13. Obeisance to one taking delight in cremation-ground; obeisance to the bestower of boons (staying) in the cremation ground; obeisance to the destroyer of the rude and the impolite. Obeisance to the deity devoid of garment; obeisance to the deity who laughs as boisterously as hundred thunderbolts; obeisance to the lord of mountain.

14. Obeisance to the householder saint, obeisance to the perpetual wearer of matted hair; obeisance to the celibate one; obeisance to one with shaven head, obeisance to one with partially shaven head; obeisance to the lord of Paśus.[1]

15. Obeisance to one who performs penance in the water; obeisance to one who bestows Yogic lordship and prosperity; obeisance to one who is calm and tranquil; obeisance to one who has controlled his sense-organs. Obeisance to one who causes dissolution.

16. Obeisance to one who causes blessings; obeisance, obeisance to one who sustains the world. Obeisance to Rudra; obeisance to Vasu, obeisance to Āditya; obeisance to Aśvin.

17. Obeisance to the father of all; obeisance to the supreme being of perfect knowledge; obeisance to Viśvedevas; obeisance to Śarva, Ugra, Śiva, the bestower of boons.

18. Obeisance to the terrible one; obeisance to the commander-in-chief; obeisance to the lord of Paśus; obeisance to the pure; obeisance to the destroyer of enemies; obeisance to Sadyojāta.

19. Obeisance to Mahādeva; obeisance to the wonderful, obeisance, obeisance to the trident-bearing deity; obeisance to Pradhāna; obeisance to the incomprehensible; obeisance to the effect; obeisance to the cause.

20. Obeisance to you—Puruṣa; obeisance to one who causes the wish of Puruṣa; obeisance to one who causes the contact of Puruṣa and the Guṇas of Pradhāna.

21. Obeisance to one who makes Prakṛti and Puruṣa function; obeisance to one who commits what is done and what is not done; obeisance to one who bestows union with the fruit of actions.

22. Obeisance to the knower of the time of all; obeisance

1. *Lord of Paśus*—lord of Jīvas or individual souls.

to one who restrains all; obeisance to one who disturbs the equilibrium of Guṇas; obeisance to one who bestows means of subsistence.

23. Obeisance to you the lord of the chiefs of Devas; obeisance to you the creator of living beings; O Śiva be gentle in face to be looked at, O lord, be gentle to us."

Brahmā said :

24. On being eulogised thus by all Devas, the lord of the universe, the lord of Umā spoke thus to the immortal beings.

Lord Rudra said :

25. O Devas, in regard to Devas I am both harsh and gentle. Tell me the boons you wish to choose. I shall grant them undoubtedly.

Brahmā said :

26-30. Thereafter, Devas bowed down to the three-eyed lord and said to him :

"O lord, let this boon be retained by you alone. When there is any task, you will grant the boon desired by us."

Brahmā said :

After saying "Let it be so", the lord bade forewell to Devas and other people. Thereafter he entered his abode together with the Pramathas.[1]

He who recites this wonderful episode of festivities in the presence of Devas and brahmins shall become equal to Gaṇeśa, who has no parallel. After death he shall become happy.

O leading brahmins, he who listens to this hymn or reads it shall go to the world of the lord. He shall be worshipped by Devas, Asuras and others.

1. *Pramathas*—gaṇas, Śiva's attendants.

CHAPTER THIRTYSIX

Umā and Śaṅkara leave Himālayas

Brahmā said :

1. When the lord entered his abode and was seated comfortably in an excellent seat, his ruthless enemy the cupid was ready to hit and pierce him with his shafts.

2-4. He was notorious for neglect of good conduct. He was evil-minded and of base family. It was he who harassed the worlds. Concealing his body by covering up his limbs, he put obstacles in the rites of sages. He had come there accompanied by Rati.[1] Both had assumed the forms of ruddy geese. As an assailant O brahmins, he was ready to hit and wound the lord. Hence, the lord of Devas glanced at him contemptuously by opening his third eye.

5. Then, with thousands of clusters of flames, the fire originating from his eye burned immediately the spouse of Rati together with his attendants.

6. On being burned he became distressed and lamented piteously and out of tune. Propitiating that lord he fell down on the ground.

7. With his limbs encompassed by fire the cupid, the scorcher of the world fell down into a swoon instantaneously.

8. His excessively distressed wife lamented piteously. In great agony she ruefully requested the lord and the goddess for mercy.

9. Realizing her pathetic plight, the sympathetic lord and the lady Umā glanced at the desolate Rati consolingly and said.

Umā and Maheśvara said :

10. Indeed, O gentle lady, he has been burned up. His resuscitation here, is not desired. Bodiless though he be, O gentle lady, he will carry out your tasks.

11. O splendid lady, when lord Viṣṇu incarnates as the son of Vasudeva, your husband will be reborn as his son.

Brahmā said :

12. After securing that boon, the fair-faced wife of Kāma

1. Rati—wife of Kāmadeva, god of love.

went back to the land of her choice. She was pleased. She was free from languor.

13. O brahmins, after burning up Kāma the delighted bull-bannered lord sported about on the Himālaya mountain in the company of Umā.

14-17. Accompanied by the goddess, the three-eyed lord sported about in various places such as—beautiful caves, lotus-ponds and lakes, charming places free from crowds of people, Karṇikāra forests, lovely banks of rivers frequented by Kinnaras,[1] peaks of the lord of mountains, tanks and lakes, different parks and groves, amongst Campa bushes, places, resonant with the chirpings and cooings of different birds, holy centres, sacred waters, lawns studded with jewels, etc, etc. In all these holy and charming spots embellished by Vidyādharas and frequented by Gandharvas, Yakṣas and the immortal beings, the three-eyed lord sported about along with the goddess.

18. Surrounded by Devas led by Indra, sages, Yakṣas, Siddhas, Gandharvas, Vidyādharas, leading Daityas and others of various sorts, the couple derived great pleasure on that mountain.

19. There the celestial damsels and the leading Devas danced; the delighted Gandharvas sang; the brahmins meditated; some hurriedly played on the musical instruments and some eulogised the excellent qualities of the lord.

20. The noble lord, who destroyed the eyes of Bhaga, who was accompanied by his powerful attendants comparable to Indra, Yama and fire-god, did not leave off that mountain just for pleasing the goddess.

The sages said :

21. What did the great lord the destroyer of Kāma do, staying there accompanied by Umā ? We wish to know this.

Brahmā said :

22-23. On the peak of the Himavān, the lord with the crescent moon for his caste mark on the forehead delighted the

---

1. *Kinnara*—a mythical being with a human figure and the head of a horse or with a horse's body and the head of a man, originally perhaps a kind of monkey, in later times reckoned among the Gandharvas or celestial choristers and celebrated as musician.

goddess and diverted himself. Desirous of pleasing the goddess he cut jokes and provoked mirth along with the leading Gaṇas of different shapes and sizes, who were omniscient, magnanimous and splendid and who could assume any form they liked.

24-25. Once it so happened that Umā went to her mother Menā who was seated in a bright and wonderful golden seat. On seeing the chaste blameless goddess who came there in a divine form, the mother greeted her by offering a valuable seat. Then, Menā the lotus-eyed beloved of Himavān spoke to her when she was comfortably seated.

Menā said :

26-27. O my daughter of splendid eyes, you have come after a long time. Now tell me why do you play sports with poor wretched persons in the company of your husband ? Only the low people sport about as your husband does, my precious girl. Those who are poor and those who have no support sport with such wretched and poor people, O Umā.

Brahmā said :

28. On being bluntly told thus by her mother Umā was not pleased. Endowed with enormous patience she did not say anything to her mother. Dismissed by her mother she went straight to her lord and said :

Pārvatī said :

29. O lord of the chiefs of Devas I will not stay on this mountain. O lord of massive splendour, make another residence for me in any of the three worlds.

The lord said :

30-31. You were being told always by me to go in for a separate residence, O goddess, but, O gentle lady, the proposal did not appeal to you at all. But now, O gentle lady, O splendid one, why do you seek a residence elsewhere ? Tell me O lady of pure smiles the cause for the change of your view.

The goddess said :

32-34. O lord of Devas, today I had been to the abode of my noble father. O creator of the worlds, my mother met me in a room where there was no one else. After honouring me by offering seat etc. she spoke to me thus "O Umā, my auspicious girl your husband sports with the poor wretched people. Sports and pastime of Devas are never of that sort."

O bull-bannered lord Śiva ! the fact that you sport about with the attendants of poor status is not approved of by my mother."

Brahmā said :

35-38. Then, in order to humour the goddess and make her laugh, the lord laughed biosterously and said :

The lord said :

This is true. There is no doubt about this why were you angry ? O lotus-eyed one, I do roam about in the forests and mountain caverns, surrounded by naked Gaṇas.[1] Sometimes I wear the hide of an elephant. Sometimes I have no cloth to wear. Sometimes I stay in the cremation ground and have it as my abode. I have no permanent abode anywhere.

O gentle lady, do not be furious with your mother. Your mother has spoken the truth. Unto all creatures in the world there is no other kinsman on a par with one's mother.

The goddess said :

39-40. O destroyer of three cities[2], I have nothing to do with my kinsmen. O great lord, do such things as will enable me to derive happiness.

Brahmā said :

On hearing the words of the goddess the lord of Devas left his father-in-law's residence for pleasing her consort. Accompanied by his wife and Gaṇas he went to the Meru mountain frequented by Devas and Siddhas and other Beings.

---

1. *Gaṇas*—attendants of Śiva under the special superintendence of god Gaṇeśa.

2. *Destroyer of three cities*—The three strong cities, triple fortification built of gold, silver and iron in the sky, air and earth, by Maya for the Asuras and burnt by Śiva.

CHAPTER THIRTYSEVEN

Destruction of Dakṣa's Sacrifice

The sages said :

1-2. O Brahmā, how was the horse-sacrifice of Prācetasa Dakṣa the Prajāpati destroyed in the Vaivasvata Manvantara ? How did the lord, the soul of all, become infuriated after knowing that the goddess had been made angry ? How was the sacrifice of Dakṣa of unmeasured splendour destroyed by the great lord in rage ?

Brahmā said :

3. O brahmins, I shall describe to you how the sacrifice was destroyed in rage by the great lord in retaliation of the treatment meted out to his consort—Satī.

4-6. O excellent Brahmins, the wonderful peak of Meru, Jyotiḥsthala by name, is worshipped in the three worlds. It is adorned by precious jewels. It is incomprehensible, unthwartable, and bowed to by the people. Formerly, the lord was seated there on the ridge of the mountain wonderfully beautified by all sorts of minerals. He shone well and was as comfortable as he was seated in a palanquin. The daughter of the lord of the mountains stood away by his side.

7-17. He was served by the following: The noble-souled Ādityas, Vasus of great prowess, Aśvins, the noble and excellent physicians, Vaiśravaṇa[1] the lord of Yakṣas, the glorious lord whose abode was in Kailāsa and who was surrounded by Guhyakas, Uśanas, the great sage Sanatkumāra and other great sages, Aṅgiras and other celestial sages, Viśvāvasu the Gandharva as well as Nārada and Parvata.[2] Many groups of Apsaras came there. The pure, auspicious and pleasant breeze blew wafting different kinds of fragrance. The trees of the forest were laden with flowers of all seasons. The Vidyādharas, Sādhyas, Siddhas and ascetics worshipped and served the great lord, the lord of Paśus. Similarly, there were other living beings

1. *Vaiśravaṇa*—Kubera, son of Viśravas.
2. *Nārada and Parvata*—Two sages expert in music who lived for a long time as inseparable friends.

that had assumed different forms. There were extremely terrible Rākṣasas, and Piśācas of great strength who were very bold, who assumed many forms and who held different sorts of weapons and means of striking. The followers of the lord comparable to the fire-god also stood there. Nandīśvara, permitted by the lord was also there holding a blazing trident brightly illuminated by its own radiance. Gaṅgā, excellent of all rivers and the source of all sacred waters attended upon him in her embodied form. Thus the great lord stayed there worshipped by the celestial sages and the highly blessed Devas.

18-27. After the lapse of some time the Patriarch Dakṣa resolved to perform sacrifice in the manner laid down and mentioned before. Led by Indra, Devas came from their heavenly abodes to his sacrifice at Gaṅgādvāra[1]. Noble-souled Devas who had fiery lustre came there on shining aerial cars. The Gaṅgādvāra was thronged by Gandharvas and Apsaras. It abounded in trees and creepers. Dakṣa the most excellent among the virtuous ones was surrounded by groups of sages.

The residents of the Earth, firmament and heavenly world joined their palms in reverence and stood near him. The Ādityas, Vasus, Rudras, Sādhyas, Maruts and Viṣṇu came there to partake of their shares in the sacrifice. The excellent Devas, Ājyapas, Somapas, Aśvins, Maruts and different groups of Devas came there. These and other congregations of living beings, the four species of living organisms such as the ovoviviparous, viviparous, the sweat-born ones and the shorting ones (plants) came there. Devas had been invited along with their womenfolk and the sages. Seated in the aerial chariots (or lofty chambers) they shone like blazing fires.

On seeing the raised platform devoid of Rudra, Dadhīci, the great sage, spoke to the sages :—

"O sages, Śaṅkara the leader of all, is not seen in this great sacrifice; the sacrifice does not shine without him.

28. By worshipping those who should not be worshipped and by not worshipping those who are worthy of being worshipped a man undoubtedly incurs great sin.

1. *Gaṅgādvāra*—A locality into the Indo-Gangetic plane where the river Gaṅgā falls from the Himālayas. This place is known as Haridvāra.

Brahmā said :

29-33. After saying this, the brahminical sage said to Dakṣa again.

Dadhīcī said :

Why do you not worship the lord of Paśus ?

Dakṣa said :

I have many Rudras of my own; they have matted hairs and they are armed with tridents. They are eleven in number and they stay in eleven abodes. We do not recognize any other Maheśvara beside them.

Dadhīci said :

This is the warning I shall give you all. My lord has not been invited. Just as I am sure that I do not see a deity above Śaṅkara so also I am sure that this elaborate sacrifice of Dakṣa will not attain completion.

Dakṣa said :

This entire offering has been sanctified by the due chanting of Mantras. It is dedicated to the lord of sacrifice. O brahmins, by means of gold vessels I offer this to the unparalleled god Viṣṇu as his share in the sacrifice and not to Śaṅkara.

O Dadhīca, this is duly offered as the permanent share to Viṣṇu, the lord of the universe. I give this share in the sacrifice to that excellent deity and not to Śaṅkara.

Brahmā said :

34. Knowing that Devas were going somewhere, the chaste daughter of the king of mountains spoke these words to lord Śiva her husband.

Umā said :

35. O lord who know all facts, where do these Devas with lord Indra at their head go ? Tell me truthfully. I entertain great doubts on that count.

Maheśvara said :

36. The highly blessed, the most excellent patriarch Dakṣa is performing a horse-sacrifice. Those heaven-dwellers are going there.

The goddess said :

37. O blessed one, why don't you go to this sacrifice ? By what ban is your departure prevented ?

Maheśvara said :

38. O highly blessed lady, all this has been manipulated by Devas alone. No share is allotted to me in any sacrifice.

39. O fair-complexioned lady, following the path of previous precedent in the allotment of shares Devas do not offer me the rightful share in the sacrifice.

Umā said :

40-42. O lord, among Devas, you are superior in power and good qualities. You are invincible and unthwartable by virtue of splendour, fame and glory. O highly blessed one, on account of this ban in respect to the share (in sacrifice) I am extremely distressed. I tremble excessively. What sort of charitable gift, holy observance or penance shall I perform, whereby my husband, the infinite lord shall now obtain a substantial or an appropriate share ?

43-45. As she spoke the delighted lord thought that his wife was most agitated. He said :— "O gentle lady of slender belly and limbs you do not know me fully. Do you speak these words in propriety ? O lady of large eyes, I know and all good people know through meditation. Due to your anger all Devas, the three worlds, have been destroyed. They highly praise me as the lord of sacrifices; they sing the Rathantara hymn for my sake; they worship me by means of sacrifices. The priests who perform sacrifices allot share unto me.

The goddess said :

46. O lord, even a vulgar person behaves like a lofty-minded person in the assembly of people. Particularly in front of ladies he praises himself and arrogates.

The lord said :

47. O goddess of Devas, I do not praise myself as you seem to think. O beautiful fair-complexioned lady, I shall create a being and assert my right to this share.

Brahmā said :

48. After saying this to Umā his wife, whom he loved more than his vital breath, the lord created a goblin from his mouth. It arose from the fire of his fury.

49. The lord said thus to him :—"Go and destroy the sacrifice of Dakṣa. With my permission, immediately destroy that holy rite of Dakṣa."

50. That goblin knew that Dakṣa was the cause of Mother's indignation. Hence, he destroyed the sacrifice of Dakṣa playfully. This he did by the order of Rudra to assume the form of a lion.

51. The extremely terrible Bhadrakālī[1] the great goddess was created from that indignation. As a witness to the actions of her lord she accompanied him.

52. In fact, the goblin was the lord himself, who assumed the form of the fury of the lord and took up his abode in the cremation ground, the resting place of ghosts. He is known as Vīrabhadra.[2] Eventually he wiped off indignation and sorrow of his consort Umā.

53. From the pores of his bodily hairs he himself created some leading Gaṇas, the terrible followers who had virility and exploit akin to that of Rudra himself.

---

1. *Bhadrakālī*— form of Pārvatī. Lord Śiva, on hearing about the self-immolation in fire of his wife Satī, at the famous sacrifice conducted by Dakṣa, rushed in all anger to the spot and beat the earth with his matted hair, and there ensued two forces called Vīrabhadra and Bhadrakālī. This Bhadrakālī was really Satī in another form.

2. *Vīrabhadra*—There are two different opinions in the Purāṇas regarding the origin of Vīrabhadra. According to the Purāṇas his birth was due to the anger of Śiva. When Śiva knew that his wife Pārvatī jumped into the fire and died at the sacrifice of Dakṣa, he struck his matted hair on the ground and from that, Vīrabhadra and Bhadrakālī came into being. But according to *Mbh.* (Śānti Parva, Ch. 284) Vīrabhadra was born from the mouth of Śiva to destroy the sacrifice of Dakṣa. From each of the hairpores of Vīrabhadra a fearful monster was born, all of whom formed a group of ghosts called Gaṇas.

54. These followers of Rudra, who had the valour of Rudra himself, jumped out of his pores in hundreds and thousands.

55. O brahmins, the tumultuous sound produced by those Gaṇas of Rudra was extremely sonorous and appeared to fill the entire firmament.

56. The heaven-dwellers were frightened by that loud tumult. The mountains crumbled down and the earth quaked.

57. Gusts of wind blew ruthlessly. The abode of ocean became stirred up and excited. Fires did not blaze nor did the sun shine.

58. Neither did glimmer the planets nor the stars nor the constellations. Neither sages nor Devas nor Dānavas had any lustre in their faces.

59. When darkness enveloped everything thus, those seated in the aerial chariots were burned up. Terrible stormy gusts of wind blew ruthlessly with the stinking odour of rotting ordure.

60. Some of the goblins shouted and cried aloud; others crashed and thrashed. With the velocity of the wind and the mind they ran helter-skelter in hurry.

61. The ritual vessels were broken to pieces and reduced to powder. The sacrificial chambers crumbling down appeared like the stars fallen from the sky.

62-65. Various sorts of foodstuffs and beverages were swallowed and lapped by the goblins. Hugh mountains like masses of divine cooked rice, beverages and foodstuffs, rivers of milk, marshy sloughs of ghee and milk pudding, divine honey and watery whey and gruel, sand-like candies and sugar, rivers with floating cooked rice of all the six tastes, channels of liquid treacle and molasses pleasing to the mind, high and low heaps of meat, footstuffs of different sorts—nay all those exquisitely prepared lambatives and edibles, juices and squashes were gorged up by those enormous beings with their mouths of diverse kinds. Those beings issuing from the anger of Rudra, and comparable to fire of Death destroyed some and scattered others.

66. Those gigantic beings towering high like mountains agitated and terrified everyone everywhere. Those beings of various forms hurled the celestial damsels playfully.

67-68. Such were the Gaṇas. Accompanied by them, the valorous Vīrabhadra, impelled by the fury of Rudra, quickly burned that sacrifice well-guarded by all Devas. He burned it up in the presence of Bhadrakālī. The others produced loud crying sounds that frightened all living beings.

69. Cutting the head of sacrifice they yelled terrifically. Then Dakṣa the patriarch and Indra and other Devas joined their palms in reverence and said :—"May this be known who are you, please ?"

Vīrabhadra said :

70-73. O leading Devas, I am neither a Deva nor a Daitya. I have not come here to eat or to enjoy. I have not come here to see anything nor am I impelled by curiosity.

O excellent Devas, I have come here for destroying the sacrifice of Dakṣa. I am wellknown as Vīrabhadra. I have come out of the fury of Rudra.

(This lady) shall be known as Bhadrakālī who has emerged from the fury and indignation of the Mother. She is sent by the lord of Devas and so has come to the venue of sacrifice.

O leading king, seek refuge in the consort of Umā, the lord of Devas. Better to face the fury of the lord than to court the challenge of his attendants.

Brahmā said :

74-81. Then the planted sacrificial posts were pulled up and cost off here and there. The vultures, greedy of flesh were swooping down or flying about. The gusts of wind generated by their fluttering wings shook down everything. Hundreds of vixen howled. The sacrifice of the arrogant Dakṣa was harassed by the Gaṇas. Thus harassed the sacrifice assumed the form of a deer and jumped high into the sky.

Observing the sacrifice slipping away in that form, lord (Vīrabhadra) seized his bow and arrow and went after it. Due to the wrath of that Gaṇa of unmeasured splendour a terrible drop of sweat flowed from his forehead. The moment the drop of sweat fell on the ground, a huge fire appeared, that was comparable to the blazing fire of death. Then, O excellent brahmins, there appeared a man-like being. He was very short in stature. His eyes were red; his beard and moustache were green. He was terrific. His hair stood up on his head. His limbs were profusely covered with hair. His ears were red. He was awful and black in colour. He wore a red cloth. That Puruṣa of great prowess burned down the sacrifice like a fire that burns down a heap of straw.

82-89. The frightened Devas fled in all directions. As he moved about with long studies the Earth consisting of seven continents shook all round. When that great Being began to function like this, striking terror into the world of Devas I worshipped the great lord and said to him— "O lord, Devas will offer share unto you too. O lord of Devas; let this be withdrawn. All these Devas and thousands of sages know no peace, O great lord on account of your anger, O leading Deva conversant with virtue, the Being who was born of your sweat will be known as Jvara (Fever). He will move about in the world. O lord, the whole of this earth would not bear his vigour if he stayed as one single Being. May he be diffused in manifold forms." When the lord was requested thus by me and when the share too was allotted, the Pinākabearing lord of Devas said to me— "So be it." The Pināka-bearing lord himself derived great pleasure.

90-92. Dakṣa sought refuge in lord Śiva. He restrained the Prāṇa and Apāna winds in the cavity of the eye with great effort.

The lord, the conqueror of enemies opened his eyes fully and looked all around. He then smiled and spoke soft words— "Tell me what shall I do for you ?" When the great story was narrated to Devas accompanied by Pitṛs, Dakṣa the Prajāpati joined his palms in reverence and spoke to the lord. He was afraid, suspicious and even terrified. His face and eyes were covered with tears.

Dakṣa said :

93-97. O lord, if you are pleased, if I am your favourite, if I am to be blessed, if boon is to be granted to me (I shall request for this). Some of the food has been eaten. Some beverage is drunk. Some are simply bitten, some destroyed, some are ground into powder. This is the state regarding the requisites of sacrifice. These were acquired by me during the course of long time with great strain. O great lord, let this not go in vain in regard to me, due to your favour.

Brahmā said :

The lord Śiva who removed the eyes of Bhaga said—So be it.

The Patriarch Dakṣa bowed to the three-eyed lord Śiva the presiding deity of virtue. After securing the boon from lord Śiva, Dakṣa knelt on the ground and eulogised the bull-bannered lord by his thousand and eight names.

CHAPTER THIRTYEIGHT

The Prayer by Dakṣa

1. O excellent brahmins, on seeing the virility of Śiva thus, Dakṣa joined his palms in reverence and bowed down. Then he began to eulogise.

2. Obeisance to you, O lord of the chiefs of Devas, Obeisance to you, O slayer of Bala, O lord of Devas, you are the most excellent one in strength, you are worshipped by Devas and Dānavas.

3-63. O thousand-eyed one, O one of deformed eyes, O three-eyed one, one fond of the overlord of Akṣas, you have hands and feet all round; you have eyes, heads and mouth all round; you have ears all round; you stand enveloping everything in the world, Śaṅkukarṇa (Pike-eared), Mahākarṇa (Long-eared), Kumbhakarṇa (Pot-eared), Arṇavālaya (ocean-dweller), Gajendrakarṇa) (elephant-eared), Gokarṇa (cow-eared), Śatakarṇa (hundred-eared). Obeisance to you Śatodara (hundred-bellied), Śatāvarta (having hundred curly locks of hairs), Śatajihva (having hundred tongues), Sanātana (Eternal), One who is worshipped by the Gāyatrins, singing songs of praise, one who is worshipped by those who have stopped performing activities. Devadānavagoptā (Protector of Devas and Dānavas), Brahmā and Śatakratu (Indra). You are Mūrtimān, (Embodied),

Mahāmūrti (having physical form), Samudra (Ocean), Sarasāṁ Nidhi (storehouse of lakes), in whom Devas abide as cows in the cowpen. I see in your body the moon, fire, lord of waters, sun, Viṣṇu, Brahmā and Bṛhaspati (Jupiter). You are the action, cause and effect, the maker and the instrument. You are Asat and Sadasat (existent as well as non existent). You are the source of origin and seat of Dissolution (Prabhava and Appaya). Obeisance to Bhava, Obeisance to Śarva. Obeisance to Rudra. Obeisance to the bestower of boons (Varada). Obeisance to Paśupati (Lord of Paśus) Obeisance to Andhakaghātin (one who hit Andhaka). Obeisance to Trijaṭa (having three locks of matted hair). Obeisance to Triśīrṣa (having three heads). Obeisance to Triśūlavaradhārin (one who holds excellent trident). Obeisance to Tryambaka (three-eyed). Obeisance to Trinetra (three-eyed). Obeisance to Tripuraghna (one who destroyed the three cities). Obeisance to Caṇḍa (the fierce). Obeisance to Muṇḍa (one with shaven head). Obeisance to Viśvacaṇḍadhara (One who holds the universe fiercely). Obeisance to Daṇḍin (One who holds a staff). Obeisance to Śaṅkukarṇa (One having pike-ears). Obeisance to Caṇḍīcaṇḍa (fierce lord of the fierce goddess). Obeisance to Ūrdhva Daṇḍikeśa (One who holds the staff pointed upwards and one who has hairs growing up). Obeisance to Śuṣka (Dry). Obeisance to Vikṛta (the deformed). Obeisance to Vilohita (one who is particularly red. Obeisance to Dhūmra (smoke-coloured). Obeisance to Nīlagrīva (the bluenecked). Obeisance to Apratirūpa (one who has no replica). Obeisance to Virūpa (the deformed). Obeisance to Śiva. Obeisance to Sūrya (identical with the sun). Obeisance to Sūryapati (the lord of the sun). Obeisance to Sūryadhvajapatākin (one having the sun as flagstaff and emblem). Obeisance to the lord of Pramathas. Obeisance to Vṛṣaskandha (bull-shouldered). Obeisance to Hiraṇyavarṇa (golden coloured). Obeisance to Hiraṇyavarcas (golden coat mail). Obeisance to Hiraṇyakṛtacūḍa (Obeisance to one with golden tufts). Obeisance to Hiraṇyapati (Lord of gold). Obeisance to Śatrughāta (One who kills enemies). Obeisance to Caṇḍa (the fierce one) Obeisance to Parṇasaṅghaśaya (one who lies amidst clusters of leaves). Obeisance to Stuta (the eulogised one). Obeisance to Stuti (the eulogy). Obeisance to

Stūyamāna (one who is being eulogised). Obeisance to Sarva (identical with all). Obeisance to Sarvabhakṣa (one who eats every thing). Obeisance to Sarvabhūtāntarātman (the immanent soul in all living beings). Obeisance to Homa.) Obeisance to Mantra). Obeisance to Śukladhvajapatākin (One whose flag-staff and banner are white). Obeisance to Anāmya (one who cannot be bent). Obeisance to Nāmya (one who should be bowed to). Obeisance to Kilakila (tumultuous noise). Obeisance to Śayamāna (lying down) Obeisance to Śāyita (one who has already lain down). Obeisance to Utthita (one who has got up). Obeisance to Sthita (one who stands). Obeisance to Dhavamāna (one who runs). Obeisance to Bhūta (one who has become). Obeisance to Kuṭila (the crooked). Obeisance to Nartanaśīla (one habituated to dance). Obeisance to Mukha-vāditrakārin (one who plays with his mouth as with a musical instrument). Obeisance to Bādhāpaha (one who dispels obstacles). Obeisance to Lubdha (one who is greedy). Obeisance to Gītavāditrakārin (one who sings and plays on musical instruments). Obeisance to Jyeṣṭha (the eldest). Obeisance to Śreṣṭha (the most excellent). Obeisance to Balapramathana (one who suppresses Bala). Obeisance to Kalpana (conception). Obeisance to Kalpya (one who is to be conceived). Obeisance to Kṣama (the competent). Obeisance to Upakṣama (very nearly efficient). Obeisance to Ugra (the fierce one). Obeisance to Daśa-bāhu (ten-armed). Obeisance to Kapālahasta (having the skull in hand). Obeisance to Sitabhasmapriya (one fond of white ashes). Obeisance to Vibhīṣaṇa (the terrifying one). Obeisance to Bhīma (the terrible). Obeisance to Bhīmavratadhara (one who observes terrible holy rites). Obeisance to Nānāvikṛtava-ktra (one who has many deformed faces). Obeisance to Khaḍ-gajihvogradaṁṣṭrin (one with sword-like tongue and fierce curved fangs). Obeisance to Pakṣamāṁsalavādya (one who has huge musical instruments at his sides). Obeisance to Tumbivīṇāpriya (one fond of Tumbivīṇā, a kind of lute).

Obeisance to Aghoraghorarūpa (one who has the form of Aghora, a terrible form). Obeisance to Ghoraghoratara (one who is more terrible than the most terrible). Obeisance to Śiva. Obeisance to Śānta (calm). Obeisance to Śāntatara (calmer). Obeisance to Buddha (enlightened). Obeisance to

Śuddha (pure one). Obeisance to Saṁvibhāgapriya (one fond of classification). Obeisance to Prapañca (extensive universe). Obeisance to Ugra (fierce). Obeisance to Sāṁkhyapara (one devoted to Sāṁkhya philosophy). Obeisance to Caṇḍaika-ghaṇṭa (one having a fierce bell). Obeisance to Ghaṇṭānāda (sound of the bell). Obeisance to Ghaṇṭin (one with a bell). Obeisance to Sahasraśataghaṇṭa (one who has thousands and thousands of bells). Obeisance to Ghaṇṭāmālāpriya (one fond of a garland of bells). Obeisance to Prāṇadaṇḍa (one awarding life sentence). Obeisance to Nitya (the permanent). Obeisance to you Lohita (Red in colour). Obeisance to Huṁhuṁkāra (one shouting Huṁhum). Obeisance to Rudra. Obeisance to Huṁhumkārapriya (one fond of the sound (Huṁhum) Obeisance to Apāravān (Endless, limitless). Obeisance to Nityaṁ-girivṛkṣapriya (one who is always fond of tree on the mountain). Obeisance to Mārga-Māṁsaśṛgāla (the jackal at the way-side with a price of meat). Obeisance to Tāraka (one who redeems). Obeisance to Tāra (one who crosses). Obeisance to Yajñādhipati (the over-lord). Obeisance to Kṛta (what is done). Obeisance to Prakṛta (what is perfectly done). Obeisance to Yajñavāha (one whose vehicle is Yajña). Obeisance to Dānta (one who has controlled sense-organs) Obeisance to Tathya (truth). Obeisance to Vitatha (untrue). Obeisance to Taṭa (shore); Obeisance to Taṭya (one favourable to the shore). Obeisance to Taṭinīpati (lord of rivers). Obeisance to Annada (bestower of cooked rice). Obeisance to Annapati (Lord of cooked rice). Obeisance to Annabhuja (one who eats cooked rice). Obeisance to Sanasraśīrṣa (the thousand-headed). Obeisance to Sahasrācaraṇa (having thousand feet) Obeisance to Sahasrodyataśūla (one who has lifted up a thousand tridents).Obeisance to Sahasranayana (thousand-eyed) Obeisance to Bālārkavarṇa (one having the colour of rising sun). Obeisance to Bālarūpadhara (one having the form of a boy. Obeisance to Bālārkarūpa (one having the form of the rising sun). Obeisance to Bālakrīḍanaka (one who plays like boys). Obeisance to Śuddha (the pure one). Obeisance to Buddha (enlightened). Obeisance to Kṣobhaṇa (one who causes agitation). Obeisance to Kṣaya (one who causes decline). Obeisance to Taraṅgāṅkitakeśa (one whose hair is marked with waves). Obeisance to Muktakeśa (one whose tresses are released). Obeisance to Ṣaṭkarmatuṣṭa (one who is pleased with six types of holy rites). Obeisance to Trikarmanirata (one is engaged in the three holy rites). Obeisance to Varṇāśrama-dharma-pravartaka (one who makes castes and stages of life function duly and severally). Obeisance to Śreṣṭha (the most excellent). Obeisance to Jyeṣṭha (the eldest). Obeisance to Kalakala (indistinct but sweet sound). Obeisance to Śvetapiṅgalanetra (one who has white and tawny coloured eyes). Obeisance to Kṛṣṇarakteksaṇa (one who has black and red eyes). Obeisance to Dharmakāmārthamokṣa (virtue, love, wealth and salvation). Obeisance to Kratha (one who injures). Obeisance to Krathana (one who slaughters). Obeisance to Sāṁkhya. Obeisance to Sāṁkhyamukhya (Chief of the Sāmkhya). Obeisance to Yogādhipati (overlord of Yogas). Obeisance to Rathyādhirathya (Charioteer on the street). Obeisance to Catuṣpathapatha (having the pathway in the fourcross roads). Obeisance to Kṛṣṇājinottarīya (one having the hide of a black deer as the upper garment).

O Īśāna Rudrasaṅghāta (group of Rudras), Harikeśa (one having green hair). Obeisance to you. Obeisance to Tryambaka (three-eyed). O Ambikānātha (lord of Ambikā), O manifest and unmanifest. Obeisance to you O Kāla, O Kāmada (bestower of desires), O Kāmaghna (destroyer of desires), Duṣṭa-duritanivāraṇa (destroyer of the wicked and the violators of good conduct), O Sarvagarhita (despised by everyone). O Sarvaghna (destroyer of everyone). O Sadyojāta, Obeisance to you. Unmādana (one who causes madness. Śatāvartagaṅgā-toyārdramūrdhaja (one whose hair on the head is wet due to the waters of Gaṅgā that has hundreds of whirlpools). O Candrārdhasaṁyugāvarta (one who has war-like eddies by means of crescent moon?). O Meghāvarta (having eddies with clouds) Obeisance to you. You alone are Nānārthadānakartā (the bestower of different sorts of riches) and Arthada (bestower of riches), Annasraṣṭā (creator of cooked rice), Bhoktā (eater of cooked rice), Yajñabhuk (partaker of sacrifice), Anala (fire), the four types of creatures Jarāyuja etc. You alone, O lord of the chief of Devas, are the four types of creatures. You are the creator of the mobile and immobile beings. You are Pratikartā (one who withdraws i.e. annihilates). O lord of the universe, you alone are the Brahman. They speak of Brahman in the waters, you are the great womb of everything. You are Svadhā. You are the storehouse of luminaries. Expounders of Brahman call you *Rk*, *Sāman* and Oṁkāra. The excellent Devas and the expounders of Brahman who sing Sāman say frequently—"Hari Hari etc." or "Hara Hara etc." You are full of *Yujur* Mantras, *RK* Mantras, *Sāman* and *Atharva* Mantras. You are served by those who know Brahman, and Kalpas and Upaniṣads. The Brahmins, Kṣatriyas, Vaiśyas, Śūdras and other castes and stages of life are identical with you. You are Āśramas. You are Vidyut Stanitam (lightning and thunder). You are the year, seasons, month, fortnight, and Kalā, Kāṣṭhā, Nimeṣas, stars and Yugas. You are Vṛṣaṇam Kakudam (the chief of bulls). You are the peak of mountains. You are the lion, the chief among animals. You are Takṣaka among Nāgas, You are milk ocean among seas. You are Yajus among Mantras. You are thunderbolt among weapons. You are truth among holy rites. You are the following attributes viz. wish, hatred, lust delusion, calmness, forbearance, industry, courage, greed, love, anger, victory and defeat. You are the wielder of arrow, bow, iron club (Khaṭvāṅga), banner and chariot. You cut, pierce, strike and lead. You are considered a thinker by us. You are the Dharma with its ten characteristics; you are Artha (Wealth) and Kāma (love). You are Indra, Samudra (ocean) Sarits (rivers) Palvalas (Puddles) Sarasi (lakes) Latāvallis (creepers and winding plants) Tṛṇauṣadhayaḥ (grasses and medicinal herbs), Puśus, (animal) and birds. You are the origin of Dravyas (objects), Karmans (actions) and Guṇas (attributes). You are Kālapuṣpaphalaprada (bestower of fruits into the flower of time). You are Ādi (origin) Anta (end) Madhya (middle). You are Gāyatrī and Oṁkāra. You are Harita (green) Lohita (red) Kṛṣṇa (black) Nīla (blue) Pīta (yellow) Aruṇa (pink) Kadrū (tawny) Kapila (palebrown) Babhrū (deep-brown), Kapota (dove-coloured), Mecaka (dark-coloured). You are well known as Suvarṇaretas (one having golden semen). You are considered Suvarṇa (gold in colour), Suvarṇanāman (golden named) Suvarṇapriya (fond of gold). You are Indu (moon), Yama, Varuṇa, Dhanada (bestower of wealth i.e. Kubera), Anala (fire), Utphulla-Citrabhānu (full-fledged sun), Svarbhānu(Rāhu), Bhānu(sun), Hotra(sacrifice), Hotā (sacrificer), Homya (paraphernalia of oblation), Hutam (oblation). O lord, you are the Trisauparṇa mantra and the Śatarudrīya Mantra of Yajurveda. You are the most sacred of all sacred things. You are the most auspicious of all auspicious things. You are the mountain that destroys sins. You are Vṛkṣa (a tree), Jīva (individual soul), Pralaya (Dissolution). You are Prāṇa (vital airs) and Rajoguṇa, Tamoguṇa, and Sattva. You are Prāṇa, Apāna, Samāna, Udāna and Vyāna. You are Unmeṣa (Opening of the eye), Nimeṣa (closing of the eye), Kāla (time), Kalpa, Lohitāṅga (Red-limbed), Daṁṣṭrin (having curved fangs), Mahāvaktra (having huge mouth), Mahodara (having large belly), Śuciroman (having pure hair), Haricchmaśru (having green moustache and beard), Ūrddhva-keśa (having hair standing up), Calācala (moving and unmoving), Gītavāditranṛtyaga (Interested in singing, playing on instruments and dancing), Gītavādanakapriya (Fond of singing and playing on instruments). You are Matsya (fish) Jāla (net) Jala (water), Ajayya (Unconquerable), Jalavyāla (water-python) Kuṭicarya (Porpoise), Vikala (having adverse time), Sukala (having good time), Duṣkala (having bad time) Kālanāśana (Destroyer of Kāla Time or god of Death). Mṛtyu (Death), Akṣaya (Everlasting), Anta (end), Kṣamāmāyākarot-kara (? One who offers and carries out forbearance and deception).

64-73. Saṁvarta (Dissolution), Vartaka (one who causes whirling), Saṁvartaka and Balāhaka (the clouds at the time of dissolution), Ghaṇṭākin and Ghaṇṭakin and ghaṇṭin (having bells of different types), Cuḍāla (having tufts), Lavaṇodadhi (the briny sea), Brahmā, Kālāgnivaktra (having black fire in the mouth), Daṇḍin(having staff), Muṇḍa (having shaven head, Tridaṇḍadhṛk (one holding three staffs), Cāturyuga (of four Yugas), Caturveda of four Vedas), Caturhotra (set of four sacrifices), Catuṣpatha (set of four paths), Caturāśramyanetā (leader of the people of four stages of life) Cāturvarṇyakara (cause of division of four castes) Kṣarākṣara (perishable and imperishable) Priya (Beloved), Dhūrta (wicked) Gaṇaikagaṇya (worthy of being considered by the Gaṇas), Gaṇādhipa (the overlord of

Gaṇas) Raktamālyāmbaradhara (one who wears red garments and garlands), Giriśa (Lord of the mountain) Girijāpriya (Fond of the daughter of the mountain lord), Śilpīśa (chief of Artisans) Śilpiśreṣṭha (the most excellent among artisans) Sarvaśilpapravartaka (He who makes arts and crafts function), Bhaganetrāntaka (the destroyer of the eyes of Bhaga), Caṇḍa (fierce), Pūṣṇaḥ Dantavināśanaḥ (he who destroys the teeth of Pūṣan), Svāhā Svadhā Vaṣaṭkāra Namaskāra (Obeisance). Obeisance be to you) Gūḍhavrata (one who performs holy rites in isolation), Gūḍha (well-hidden), Gūḍhavrataniṣevitā (one resorted to by those who perform holy rites in secret), Tīrṇṇa (One who crosses), Taraṇa (one who redeems), Sarvānusyūtacāraṇa (one who has his cāraṇas (spies) spread in every place), Dhātā (creator), Vidhātā (dispenser of destiny) Sandhātā (one who joins together), Nidhātā (one who deposits), Dharaṇidhara (sustainer of the earth), Tapas (penance), Brahman (the supreme Being), Satyam (truth), Brahmacaryam (the soul of living beings), Bhūtakṛt (the creator of living beings), Bhūta (one who has become Bhūta), Bhavya Bhavodbhava (the source of origin of every thing past, present and future), Bhūrbhuvaḥ svar (one who has gone to the worlds Bhuḥ, Bhuvaḥ and Svaḥ, Vṛta (Surrounded), Agni (fire), Maheśvara (great lord), Rekṣaṇa (having fiery vision) Dvīkṣaṇakānta (lover of one with two eyes), Dānta (one who has self control) Adāntavināśana (Destroyer of those who have not conquered their sense organs) Brahmāvarta (one who has turned out from Brahma?) Surāvarta (one who makes Devas revolve), Kāmāvarta (one who makes Kāma revolve), obeisance to you. Kāmabimbavinirhantā (one who destroys the idol of Kāma) Karṇikārasrajapriya (one fond of the garland of Karṇikāra flowers) Gonetā (leader of cow), Gopracara (one who makes rays spread, or one who makes cows graze), Govṛṣeśvaravāhana (one who has, as vehicle, a cow and a leading bull), Trailokyagoptā (the protector of three worlds), Govinda, Goptā (Protector), Gogarga.

74-80. Akhaṇḍacandrābhimukha (one who is face to face with the full moon), Sumukha (having good face) Durmukha (having bad face) Amukha (having no face) Caturmukha (four-faced) Bahumukha (many-faced) Raṇeṣvabhimukhaḥ sadā (Always face to face in battles), Hiraṇyagarbha, Śakuni, Dhanada (bestower of wealth), Annapati (Lord of cooked rice), Virāṭ (Immense being), Adharmahā (Destroyer of evil), Mahādakṣa (very efficient), Daṇḍadhārī (Holder of staff) Raṇapriya (fond of war), Tiṣṭhan (standing), Sthira (Steady), Sthāṇu (Stump), Niskampa (unmoving), Suniścala (very still), Durvāraṇa (one who cannot be checked) Durviṣaha (who cannot be borne), Durdarpa (having wisked arrogance), Duratikrama(one who cannot be made submissive), Nitya (Permanent), Durdama (one who cannot be suppressed), Vijaya (Victory), Jaya (conquerer) Śaśa (hare), Śaśāṅkanayana (having the moon as an eye), Śītoṣṇa (Bearing heat and chillness), Kṣut (Hunger), Tṛṣā (thirst) Jarā (Old age), Ādhis (agonies), Vyādhis (ailments), Vyādhihā (destroyer of ailments) Vyādhipa (the lord of sickness) Sahya (Bearable) Yajña-mṛgavyādha, (Hunter of Yajña in the form of a deer), Vyādhīnām Ākara (mine of ailments), Akara (handless) Śikhaṇḍī (tufted), Puṇḍarīka (lotus), Puṇḍarīkāvalokana (one who looks at lotuses), Daṇḍadhṛk (holding staff), Cakradaṇḍa (holding wheel and staff), Raudrabhāgavināśana (Destroyer of terrible share), Viṣapā (one who drinks poison), Amṛtapā (drinker of nectar), Surāpā (drinker of wine), Kṣīrasomapā (drinker of milk and some juice), Madhupā (drinker of honey) Apapā (drinker of water, Sarvapā (drinker of everything), Balābala (strong and weak).

81-90. Vṛṣāṅgavāhya (one who is to be carried over the body of the bull), Vṛṣabha(Bull-leading deity), Vṛṣabhalocana (bull-eyed). You are well known as the leader of all worlds, Lokasaṁskṛta (consecrated in the world). The moon and the sun constitute your eyes, Brahmā is your heart, Agniṣṭoma sacrifice is your body and it is embellished by virtuous holy rite.

O Śiva, neither Brahmā nor Viṣṇu nor the ancient sages are competent to know your greatness precisely like a father protecting his son.

O Śiva, always protect one with the help of your physical subtle forms. Let them come into my vow.

O sinless one, protect me. I am worthy of being protected by you. Obeisance be to you. You are sympathetic to the devotees and I am always your devotee.

May he be my continuous protector, he who stands alone on the shore of the sea after encompassing the miserable state of many thousands of men.

Those who have conquered sleep, those who have mastered their breath, those who abide by the Sattva Guṇa, and those who have similarity of vision and those who perform Yoga, see that brilliance. Obeisance to that Yogic Ātman.

When the close of Yugas is imminent he devours all living beings and he lies down in the middle of waters. I resort to him who lies down in the waters.

It is the fire of the Soma juice that enters the mouth of Rāhu and drinks the nectar of the moon at night. As Rāhu, it devours the sun.

Puruṣas (souls of individuals) of the size of thumbs are stationed in the bodies of embodied persons. Let them protect me always. Let them always nourish me.

91. Devas are procreated by Svāhās and Svadhās. To those who attain death Svāhās and Svadhās are offered. Svāhā, Svadhā and Ahar eulogise you.

92-96. Where the embodied persons ascend to and where the living beings descend from, those who delight but do not drag one—obeisance be to them, obeisance to them. Obeisance to those who are in the ocean, to those who are on mountains, to those who are in the impassable rivers, to those who are in caves, at the roots of trees, in cowpens, in dense forests, in the four cross-roads, in streets, in jungles, in assemblies, in chambers of elephants, horses and chariots, in old and dilapidated parks and temples. Obeisance to those who are in five elements, in quarters and intermediary junctions, to those who are in between Indra and the sun, to those who are in the rays of the moon and the Sun, to those who are present in the nether worlds and who have gone beyond that (I make obeisance always).

97. You are identical with all. You are the omnipresent lord, the lord of all living beings, and the immanent soul in all living beings. Hence you have not been invited.

98. O lord, you alone are worshipped in sacrifices with various sorts of gifts. You alone are the doer of everything. Hence you have not been invited.

99. Or O lord, I have been deluded by your subtle Māyā. For that reason too, you have not been invited by me.

100. O lord of Devas, be pleased with me. You alone are my refuge. You are the goal and the foundation. It is my opinion that no one else is so.

Brahmā said :

101. After eulogising the great lord thus the highly intelligent Dakṣa stopped. The delighted lord spoke to Dakṣa once again.

The lord said :

102. O Dakṣa of good holy rites, I am delighted with this hymn of yours. Of what avail is much talk ? You will come to my presence.

103. After uttering the words of consolation the omniscient lord of the three worlds spoke the following words succinctly put in good sentences.

Lord Śiva said :

104. O Dakṣa, you should not feel sad by this destruction of sacrifice. O sinless one, I am the destroyer of sacrifice and this has been seen by you formerly.

105. O one of Good holy rites, accept this boon from me. Wear a happy and pleasant face and listen to me attentively.

106. O Patriarch, by virtue of my favour, you will derive the fruit of a thousand horse and a hundred Vājapeya sacrifices.

107-110. The holy rite of Pāśupata has been prescribed by me. The Vedas and their six ancillaries are to be understood along with the schools of philosophy—Sāṁkhya, Yoga etc. A penance too difficult to be performed even by Devas and Dānavas should also be undertaken. Thus during the course of twelve years this holy rite has been prepared. It is subtle and no intelligent man shall censure it. In some respects it may conform to the disciplined life of four castes and four stages; in some respects it may not. But its aim is the liberation of individual soul from bondage. This holy rite of Pāśupata has been prescribed by me, O Dakṣa, for people of all stages of life. It releases one from all sins. If this holy rite is performed well, the benefit is splendid. O highly blessed one. may it befall you. May this mental ailment be eschewed.

Brahmā said :

111. After saying this to Dakṣa of unmeasured splendour the lord of Devas vanished along with his wife and attendants.

112. O sages who are conversant with holy rites, after acquiring his share as mentioned before, the lord classified (ailments, fever etc.) into various divisions, in the company of Umā.

113. It is for peace among all living beings that he classified thus. O brahmins, listen. For Nāgas (elephants) it is the scorching of the tuft; for the mountains it is bitumen.

114. It is Nīlikā (for water). For the serpents it is slough (limping). For the cow it is Khoraka (limping), For Earth it is the barren soil.

115. O sages conversant with virtue ! for dogs it is the obstruction of the vision; for horses it is the entanglement with the cavity. For peacocks it is the splitting of their tuft-like flower on the head.

116. Redness in the eye is the fever of cuckoo. Split is the fever among noble persons.

117. Hikkikā (coughing) is the fever of parrots. O brahmins, among lions fatigue is the fever.

118. O sages conversant with virtue, such are the fevers among living beings. It occurs at the time of birth, death and in the intervening period.

119. What is called fever is the refulgence of the great lord. It is very terrible. The supreme lord should be bowed to and honoured by all living beings.

120. He who reads this narrative about the origin of fever with great attention without any wretchedness of mind shall be liberated from ailments. He will be gay and joyous. He will get the benefit of his wishes.

121. He who repeats the hymn of Dakṣa or he who listens to it will never have any thing inauspicious. He will obtain a long life.

122. Just as Lord Śiva is the most excellent among Devas so also this hymn of Dakṣa is the most excellent among all hymns.

123. With great devotion this hymn should be repeated

assiduously by those who seek fame, heavenly pleasures, divine riches, glory, victory, knowledge and other things of a similar nature.

124. He who is sick, he who is miserable, he who is in a wretched state, or employed in a dengerous task by the ruler—all these are liberated from danger and fear.

125. From the supreme lord he derives happiness and with this body itself he becomes the lord of Gaṇas.

126. In the house where the lord is eulogised, neither Yakṣas nor Piśācas nor Nāgas nor Vināyakas will create any obstacle.

127. A women who listens to this with devotion and is sanctified by the lord shall be honoured in her parental abode as well as in the abode of her husband.

128. The holy rites of that person who listens to this or narrates this frequently, shall fructify without any hindrance.

129. By repeating this hymn, whatever one desires mentally or utters orally shall be realized.

130-131. The devotee shall maintain holy observances with the complete control of his sense-organs. According to his capacity he shall offer oblations to the lord, to his consort Pārvatī and their son Kārttikeya and Nandīśvara. Thereafter, he shall repeat the manes in due order. The man will attain his desired objects. He shall enjoy his cherished pleasures.

132-137. After death he will go to heaven where he will be surrounded by thousands of beautiful women.

If a person is endowed with all desires or defiled by all sins, if he reads this hymn of Dakṣa he will be liberated from sins. On death he will attain identity with the Gaṇas. He will be honoured by Devas and Asuras. He enjoys a trip in an aerial chariot yoked to a bull. He will be a follower of Rudra and stay in the region of Śiva till the dissolution of the universe. This has been mentioned by lord Vyāsa the son of Parāśara. No one knows this nor should it be narrated to any one or every one. By listening to this secret, those who are of sinful origin viz. Vaiśyas, Śūdras and women will attain the world of Rudra.

There is no doubt that the brahmin who narrates this on Parvan days attains the world of Rudra.

CHAPTER THIRTYNINE

The holy Centre of Ekāmra

Lomaharṣaṇa said :

1-5. Thus, the excellent sages heard the meritorious story about the fury of Rudra that destroys sins, as Vyāsa recounted it, O brahmins. They heard about the fury and indignation of Pārvatī, the anger of Śiva, the origin of Vīrabhadra and the nativity of Bhadrakālī.

They then heard about the destruction of Dakṣa's sacrifice and the wonderful valour of Śiva. They also heard about the propitiation of the lord by Dakṣa the great soul, the allotment of share to Rudra, the benediction of Dakṣa that confers the fruit of all sacrifices. Those brahmins became surprised and pleased in turns. They asked Vyāsa for the rest of the story. Thus asked by them Vyāsa described the holy centre of Ekāmra.

Vyāsa said :

6. On hearing the story mentioned by Brahmā, the leading sages were delighted. Their hairs stood on ends. They praised the lord.

The sages said :

7-8. Wonderful indeed is the glory of the lord, eulogized by you. O most excellent one among Devas, the destruction of the sacrifice of Dakṣa (is also wonderful). Now it behoves you to recount Ekāmra, the most excellent of holy centres. O Brahmā, we wish to hear about it. Our eagerness is beyond measure."

Vyāsa said :

9. On hearing their words, the fourfaced lord of worlds recounted that holy centre of lord Śiva which yields worldly pleasures and salvation on this very earth itself.

1. *Ekāmra*—A holy centre in the land of Utkala distinct from one in South India.

Brahmā said :

10-11. Listen, O leading sages, I shall succinctly mention. There is a great holy centre known as Ekāmra. It dispels all sins. It is extremely inaccessible to ordinary persons. It is as auspicious and splendid as Vārāṇasī. It has a crore of Liṅgas and eight holy water spots in it.

12. O excellent brahmins, in the previous Kalpa, there was a single Mango tree there by which name, the holy centre came to be known as Ekāmra.

13. It was full of delighted and well-nourished people, both men and women. Most of the people there belonged to the learned group. It abounded in riches and foodgrains and similar things.

14. There were many houses full of cattle. It was well decorated with towers and minarets. There were many traders and businessmen and variety of jewels beautified it.

15. The city was beautified by streets and embellished by palaces as white and pure as royal swans. There were many lofty mansions with upper apartments.

16. It contained massive doorways arranged in groups of three. A white outer wall enhanced its beauty. It was well guarded by weapons and beautified by moats and trenches.

17. It was adorned by various flags and emblems of variegated colours such as white, red, black, dark or yellow. They were wafted and waved to the winds.

18. The people were gay and joyous in perpetual festivities with various kinds of musical instruments such as the lute, flute and drums. The area was adorned with slings for hurling missiles.

19. There were many temples of gods embellished by outer walls and gardens. The ways of worship therein were wonderful and they enhanced the beauty of the holy centre.

20-27. The women were slender-waisted and joyous. Their necks were adorned by necklaces. They had large eyes like the petals of the lotus. Their breasts were plump and lifted up. These ladies were dark-complexioned with faces shining like the full moon. Their forelocks were steady. Their cheeks were fine. Their girdles and anklets sounded sweet. They had good tresses of hair; their buttocks were beautiful and their eyes were large extending as far as the ears. They were richly endowed with all characteristic signs and bedecked in all ornaments. They wore white and lustrous garments. Some were golden-coloured. Their bodies bent down due to the weight of their breasts. Their mode of walking was like that of the swans and elephants. They had smeared their limbs with divine scents and unguents. They felt sweet languor due to intoxication. They had ample and beautiful buttocks. They had ever-smiling faces. Their teeth appeared like lightning streaks. They had lips like the Bimba fruits. They had sweet voice. Betel leaves added colour to their mouths. They were artful, beautiful to look at. They were fortunate. They spoke pleasing words to everyone. They were proud of their perpetual youthful bloom. They wore divine garments. They were embellished by their chastity. They resembled the celestial ladies and they sported about in their respective houses. They remained gay and jolly by day and night.

28. The men too were richly endowed with their noble traits and bedecked in all ornaments. They appeared to be haughty by virtue of their youth and handsome features.

29. O excellent sages, they were brahmins, Kṣatriyas, Vaiśyas and Śūdras. Those who lived there were very virtuous and engaged in their respective profession.

30-32. There were many bright-eyed courtezans comparable to Ghṛtācī, Menakā, Rambhā, Tilottamā, Urvaśī, Vipracitti, Viśvācī, Sahajanyā and Pramlocā. They had smiling faces and they spoke pleasing words. They were clever and skilled in arts and crafts. They were endowed with good qualities.

33. O excellent sages, the women were experts in dancing and singing. They were proud of their feminine virtues.

34. These beautiful women, pleasing to behold were experts in conversation and side-glancing at people. None of them was bereft of beauty, none harassed others, none could be called wicked or evil in their activities.

35-37. Men were fascinated the moment their side-glances fell on them.

Among the males there were no impoverished, foolish, inimical, sickly, dirty, miserly or deceptive persons. None of them lacked in handsome features. None wilfully harassed others. None could be called evil or wicked in his activities. These men lived in that holy centre which was reputed allover the world. The holy centre could be traversed comfortably; it was very pleasing to the people who resided there.

38-50. The holy centre was thronged with different sorts of people. It was full of many kinds of plants and trees such as Karṇikāras, Panasas, Campakas, Nāgakesaras, Pāṭalas, Aśokas, Bakulas, Kapitthas, Dhavas, Cūtas, Nimbas, Kadambas and other trees in full bloom; it was bedecked in Nīpaka, Dhava and Khadira trees with creepers growing over them. There were other trees such as Śāla, Tāla, Tamāla, Nārikela (cocoanut), Śubhāñjanas, Arjunas, Saptaparṇas, Kovidāras, Pippalas, Lakucas, Saralas, Lodhras, Hintālas, Devadārus, Palāśas, Mucukundas, Pārijātas, Kubjakas, plantains, Jambus, areca palms, Ketaki, Karavīras, Atimuktas, Kiṁśukas Mandāra, Kundas and other flowering plants. The gardens were comparable to the Nandana garden by the chirping of different birds, the trees laden with fruits that made them bend down and other living beings such as Cakoras, Śatapatras, royal bees, cuckoos, partridges peacocks, crows and parrots. There were many other birds such as Jīvañjīvakas, Hārītas, and Cātakas. They encompassed the forests. There were other birds chirping very sweetly. The holy centre abounded in long tariff lakes, ponds, sacred water spots adorned with clusters of lotus plants. The lakes looked beautiful with clear water. There were lilies, white lotuses, blue lotuses, Kadamba birds, ruddy geese, water hen, Kāraṇḍava birds, swans and other aquatic animals. The spot was made highly beautiful with different kinds of trees, excellent flowers and water spots. It appeared splendid all round. There the lord with the full-emblem and elephant hide garment was present directly.

51-58. Śiva who yields worldly pleasures and salvation to the people sat among Devas and Sages who brought water severally from the sacred rivers, holy water spots, lakes, lotus-ponds, tanks, wells and oceans on the earth. For the welfare of the people Śiva evolved the holy lake Bindusaras in that holy centre, O excellent brahmins. It was on the eighth day in the dark half of the month of Mārgaśīrṣa, O excellent brahmins, that the lake was created by the lord.

The devotee who undertakes a pilgrimage to that place on the day of equinoctical transits shall duly take his bath in the Bindusaras in faith. He shall perform Tarpaṇa rites unto Devas, sages, human beings and Manes assiduously. Repeating their names and Gotras he shall perform the libation of water with gingelly seed. By taking ablution duly in that holy water he shall attain the benefit of horse sacrifice. Those who offer charitable gifts to the brahmins on the following occasion derive hundred times the benefit which they may receive from other holy centres.

59-63. There is no doubt that the devotees will accord an everlasting satisfaction to the Pitṛs if they offer balls of rice to them on the bank of this lake.

He shall then go to the abode of lord Śiva observing restraint in speech and control on sense-organs. After entering the shrine he shall circumambulate thrice. Pure (in his mind and body) he shall bathe Śiva with ghee, milk etc. He shall apply sandal paste and sweet scent. He shall worship the moon-crested lord, the consort of Umā with different kinds of flowers worthy of being used in holy rites such as Bilva, Arka, lotus, etc. He shall eulogise the deity with the Mantras mentioned in the Vedas or Āgamas.

64-73. A man who has not undergone the formal initiation shall worship by pronouncing the name and the basic Mantra. After worshipping the lord with scents, fragrant flowers, garments etc, with incense, lights, food offering and presents, by means of eulogies, prostrations on the ground, by sign songs, accompanied by musical instruments, by dances, repeated obeisances, shouts of victory, and circumambulations, the devotee becomes liberated from all sins. By worshipping the lord, the consort of Umā, the lord of Devas, the devotee gets rid of sins. They are endowed with handsome features and youthfulness. He can redeem twentyone generations of his family in this way. He is bedecked in divine ornaments. He will be born as a performer of sacrifices, a liberal donor of charitable gifts and an overlord of the earth.

After taking bath in the waters of Bindusaras, the devotee shall visit the following shrines—Muktīśvara, Siddheśa Suvarṇa jāleśvara, Parameśvara and the subtle lord Āmratikeśvara. He shall duly worship them. He will be going to the world of Śiva on the golden aerial chariot with clusters of tinkling bells. Gandharvas and Apsaras will be singing in his praise and embellish him. He will brighten up quarters. O brahmins, along with the people who habitually reside in that world, he will enjoy all pleasures there pleasing to the mind, until the dissolution of all living beings. When the merits decrease he will return to the earth. O excellent brahmins, he will be reborn in the abodes of Yogins. He will become the master of the Vedas. After attaining the Pāśupata Yoga he will attain salvation.

74-75. Those who visit the temple of lord Śiva on the following days go to the world of Śiva on the aerial chariot having solar lustre. The holy occasions are—the day of Śayana (lying down), the day of Utthāpana (rising up), the monthly transit from one sign of zodiac to another, on the days of tropical transits, on the Aśokasaptamī and on the day of Pavitrāropaṇa.

76. The intelligent people who visit the lord at any time, are liberated from their sins. They go to the world of lord Śiva.

77. The holy centre extending to two and a half Yojanas to the West, East, North and South of the lord is an area that yields worldly pleasures and salvation.

78-83. In that excellent holy centre there is a Liṅga named Bhāskareśvara. It had been worshipped by the Sun-god previously. The devotees shall take bath in the holy ditch and then worship the three-eyed lord of Devas. They will be liberated from all sins. Seated in an excellent aerial chariot they will go to the world of lord Śiva. The Gandharvas will sing in their praise. O excellent brahmins, full of joy they remain there for the period of a Kalpa. After enjoying extensive pleasures in the world of lord Śiva, when their merits dwindle, they come down to the Earth and are born in an excellent family. Or they are born in the abodes of Yogins. They will be masters of Vedas and Vedāṅgas. They will be born as excellent brahmins engaged in the welfare of living beings. They will become experts in the science of Salvation and will have equal consideration for all. After attaining the excellent Yoga of Śiva they derive salvation.

84-87. O brahmins, the devotee shall worship any Liṅga he sees in that holy centre. Wherever that Liṅga is seen whether it is worthy of worship or not, whether it is obtained from forest or in the street, in the cremation ground or in the main cross-roads the devotee shall bathe that Liṅga with devotion and faith. He must assure himself that the Liṅga has no cracks. He shall then worship the Liṅga with scents fragrant and charming flowers, incense, height, food-offerings, obeisances, eulogies, prostrations, dances, songs etc. By worshipping thus in accordance with the injunctions he shall go to the world of Śiva.

88. Even a woman, O leading brahmins, attains the benefit if she worships in due faith. No doubt need be entertained in this respect.

89. Excepting lord Śiva, O excellent sages, who can recount the good qualities of that excellent holy centre ?

90-92. Whether a person possesses faith or not whether it is a male or a female person, the pilgrim shall go there on any day in any month. O brahmins, after taking bath in the waters of Bindusaras, he or she shall visit the temple of three-eyed lord Śiva and the goddess Umā the bestower of boons, as well as Caṇḍa, the Gaṇa, Kārttikeya, Gaṇeśa, the bull, the Kalpa tree and Sāvitrī. He goes to the world of lord Śiva immediately.

93-95. By taking bath in the Kapila Tīrtha that is destructive of sins, one obtains all cherished desires and goes to the world of lord Śiva. He who performs pilgrimage in accordance with the injunctions after controlling the sense-organs, shall uplift twentyone generations and then attain the world of lord Śiva.

He who takes his holy dip in Ekāmra, the holy centre of lord Śiva, that is as splendid as Vārāṇasī, will certainly attain liberation.

CHAPTER FORTY

The holy centre Utkala

Brahmā said :

1. Mother Virajā, my mistress, is firmly established in Virajā. By visiting her a man protects his family upto the seventh generation.

2. By visiting that goddess even for once and by worshipping and bowing to her with devotion a man redeems his family and goes to my world.

3. The other mothers of the world who stand in Virajā are goddesses who dispel sins and bestow boons. They are favourably disposed to the devotees.

4. There is the river Vaitaraṇī there. It dispels all sins. By taking holy dip there, the excellent man is liberated from all sins.

5. The self-born lord Viṣṇu stays there in the form of a Boar. By visiting him and bowing to him with devotion, man goes to Viṣṇu's abode.

6-8. There are eight holy sites in the holy centre of Virajā viz—Kapila, Gograha, Somatīrtha, Alābutīrtha, Mṛtyuñjaya, Kroḍatīrtha, Vāsuka and Siddhakeśvara. The intelligent pilgrim shall visit all these holy sites and take a holy dip therein in the Virajā with all his sense-organs controlled. By bowing down to the lords he shall be liberated from all sins. Seated in an excellent aerial chariot he goes to my world. The Gandharvas sing in his praise and honour him.

9. He who offers balls of rice in Virajā, my holy centre, shall undoubtedly accord ever-lasting satisfaction to the manes.

10. O excellent sages, men who cast off their body in Virajā my holy centre, do attain salvation.

11. He who takes a holy dip in the ocean and visits Kapila, Viṣṇu and Varahī, goes straight to heaven.

12. O excellent sages, there are many holy sites and shrines. They should be known as equal to that (Virajā).

13. O excellent brahmins, there is a secret and great holy centre which bestows salvation and destroys sins, in the land on the northern shore of the sea.

14. It is covered with sands. It is sacred. It bestows all desires. It extends to ten Yojanas. This is one of the rarest of holy centres.

15-21. That holy centre contains many trees such as Aśoka, Arjuna, Punnāga, Bakula, Sarala, jack tree, coconut tree, Śālas, palmyra, the wood apple, Campaka, Karṇikāra, mango, Bilva, Pāṭala, Kadamba, Kovidāra, Lakuca, Nāgakesara, Śami, Āmalaka (Embylic myrobalan), Lodhra, Citron, Dhava, Khadira, Sarja, Bhūrja, Aśvakarṇa, Tamāla, Devadāru, Mandāra, Pārijāta, Nyagrodha, Aguru, Sandal, Kharjūra, Āmrātaka, Siddha, Mucukunda, Kiṁśuka, Aśvattha, Saptaparṇa, Madhudhara, Śubhāñjana, Śiṁśapa, Nīpa, Nimba (Margose), Tindu, and Vibhītakas. These trees were laden with fruits and fragrant flowers of all seasons. They were delightful to the mind. They were splendid. Many types of birds made the atmosphere resound. The sounds produced by the birds were pleasing to the ears. They were very sweet and excited love pangs powerfully. They afforded great pleasure to the mind.

22-23. The place was full of various birds such as Cakoras, Śatapatras (woodpeckers), Bhṛṅgarājas, (bees), parrots, cuckoos, partridges, Hārītas, Jīvajīvakas, Cātakas, and other birds of sweet voice. They were chirping and their sounds were pleasing to the ears. They delighted everyone and they were beautifully perched (on the branches).

24-31. There were clusters of Ketaki plants, Atimuktas, Kubjakas, Mālatīs, Kundas, Banas, Karavīras of black varieties, Jambīras, Aruṇas, Kaṅkolas, Dāḍimas, Bījapūrakas, Mātuluṅgas, Areca palms, Hintālas, groves of plantain trees and many types of flowering trees pleasing to the mind. There were creepers, and bushes spreading like canopies. There were different kinds of water reservoirs such as oblong ponds, lakes lotus ponds, and tanks. The different water reservoirs were holy and decorated with lotus-clusters. The lakes were beautiful with clear water lilies, white lotuses, splendid blue lotuses, Kalhāra flowers, and similar flowers abounded in those lakes all round. There were Kadambaka birds; Cakravākas and water fowls. There were floating Kāraṇḍava birds, swans, tortoises, fish, Madgus, Dātyūhas, Sārasas, Koyaṣṭis and cranes and these enhanced the beauty of the place. There were other birds living in water, flying in the air or walking over the land. There were aquatic flowers; thus the whole holy centre looked very beautiful with different sorts of trees and flowers both on land and in water. There were aquatic and other types of elephants beautifying the place.

32-35. The place was adorned by religious students, householders, forest dwellers and recluses. They were engaged in their virtuous duties. There were other people as well adorning it. The place was filled with delighted and well nourished people. It was thronged by men and women. The place was the abode of all lores. It was a mine of all holy rites and virtues. Thus, the holy centre, endowed with all good qualities, was the rarest of all holy centres.

O excellent sages, the famous lord Viṣṇu abides there. As far as the boundary of the land of Utkala extends, the place is very holy due to lord Kṛṣṇa's favour.

36-43. Everything is well established in the place where the supreme lord who pervades the universe is present. He is the lord of the universe and the soul of all. O excellent sages, we always stay in that land. Rudra, Indra, Devas led by Agni and I too stay there. So also the following too stay there : Gandharvas, Apsaras, Pitṛs, Devas, human beings Yakṣas Vidyādharas, Siddhas, sages of praiseworthy holy rites, Vālakhilyas and other sages, the Patriarchs—Kaśyapa and others, Suparṇas, Kinnaras, Serpents and other celestial beings; the four Vedas with their ancillaries, the different sorts, sacred treatises, the Itihāsas and Purāṇas, the sacrifices with excellent monetary gifts and the different sorts of holy rivers. Tīrthas and shrines, oceans and mountains too were established in that land. Who will not like to stay in such a place which is the holiest of the holy, which is frequented by Devas sages and Pitṛs and which is blessed with all means of pleasures.

Which land can surpass it in excellence ?

44-49. It is the place where lord Puruṣottama stays as the bestower of salvation.

Blessed indeed are those men who live in Utkala like Devas. They take their bath in the waters of the most excellent of holy centres and see Puruṣottama. They are actually the dwellers of heaven. They never go to the abode of Yama.

Fruitful indeed is the life of the people who stay in Utkala which is the holy centre of Puruṣottama. The residents of Utkala are highly intellectual because they see the lord in all these attributes. He is the most excellent of Devas, his eyes are large and pleasant; his brows, tresses and the crest are beautiful; he has a beautiful piece of ornament embellishing his ears, his smile is beautiful, his teeth are exquisitely fine, his ear rings adorn him beautifully; his nose and cheeks and forehead are very beautiful and possess good traits. The lotus-like face of lord Kṛṣṇa is the cause of delight to all.